FROM HEYDAY TO MAYDAY

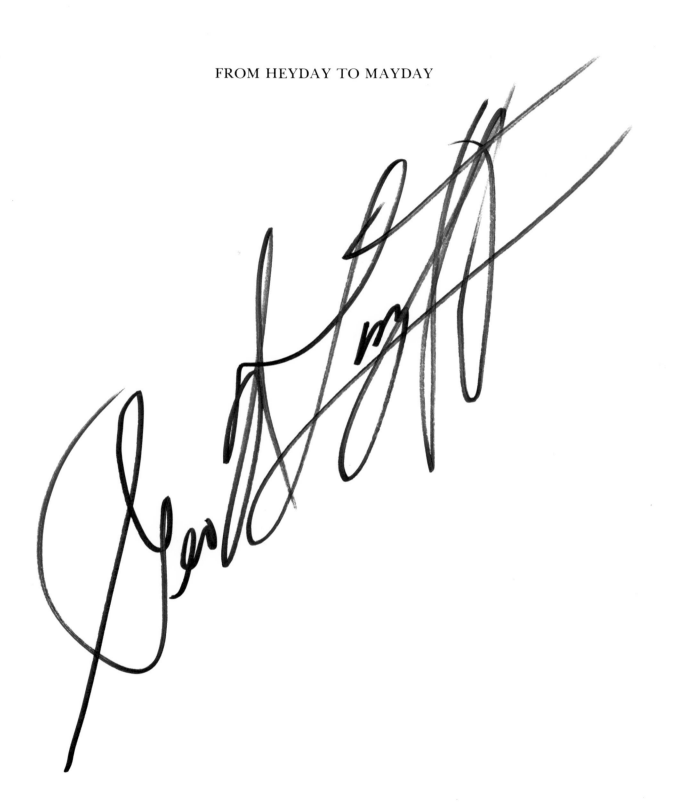

FROM
HEYDAY to MAYDAY

GEORGE H. LONGSTAFF

1983

Valkyrie Publishing House
6236 12th Street South,
St. Petersburg, Florida 33705

DEDICATION

This book can only be dedicated to my mother, Carrie Snyder Longstaff. She gave me my love of the Adirondacks and my hotel training, and then financed the purchase of the Moss Lake Tract and the development of the camp. Her wise counsel and generous support continued until her death in 1937.

ISBN 0-912589-00-0
LC 83-080424

First Edition, First Printing . . . April 1983

Printed in the United States of America

CONTENTS 🙌

INTRODUCTION

This book is being written so that others of my generation may realize how gracious the gods have been in allowing us to stretch our lives over this special period of American history. It is based on memory, not research.

As I dictate, the first chapters have developed into an autobiography and an account of what I consider to be the most important educational development of the 20th century—children's camps.

Also, since the main location is the Central Adirondacks, the book traces the resort history of that area from its heyday in the first quarter of the century through its decline in the forties and fifties, and its near extinction in later years.

As it deals with several properties and many people and includes time overlaps that have a built-in confusion, two chapters deal with people and miscellaneous events, and one with my Florida Boarding school, with no attempt to relate them to the general flow of the narrative.

Unfortunately the "From Heyday to Mayday" concept covers not only our northern resorts, but the whole state of the nation. Our educational system from the lower grades through college is in shambles; our immigration policy and our foreign policy seem to no longer operate with the good of our own country in mind; our welfare, medical, and correctional costs threaten to destroy our economy, and this is hastened by a free trade policy that fails to protect our workmen and our industrial machine. Drugs, declining patriotism, and rampant crime complete a sorry picture, yet I feel a few, perhaps rather drastic, reforms could turn our ship around. I hope many may agree with me.

PART ONE

CHAPTER I

The Early Adirondack Years

My paternal grandfather came from England in 1840, bought several pieces of land (Royal Grants) in Newport, New York, and while a blacksmith and farmer by trade he soon found himself running an express service between that town and the county seat of Herkimer. At its peak it required a dozen teams, justified the building of a plank toll road between the two communities, and became his chief source of income.

He had five sons and two daughters—my father was the youngest. Three brothers moved to Huron, South Dakota, where one owned a pharmacy, one ran a newspaper and was a state senator, and the other was an attorney and real estate developer. Except for my son, who is now president of the Flagship Banks in Broward County, Florida, and myself, the male descendants bearing the family name stem from this western group.

My maternal grandparents trace back to Dutch Colonial days. My grandfather lost his only brother in the Civil War (both of them served in the navy). My grandmother had two sisters and a brother living in Columbia County, New York, all of whom died before I went to college.

My grandfather Snyder had a scale factory in Mechanicsville, and probably would never have left Columbia County had my grandmother not developed tuberculosis. As the only treatment at that time was migration to the Adirondacks or other similarly high and dry areas, he sold his factory and took a position as chief engineer of the steamboat transportation on Raquette, Eagle, Utowana, and Blue Mountain Lakes with William West Durant, who at that time was the Adirondacks' largest and most active land developer. The cure took nearly ten years, but it worked and they returned to "civilization."

By this time my mother was the primary principal of the Herkimer schools, but in love with the Adirondacks. The next spring she and my grandfather purchased summer property on Fourth Lake.

Some years before, my father had embarked on a dental career that was to cover seventy-five years of active practice—approximately twenty-five each in Herkimer, Brooklyn, and Jamaica. I can remember the old red gas generator which made his nitrous oxide extractions the talk of the town, and the way teeth literally flew around the operating room. It would be some time before anyone would think of adding oxygen to the gas to control and prolong the anesthesia. The procedure was to have the patient inhale the nitrous oxide until he started to breathe hard, stiffened, turned blue, or showed the eye signs of deep anesthesia. The gas was then discontinued, and the dentist could count on about a minute before consciousness returned. My father would let me pick up the teeth as they flew around the room and, of course, I counted them. Sometimes there were over a dozen.

The Fourth Lake cottage or camp was soon turned into a guest house but within ten years it had burned, been replaced with a larger one, and had sired about eight cottages—Camp Mohawk.

In Herkimer my father was politically active and a few years after his arrival was elected Mayor or, more accurately, Village President. It was a city of ten thousand

The Longstaff Homestead
← *Newport, N.Y. circ. 1875*

Entrance to plank road an early Longstaff project.

Rocky Point Inn showing the boat house built in 1909.

Herbert Henry Longstaff 1860–1953

Carrie Snyder Longstaff with her parents, George and Lucina Snyder at Camp Mohawk. circ. 1898

Original Fourth Lake Camp on the Mohawk site destroyed by fire 1897.

Camp Mohawk circ. 1905

Early transportation by water and wagon road

"One Day Cottage", 1900

Typical cottage at the Mohawk, 1900

then and the figure is approximately the same today, but it has elected not to incorporate as a city.

By the summer of 1900 I had been born. To prepare for my transfer to the Adirondacks, my father made a weekend visit to camp before the season opened, and with one assistant went by boat to the Fifth Lake sawmill, bought lumber, started a cottage 10 feet by 18 feet, and completed it before returning by steamer and train to Herkimer to open his office on Monday morning.

Six or seven years later he purchased Rocky Point Inn, a hotel for one hundred and twenty-five guests at the eastern end of Fourth Lake, and in 1909 he performed a much more astounding construction feat. Camp Mohawk was doing so well that my parents decided on a major expansion program, which stands as the best example of my father's incredible energy, versatility, and organizing ability.

In the spring he brought in a gang of men to start preparation for construction of the main Mohawk building. Most were men from Herkimer whose skills and energies he already knew, and they came through for him in fine style.

The plan was to tear down part of the existing main building and move the balance to a location that would not interfere with the view of the new hotel then envisioned. This change also necessitated moving four of the cottages, the boathouse, and the laundry. It likewise involved new interiors for the boathouse and the laundry and new fireplaces and plumbing for the cottages.

The hill behind the old "Main House" required much grading before construction could start, and a team and two men worked on this through most of the summer. The hotel season was shortened to close on Labor Day, with the residual guests transferring to Rocky Point. The next day a local contractor, Nick Ginther, his capstan, and his horse appeared and with the help of a few men started jacking up and moving the six buildings. My father had other men preparing their new piers, and when they were finished transferred them to the foundation walls and piers for the new building. The moving happened so quickly that in retrospect I would assign only two weeks for this part of the work. Before it was completed, my father had brought in carpenters and laborers from Herkimer and had them work on the cottages until the foundations for the new structure were ready.

The wages of the day are interesting: three dollars per day for the carpenters and lathers, two for the hammer-and-saw men, one for the common laborers, three for the plasterers, five for the plumber (he and his helper put in twenty-two bathrooms that spring), and a shocking seven for the stone mason who built the fireplaces. Room and board were included, but the men worked ten-hour days and took real pride, not merely in their individual accomplishments, but also in the speed with which the job as a whole progressed. The hotel, rechristened THE MOHAWK, opened on July fourth, and my father retired to Rocky Point.

As the newest hotel in the region The Mohawk, with its electric lights, many private baths and a lavatory in each room, was also the most modern, yet it kept the atmosphere of the old Adirondacks and quickly acquired a select and loyal clientele. The cottages were rented to various families for a season that started when schools let out in the spring and ended on Labor Day.

Fathers commuted on weekends, chiefly from New York where an 8:00 p.m. train out of the Grand Central pulled into our own Skensowane Station, a quarter of a mile from our back door at 6:00 the next morning.

Most of the thirty-two bedrooms in the main building were occupied by childless couples, widows, and the two-three-week vacationers whom we considered our transients. There also were bachelor quarters over the boathouse that were less expensive, but proved to be a real asset to the hotel. My mother screened their occupants with great care and the pattern was for them to return year after year until they were married and brought their brides to The Mohawk. They were a social asset so substantial that unlike similar hotels which had at least one hostess to plan activities, The Mohawk seemed always to have some talented, gregarious guests nicely able to keep the social ball rolling.

The tennis courts, a large boat livery, and a music room with a fine dance floor were our official contributions and they proved to be most adequate. My mother had some musical ability and was able to secure truly fine musicians year after year—always a piano and violin and sometimes a horn—chamber music for lunch and dinner and dance music from eight to eleven. The floor was seldom crowded but never deserted, yet during the last hour one would generally find more people gathered around the lakeside campfire that was started each properly clement night.

Most days one or more trips would be scheduled—short hikes to nearby lakes, mountain climbs, a picnic on an uninhabited island, and once a week the marvelous Blue Mountain excursion.

The Fulton Chain comprised eight lakes. The first four were navigable for the large steamers that provided a central focus for our resort area and made the twenty-five hotels scattered over its thirty or forty miles of shoreline a quite homogeneous community. The queen of the line, the Clearwater, was a double-decker with a capacity of three hundred, the Nehasane and the Uncas were similar in design but slightly smaller and licensed for about two hundred each. In addition there were two single-deckers, the Mohegan which was sizable and largely enclosed and the Irocosia which was little more than a large launch, and, most interesting of all, the Old Forge which was our floating postoffice. It made two round-trips a day, dropping and picking up mail at each dock, and even stopping to sell stamps. With the postoffice in the rear of the boat and the engine in the middle, it still had room for fifteen or twenty passengers. It provided the finest way of all to see the lakes for the round trip would bring you near enough to each dock for an exchange of mail bags—yet would require only three to three and a half hours. We have some excursion launches today sailing from Old Forge to Inlet for sightseers, but they do not come near the shore, make the trip in half the time, and lack the atmosphere of these early steamers, pilots, and engineers.

The finest trip of all was the Blue Mountain Excursion which continued through the pre-depression years and was surely one of the best bargains ever offered to vacationers. The excursion first ran through the lower four lakes of the Fulton Chain and one of the larger steamers would stop at the Mohawk dock between 8:30 and 9:00 in the morning, take the passengers to Eagle Bay, where they would walk two hundred yards to the railroad station, entrain to ride the ten miles to the eastern terminus, and then entrust themselves to the Raquette Lake Navigation Company.

There, steamers would take them through Raquette Lake and the Marion River to the Carry, the Adirondack term for portage. Here there was a full gauge railroad a half mile long with an engine, two old Brooklyn streetcars, and a flat car for boats and other freight. Its capacity, of course, was less than that of the boats, and it usually needed to make more than one trip. The steamers which waited at the other end took their passengers through Utowanna, Eagle, and Blue Mountain Lakes. At the eastern end of Blue Mountain Lake the excursionists were allowed two and a half to three hours. The more energetic used this time to climb the 3800 foot Blue Mountain, the highest in the area, with a packed lunch and return to the boat. The less robust would usually repair to Merwin's Blue Mountain House, which had one of the finest views in the Adirondacks. It was at the present location of the Blue Mountain Museum.

The return trip brought our guests back to the hotel about twelve hours after they started, and while many would be both stiff and tired the next morning, there was no evidence of this the previous night. You could tell when the boat rounded Eagle Point because the group seemed always to be in good voice and high spirits. As I recall, the round trip fare was $3.50.

This was the central Adirondacks before the intrusion of the automobile. Until 1919 we did not even have a hotel car and our local excursions were by buckboard. That year we purchased a Buick touring car and a much-used International Harvester truck with four-foot wheels, hard rubber tires, a two-cylinder horizontal air-cooled engine, mounted under the seat and cranked from the side, and a progressive transmission that looked like an emergency brake. It was obsolete before we bought it but it was intended only for the quarter-mile run from Skensowane Station to the hotel. It was never licensed but it took care of the baggage and its antiquity added much color. All roads were dirt through the early twenties and in the spring they were almost impassable. When Route 28 was paved as far as Inlet in 1928 the character of the resorts changed sharply, and in most cases they became enmeshed in a struggle for survival. Ten years later the road was extended to connect with the one between Lake George and Lake Placid, and we found ourselves thinking of the vacationers who settled down for two or three weeks as our long-staying guests. This was not merely The Mohawk picture, but typical of all the resorts in the area. Even before World War II many were in serious trouble, were auctioned off in small parcels, and ceased to exist in recognizable form.

The Mohawk had two, and later three, tennis courts and inter-hotel matches were popular. There was a large boat livery, but strangely no sailboats until I introduced them to the area at my Cedar Isles boys' camp in the mid-thirties.

My mother intended that I learn the hotel business quite thoroughly and from an early age I was dishwasher and troubleshooter, but whenever we had a new chef I was assigned to be his assistant for at least a fortnight.

During this period my grandfather operated our laundry and the gasoline electric light plant, which was the first in the area. Rocky Point and the other hotels were lighted by gas to or through the World War I period. From time to time I was allowed either to assist or to temporarily replace my grandfather and this was an especial thrill.

Probably nothing was more characteristic of the crew that my mother seemed to be able to assemble year after year than their willing versatility. The bellboys and gardener would meet the trains at the railroad station with wheelbarrows, take the baggage, including trunks—some of them were large wardrobes—the quarter mile to the hotel and then up to the rooms or down the hill to the various cottages.

The morning would start with waitresses sweeping the sidewalks and then ringing first a rising and later a breakfast bell. Each waitress had only two tables, but that was less than half the day's work. Some cleaned and re-set the dining room. Some washed the dishes and silver with the help of a boy and a mechanical dishwasher which my father had invented and which was made by a local tinsmith. It became quite popular in the neighborhood. In fact, I continued to use three at my girls' camps for fifty years. Other waitresses were assigned to the laundry where they would hang up the wash, take it down, mangle it, and return it to the various linen rooms. Still others cared for the public rooms and served as chambermaids. For the most part, they were not college girls, but school teachers—yet I have never seen a harder working or happier group of women.

My mother and the head waitress spent much time during the month of June coaching the new girls on the fine points of dining room service. The tables had to be set meticulously and even slightly soiled linen brought sharp reprimands. The girls were expected to reach their tables by the time the head waitress had finished seating a party unless they were busy with another table—each girl had one table of six and one of four. If she was not immediately available the head waitress supplied menus and filled water glasses. The proper waitress was quite sure to appear by that time, but if one did not another girl would be asked to take the order for the first course.

When a girl was not in the kitchen filling an order she stood in a designated spot from which she could watch her tables and where guests could readily catch her eye. Water glasses were never allowed to get empty and all other service details were closely watched. There was no tipping until the guests left for the season, but then most were quite generous and by the end of summer each girl had from one to two hundred dollars in addition to her wages of thirty dollars a month.

In the last forty years I have found comparable service only at the Fort Nelson Hotel in Cape Town, South Africa, and rarely an American plan menu that could match our three meals with their chops and steaks for breakfast and their six-course dinners.

When I reached my upper teens I commonly was entrusted with the job of closing up the hotel at night and doing some of the clerical work during this period. As I tell this, it sounds as though I also was working rather hard, but that was not exactly the picture for my mother had my social development very much in mind and planned things each summer to give me much, though spasmodic, playtime. These hours I would spend watching or participating in tennis and the waterfront activities, or "exercising" a motor canoe my father gave me when I was ten. These were truly idyllic summers with work and play nicely balanced and wonderful associates.

Although my father had many outside interests his dental career was most notable. It started with twenty-five years in Herkimer during which he dabbled in politics, a Puerto Rican orange grove, and the hotel business.

When he completed The Mohawk and returned to Rocky Point the word "retirement" which I used to describe the transition should have been appropriate for through the previous ten months he had been trying to take care of the off-season needs of his own hotel, maintain his Herkimer dental practice and give "full time" to the Mohawk construction through all but the most severe winter months. However, his pleasure in the results of his efforts there made it painful for him to compare the new Mohawk with the twenty-year-old main building at Rocky Point. He had built a large boathouse with a second floor dancing area, a few small cottages, and a tennis court in his first years there, but the 1910 patronage was down instead of up, probably because it had had so little attention through the winter and spring, and he felt it could be brought up only by razing the main structure and replacing it with another as modern as the one he had built at The Mohawk.

Funds were lacking so he decided to collect some old political "markers" and run for county clerk—a fee-sustained office that netted its holder twenty-five to thirty thousand a year. He secured the Republican nomination and campaigned as though he were running for governor, even hiring a team and driver for a tour of the county's lumber camps. Success eluded him by a single vote. Of course, the time he gave to the campaign and to the hotels had punished his dental practice and his financial world collapsed.

To avoid family bankruptcy my mother accepted a $36,000 mortgage on The Mohawk that called for principal payments of $6,000 a year. Toward the end of those six years I began to realize how hard she was working to meet those payments and can only hope my reactions were helpful. No payments were missed and before the war broke out her bank accounts were healthy and her credit more secure than ever.

These Rocky Point years were pure magic for me. The hotels were only two miles apart, but just going from one to the other was an adventure. At seven and eight I was allowed to drive Kit our elderly gray mare from Camp Mohawk to Rocky Point,

View of 4th Lake
from the porch of
the Mohawk circ. 1914

Eastern cottages
at the Mohawk

The Mohawk southern facade and lobby

... Dinner ...

At " THE MOHAWK," July 21, 1912

Consomme an Royale

Celery   Olives   Gherkins   Fig Relish

Baked Lake Trout with Tomatoes

Macaroni au Gratin
            Fried Egg Plant, Tomato Sauce
                            Compote of Fruit

Roast Turkey, Dressing, Cranberry Sauce
                    Roast Ribs of Beef, au Jus

Mashed and Boiled Potatoes
Creamed Onions   Wax Beans   Steamed Rice

Fruit Salad

Prune Whip, Whipped Cream
Apple Pie   Pineapple Cream Pie

Strawberry Ice Cream   Sponge Cake
                    Peaches
            Cheese   Crackers
        Mixed Nuts   Layer Raisins
Tea   Coffee   Iced Tea   Milk   Cocoa

Typical Mohawk menu of this era

Dining Room and Music Room at the Mohawk, 1912

turn her around, and start her home. The next day I would take myself home by steamer (25¢) and start looking forward to my next trip. My aunt was in the Rocky Point office so I guess I was little trouble to others. When she was busy there was always Fisher, the matronly housekeeper who later spent several years at The Mohawk and helped raise my sister. With the arrival of the motor-canoe that was to give me more pleasure through the years than any youngster could really deserve I was able to commute at will.

Of course Mohawk was my home, but Rocky Point with its rugged terrain was a place of never-ending interest. There was a toboggan slide on the beach that seemed, and probably was, very high, but my father never let me try it and soon condemned it. The large gas tank that rose and fell several feet each day was always intriguing as were the brightly colored lights that gave the grounds a very special life at night and which I was allowed to help light. There were speaking tubes that connected the office with the working areas and a callboard that would come to life when guests wanted ice water, a maid, or a bellboy. The need was indicated by the number of rings and a hand moved to show the room from which the call came. At the northern end of the property there were two rams that boosted the stream water to the height needed for the hotel use. These drew me on more than daily inspection trips. I could not understand their magic then and am not quite sure I do even now. There was a thirty-foot gasoline launch operated by the son of one of our Herkimer physicians and he occasionally allowed me to be his crew. Less exciting, but no less pleasurable, were the times I could have "Central Park" to myself. This was a small, level grassy space at the foot of the cliff on which the hotel was built. It was completely secluded, but with a good view of the lake and the Inlet hotels.

After his financial debacle my father decided that he should start afresh and make dentistry a full-time profession in another city. I think he chose New York because he had reports of the first successful local anesthetic. It was proprietary and had made its owner famous and prosperous. The dentist operated under the name of "Painless Parker" and my father signed up for two years in one of his offices with the understanding that he was to be given the formula at the end of that time. Parker himself was an excellent extractor but spent much of his time bringing in business to his various offices by running what sounds like a curbside medicine show. Whether this demonstration office was mounted on an early car chassis or was horse drawn, I do not remember, but he would collect crowds and remove teeth without charge—counting on the enthusiasm over the then incredible painless operation to steer patients to his offices in large numbers. Until this time only nitrous oxide in crude machines like my father's had been available; so his product and his skill were a sure-fire sensation.

My father undertook this "apprenticeship" not just to acquire the formula, but partially because he wanted to be sure he selected a good location for his own office, and to gather the necessary funds. He sent thirty-five dollars home per week, lived in a YMCA, and had the funds ready when the time was up and he was given the formula. He selected the Bushwick section of Brooklyn as the site for his office.

This magic formula, coming as it did in the earliest days of local anesthesia, let him build a better than $20,000 practice almost immediately. Of course, this would be a very nominal figure by today's standards but it was a generous income in those pre-World War I times. Incidentally, the magic formula astounded me when a dozen years later I started to practice with my father for it was cocaine, glycerine, and, of all things, the very strong caustic poison, phenol. As I used it, I realized that the phenol must be a very important ingredient and I found nothing nearly as effective in preventing post-operative infection during my twenty-five years of practice. I believe it was added originally so the solution itself would not become contaminated, but its effect certainly carried over into the post-operative period. It also acted as a vaso-constrictor and localized the anesthesia in the operating area.

The Parker solution produced almost uniformly uneventful healing, and I continued to use it for more than five years. I finally switched, largely because of the convenience of the disposable novocaine capsules and because I had gone back to nitrous oxide for most of my extractions. Incidentally, I understand that Bob Hope played the part of "Painless Potter" in a movie produced about ten years ago. I hope Parker was not lampooned, for his contribution to dentistry was an important one.

Brooklyn at that time was largely a Manhattan bedroom, but the more affluent families were starting to desert, and when my father realized that nearly half of his old patients had moved to Long Island, we opened a Jamaica office. We signed a lease in a building that was still under construction and were able to draw our own floor plan. The result was the most gracious dental suite I have ever seen, a foyer, a large waiting room, three operating rooms, a sterilization room, a laboratory. It included an office for my camp work and a storeroom for the literature and records necessary for that enterprise, as well as a secretary's office.

Instead of closing the Brooklyn office at once, my father decided we should continue it long enough to switch the clientele to Jamaica. This would have been a good idea if I had stayed in Brooklyn and my father had operated only in Jamaica. Most were his patients rather than mine, and those still living in Brooklyn preferred not to make the trip to Jamaica. For those on the Island that office was a great convenience and the result was that one and a half dentists were running two offices. Their gross ran neck and neck, and it was some years before we finally closed the Brooklyn office. Then my father agreed to it only because the neighborhood and our building had deteriorated badly.

My father had had an early interest in horses and during the Jamaica years they became his main hobby. He selected most of the camp horses, boarded two of them at a local stable each year and rode at every opportunity. Sunday was his big day. He would ride before breakfast with some other men who kept horses at the same stable, with me until dinner time, and then would take my mother in the afternoon. I credit his devotion to this hobby with doing much toward making his dental career of seventy-five years physically possible. Incidentally, even in his last years he never used an operating stool.

In 1915 both The Mohawk and my father's Brooklyn practice were flourishing and we moved to Jamaica for the winter months—first in a residential hotel and then an apartment. I intended going to Brown University largely because I had played tennis the previous summer with the captain of their tennis team, had enjoyed him as an individual, and was very much intrigued by his unorthodox but highly effective style.

By the summer of 1916 I was ready for college and matriculated at Brown, but two of our guests were seniors at Hamilton College in Clinton, N.Y. and when one suggested my going there for the opening "Rush Week," I went along with the idea, liked the college very much, and wired Brown to re-ship my trunk. It was a decision I have never regretted. At that time Hamilton was a college of about two hundred and twenty-five, and each boy knew every name and face on the campus within two weeks. As I was a small-town lad and younger than a freshman should be, the support this and the fine fraternity system made possible was extremely helpful. In addition, the classes were small, and the professors a group of talented and dedicated teachers with personalities so rich and varied that being in their classes would have been a rare privilege even if all subjects had been designed for juvenile instruction. President Melancthon W. Stryker taught freshman Bible, which struck me as odd, but I ended the year a complete punster, able to talk extemporaneously, with well crystallized ideas of right and wrong and with a deep respect for Christianity as a force in world development. He had interviewed most of us before admission and while he was basically an arch conservative these initial five minutes in his office gave me an advance reading on the way his mind worked. My credentials had been sent to Brown and I had no duplicates. He questioned me for less than a minute, picked up his telephone, and talked with Miss Foley, my Herkimer High School principal. There were three questions that elicited but brief answers—"Is he of good stock?"—"Can he do our work?"—"Will he be willing to make the necessary effort?" He thanked Miss Foley, turned to me, asked if I would be rooming in the Chi Psi House (how he knew I had been pledged there I never understood), or in a dormitory. When I indicated it would be the latter, he said, "See the Bursar—good luck."

I was housed next door to the chapel with one of our seniors in a three-room suite with a nice fireplace. There were services each morning at eight and the proximity was most convenient. I found that I could do the traditionally demanding classwork without difficulty, and this fact should have set the stage for one of my finest years, but I apparently elected to coast with plans to dig in both scholastically and athletically my sophomore year.

I fear I gave the school little in return that year, and my good sophomore resolutions were voided when my mother's health dived suddenly and her physician advised some months in Kellogg's Battle Creek Sanitarium. I was deeply concerned, transferred to the University of Michigan, and took classes that required my being on campus only Tuesday, Wednesday, and Thursday. Four months in the sanitarium were most beneficial and my mother returned to Jamaica.

At this point I started thinking about the war. As I dreaded life in the trenches, the Air Corps seemed to be the answer, and I persuaded Dean Effinger to give me six weeks leave (without loss of academic credit if I passed my final exams) around our April vacation to take flying lessons in Florida. I had had no experience or basic knowledge and picked Florida because the same man who had the well-advertised Moler Barber Training Schools was starting a flying school at Pueblo Beach and was guaranteeing a license for four hundred dollars. According to his literature this was made possible by a "Tera-Tutor" he had developed to simulate flying conditions on a backyard pedestal.

Fortunately, I was slightly skeptical and decided not to enroll by mail and remit my four hundred dollars as the literature suggested, but to go down unannounced. My initial contact was with a group of students playing with the "Tera-Tutor" and waiting for the one instruction plane, a "Canuck," to be put into service. Some were disillusioned and a couple had located an acrobat by the name of Ruggles at Atlantic Beach. He was wintering there with the Jesse Willard Circus and had resurrected a Martin-Wright biplane and was starting to fly it. It was built to carry only one person; so initial flights had to be solo, but he had had no difficulty doing it himself and was willing to let some of us try at a very modest six dollars per hour.

The plane had no fuselage, was powered by a revamped Ford engine and had two chain driven propellers (pushers). We sat on a seat rigged in the front of the wings. It had initially been built for shoulder controls, but they had been replaced by a "Dep" wheel which served to make it a reasonable preliminary for the training planes then in use. Its top speed was about fifty miles per hour and the landing speed not over twenty-five. We never took it up when there was appreciable wind and no one had any trouble.

While we were doing this we were searching for a real school where we could get our pilot licenses. Incidentally, at this time licenses were not granted by the government but by the American Aeronautical Association, and the "Beginners License" involved little except taking the plane up, executing some "figure eights," and putting it down within a reasonable distance of markers. We located a school in Daytona run by a prestige flyer by the name of Stanton. He had two "Jennys," a mechanic who was a fine flyer himself and a "Graduate Assistant." The boys who located it decided to stay at Pueblo Beach, but I went on down to Daytona and enjoyed myself in a reasonably profitable fashion. Nevertheless, I had to return to school before earning my license and had to be content with a letter from Stanton saying he judged I would have been able to pass the test if the weather of the previous two days had not precluded the attempt. One plane had crashed during my month in Daytona and that had slowed our schedule.

I remember Rodman Wannamaker was a member of the student group and that I was quite embarrassed when he asked me to take his car and pick up another member of the group. I was unwilling to admit I had never driven a car and fabricated an excuse. The next day I found and paid a garage mechanic to give me a lesson. Some of the group were staying at the Clarendon Hotel, with which I was much impressed, but my funds dictated my living at a boarding house with the instructor and some other students. When I returned a few years later to secure my official license, the Clarendon was for sale at fifty thousand dollars. I consulted with my father and I think he would have come down to look it over had those been the days of air travel. I stayed there again about 1970 and, while it was no longer the hotel of my dreams, it was still functional and valued at well over a million.

When I reached Ann Arbor Dean Effinger was as good as his word and the mark "in Florida Flying," which he put on my record, gave me full credit for the year.

With my return to Hamilton and with my Student Auxiliary Training Corps (SATC) enrollment arranged, I enjoyed the most carefree summer of my life but with some lingering concern for my mother's health. Automobile roads in the region were still dirt, but cars were coming in and guests were asking for garage space. Early paint jobs were delicate and the pride of ownership high, so none wished to leave their cars outdoors. The ten-car garage solution was my first construction and that year I was allowed to purchase a 1917 Chandler. Neither my father nor mother drove and I had only my few hours in Daytona as a background, but that was par for the course in those years and I became the family and hotel chauffeur, and that added greatly to the pleasure of the summer.

The SATC trimester was a strange experience. Studies were similar but the atmosphere was very different—much less organized, and the buoyancy more fragile. A few boys were transferred to the Officers Training School at Plattsburg and others started planning their expectancies. No one had anything else in mind but I was still fearful of the Infantry and was able to use the letter from my Florida instructor to get the promise of a transfer to the Air Corps when I reached nineteen. That and the fact that I had some gun experience made it difficult for me to develop an interest in the hours of drill with the wooden guns we were issued, so I made myself the officers' errand boy with the aid of my 1917 Chandler. None of them had cars and there was only one other student on wheels so this required but little manouvering.

We celebrated both the premature and the bona fide Armistice within a few weeks of my reaching my nineteenth birthday and then settled down to "Stick Around 'Til Christmas" as our initials, SATC, promised would be the case.

The second trimester did not register a full return to normalcy but was less disorganized, and Hamilton was a college again. Somehow the last twelve months had made me feel more mature and I was eager to get on with the business of making a living.

The war had not interfered with the resort business and my mother planned to tear down part of an overly large cottage and use the material to build a new maids' quarters behind the hotel. This meant that much more time would be needed for the construction than if we were building with new material, and I decided I should leave college at the end of the second trimester. (Hamilton had always been on a semester basis but the SATC demanded trimesters.)

The war, its end, and my increased hotel responsibilities made me anxious to give full time to The Mohawk. My father knew from his experience that the hotel business was a career gamble and insisted that I first acquire a profession, suggesting law or medicine. My heart was in the Adirondacks and I figured that with my father still active dentistry would be a better bet. We settled for that and I entered what now is the dental college of Columbia University. As the academic work seemed very easy, I also carried twelve hours per semester at New York University—this because I assumed that if I later returned to Hamilton I would be one trimester short of graduation at the end of my fourth year.

CHAPTER II

The Birth and Growth of Moss Lake Camp

In 1919 both the hotel business and my father's practice were booming and in the course of the summer I had another brainstorm. We all considered Darts Lake the prize property in the central Adirondack area and I saw an ad in "House and Garden" or "Country Life" indicating the hotel was for sale. A letter from Bill Dart confirmed this and I went over to see him. He said he had no special desire to sell, but that one of his patrons, a real estate agent from Cleveland, had asked if he would part with the property. His response was to set the then-very-high price of two hundred thousand. He added that he knew my mother was too practical to consider such a figure, but he gave me the tip that was to shape my life.

We both knew the adjoining Moss Lake property was equally beautiful and almost as large, and he told me he understood the four families who held it were having a hot dispute as to whether they should remain a foursome or expand to a club of twenty members. He added that it seemed to be a deadlock and that a twenty thousand mortgage was coming due later in the month. I carried my enthusiasm back to the hotel and with my mother's blessing called my father in New York, and one of the four owners. The result was that three of them and my father came to The Mohawk that weekend, and we signed a fifty thousand dollar sales contract that stipulated an auxiliary payment of five thousand to one family who had already built, (but not quite finished), a large cottage.

A factor in this purchase was our concern about the future of Fourth Lake. Two hotels had been taken over for operation as Jewish girls' camps, and this action revived a certainly unjustified but understandable, Jewish apprehension. Several hotels, including the finest and largest of them all, had reputedly been ruined by Jewish patronage. That hotel, the Prospect House on Blue Mountain Lake, was very near us and its brief career was a spectacular one deeply imprinted on the minds of all resort owners in the area. It had been built in Durant's heyday and with most New York City hotels still using gaslights and hydraulic elevators, it was equipped with its own light plant and electric elevators. It was the hotel sensation of its time—the rates were high and the clientele affluent and select. It soon developed a sizable Jewish following, the Christians departed, the Jewish clientele was no longer interested and the hotel closed. It opened a few years later under another name, the Utowana House, and ran through the same cycle.

When I was seven or eight years old, the dream was abandoned and the contents of the hotel auctioned. I remember quite clearly my father hiring a guide to take us through the remaining lakes of the Fulton Chain, the Brown's Tract inlet, and then the route followed by the Blue Mountain excursion from Raquette Lake. Many handsome pieces of furniture went for a song, but the only material we could take back was linen. My father purchased all the guideboat could safely carry and on the return we each made two trips over the carries, but felt the especially fine linens we were able to give my mother for The Mohawk made the trip very much worthwhile.

April 28, 1920

C H Scragstaff Dear Sir
Your Information about My
Place being for Sale is correct
as I have it—in the Hands
of 2 Real Estate Men One in
New York City and One in
Cincinatta Ohio will sell
to the First Purchaser who
gives Me My Price My Health
is poor and I dont Feel Equal
to the Strain of Managing the
Place any More My Price is
$200,000 and My Place is
well worth it I have the Entire
Lake Shore Seven Hundred and
45 Acres of Land 16 Cottages
Main House Boat House Ball
room Billeard room Bachelor
quarters Boat Leivery auto Truck
and Cars Horses Cows Hen
Dairy Green House Saw Mill
I Know the Place will Double
in a few Years as with an
Energetic Manager it is Bound
to be—that—will be of No use
to me when I am Dead and
gone and I want a few Years
rest and I am willing the
Other Fellow to Make Some
thing Two Yam Sincerely
Yours

William Dart

Moss Lake and main cottage at time of purchase, 1919

My mother decided that we should approach the Moss Lake development cautiously and that no plans should be made for at least a year. Of course, our purchase of the property was soon general knowledge and guests contributed their ideas. Some reactions were favorable while others indicated they would be reluctant to leave The Mohawk. The number of the latter spawned grave doubts in my mother's mind and there was talk of selling the newly acquired tract. I was horrified and asked that I be allowed to work out some other solution. My first thought was to start a flying service and use the income to pay the taxes and interest. My family gave me a green light but I was unable to develop the project.

In the winter of '21 I secured my bachelor degree from Michigan because Hamilton thought a Thanksgiving entrance inappropriate. My hotel and Moss Lake interests had kept me in the woods until then and my dental college also was unwilling to accept me at that late date. The Dean of Michigan apparently thought I was stretching privileges no further than when I did my six weeks of Florida flying and told me that if I could arrive within twenty-four hours and would permit him to prescribe suitable tutoring he would allow me to have full credit for the fall semester and to be graduated in the spring. When I telephoned him I was in Utica with only a small bag in which I normally kept a supply of socks under my bed. To this I had added a shirt, toilet articles, and a change of underwear. Since there was not time to return to the woods and keep my Ann Arbor deadline I took that bag and climbed onto the train.

It proved to be a relaxed and happy year that included meeting my first, and for a long time my only, heart throb. She was from Chicago, the date of a friend, and the attraction was so durable that she spent the summer at The Mohawk. By the end of the season I had decided that I wished to marry her and informed my father. His gentle reply suspended that dream. It was: "It will take you a long time to find a nicer young lady and I surely will work as happily to support her as any girl we could possibly hope for." Of course, this was a forcible reminder that I would have no independent means for some years.

The next summer my mother agreed to give me a second year to try making Moss Lake pay its way and I attempted to rent it. For some weeks I thought I was being successful. A New Jersey physical education teacher who wished to open a girls' camp was most taken with the property. Our discussions were quite detailed—what buildings she needed, how many girls she felt sure of, and what the year's profits would be. However, before the contract was executed she was offered a property in the Lake Placid area which would make a 1922 operation possible.

By this time my own camp enthusiasm was running high and I had figures to back it quite convincingly. The investment was a fraction of what would be required for a hotel, yet the profits promised to be even more generous. In the fall I cleared the ground for two cabins, a recreation hall, and two tennis courts. Thus the most pleasant and stable facet of my life was launched.

Further, quick success for the camp offered my best chance of building a financial foundation for marriage and I gave the project incredibly complete concentration. In fact, it was so complete that although I invited my "prospect" to come to Moss Lake as a camper (she was twenty and two other girls were the same age), I spoke to her alone only once during the eight weeks and that for but a few minutes. She stayed on at The Mohawk for an extra ten days after the closing, but although I was still sure that I could fall in love with no one else, we could not recapture the mood of the previous summer.

In retrospect, I am certain that this early attachment contributed much to the success of Moss Lake. Other girls remained out of focus in spite of the several years during which I was as young as the average counsellor. No happily married man could have treated them any more objectively and this paved the way for complete dedication to my new project.

I still had two years of dental college ahead, but being back in New York with a not-too-heavy academic load was most favorable. This meant that by forgetting my New York colleagues of earlier years and putting my nose to the grindstone I was able to develop a purposefulness that was to set my yearly pattern. I had collected the literature of several camps and decided I could build a better one, "knew" the hotel business better than the usual teaching director, and surely had the best location. Accordingly I felt I needed only to learn how a camp should be run. My approach was a cautious one and I plied the New York educational counsellors with a barrage of questions.

My luck, which was to be so fine for the next half century, did not make itself evident with suitable promptness, and I had about decided I must try a different approach when I struck pay dirt at Barnard College.

The head of the physical education department, Agnes Wayman, was intrigued by my description of the property and agreed to drive to Moss Lake with me. We made the round trip in one day. It apparently was a case of love at first sight, and although the salary she asked was stupendous, I agreed. She said she had a young assistant whom she wished to engage as head counsellor and added that she would like to write the camp brochure. I approved and she went to work.

The assistant was Meryl Hauser. She had a fine swimming background and was a most personable girl.

St. Nicholas magazine, the popular teenage publication, had a large camp department headed by an editor and author of real stature. I guess we impressed each other and I gave him a contract for space that was second only to that of the already long-established Teelawooket. He went to work promptly and effectively for Moss Lake.

Of equal importance was his knowledge that Teelawooket enrollment success seemed to be due primarily to a fine stable of horses. I was keen on riding and as it was an area in which my father was most knowledgeable, I felt sure we could match them there and surpass them in location, equipment, and table.

The week after the first advertisement appeared I had my initial enrollment, even though as yet we had no booklet. The reason our booklet was so late was that I did not approve Miss Wayman's draft and she decided future disagreements would be too serious and withdrew. Much to my disappointment, Miss Hauser went with her and I was back at Square One.

Fortune left me hanging for only a couple of days. Helen Frost, head of Columbia University's Teachers College athletic department and for some years the director of their summer training camp whom I had contacted before meeting Miss Wayman, called to say that her plans had changed and she would be interested if the post was still open. She also wished to bring an assistant, Hazel Cubberly, with head counselor experience. Thus the lost ground was recaptured in the same week I had let it sink under my feet.

We worked out a program together, but I said nothing about staff or enrollments and we had almost no contact until she reached Moss Lake and started running the camp.

There could have been no more capable, personable, or understanding director. The atmosphere she established continued through the years, except that as the camp increased in size the approach became more formal, and in a few years we had set standards that I still feel were higher than those of any other camp or school in the country.

Despite the fact that I looked even younger than my twenty-three years and often

George H. Longstaff
1923

Moss Lake campers, 1923

Moss Lake "Ark" 1926

Moss Lake Camp Group, 1926

asked my mother to accompany me on interviews, enrollment went well and we opened with twenty-two girls.

My years at The Mohawk had left me much more competent in food and maintenance than the usual camp director, and our table in 1923 was that of a resort hotel, with steaks and chops frequently appearing on the breakfast menu. For the first five or ten years we used linen napkins and tablecloths, and even when we switched to padded oilcloth damask for table covering we continued the linen napkins for another decade.

A colorful old guide came with the place and with Miss Frost's experience we gave the girls a year that brought nineteen of the twenty-two back in 1924, and the three girls lost were all over-age.

Before Christmas Helen Frost told me she was marrying and moving to Australia.

That news was a severe blow but the camp had gained good momentum and 1923 had done much for my professional education even though I had left its direction to Miss Frost. Also I had hit upon an approach that made high staff quality almost automatic. At that time salaries in the private schools were extremely low and a summer salary of two or three hundred dollars looked very attractive to most teachers. My first year one of the counsellors was a teacher I had known for years, another taught in my sister's school, Drew Seminary in Carmel, N.Y., one in Miss Porters at Farmington, Conn., one in the Barnard School in New York City, and one at St. Agnes in Albany. Each was the head of the physical education department.

The one from Miss Porter's School was a small, but extremely polished and comely thirty-five, and I made her head counsellor.

The teacher from St. Agnes brought a friend, Edith Potter of the Berkeley Institute, whose contributions in personality and goodwill were to set standards that later staff members sometimes approached but never equaled. In 1927 twenty-five of our girls were from her school.

The teacher from Barnard, Felicia Townsend, was British, took a camp horse home for the winter and bought another that I purchased from her in the spring. It was a beautiful chestnut mare of about fourteen hands named "Goldie," and was a camp favorite for the next twenty-two years. Miss Townsend soon started working with the Oxbridge Hunt Club in Darien and went on to become one of the best known instructors in the East.

Except that I was an active director, 1924 was basically a replay of '23. We started with two extra bungalows and added a third in mid-season. To this point all my building had been done by my own men, but this last bungalow was needed for August 1st and on July 15th we did not even have the ground cleared. Three local carpenters, Alfred Nelson, John Petersen, his brother, Fred, and a particularly hardworking lumberjack, Jack Hill, who also was a good rough carpenter worked as a team. They finished the stone foundation pillars and completed the carpenter work in time for Bert Youmans, our competent Eagle Bay plumber, to have the bathroom installed by the thirty-first. We had only tar paper on the roof and did not shingle either that or the sides until fall, but inside it was complete and comfortable.

At the end of the 1924 summer I had the best physical workout of my life. Riding was emerging as the camp's major sport and since our access road from Eagle Bay to Big Moose was being paved I decided that we must put a bridle path around the lake. It was three miles of rough going and I needed real lumberjacks for the job. One had been with us through the summer and volunteered that he had three friends whom he thought would be interested. I let him go down to Utica to make the contact, and he came back with three of the finest workmen ever to be on my payroll. All were Swedish—Albert Benson, Charles Ostlund, and Oscar Berg. I doubt if I could pick three equally fine workmen if I had before me a list of the hundreds who have since been on my payroll.

I had a good teamster and a light but wood-wise team, and we started immediately. They swamped, cut the timber, blasted the stumps and boulders, and built the bridges. Amos, my teamster, and I plowed with a rugged iron-beam plow and graded with a scoop shovel. This was my daily routine until two days before Christmas, and by that time I had reached my physical peak.

My "Miracle Three" returned in the spring and had the path ready for use by the time the girls arrived, of course without my help for I was busy with my 1925 building program. These three Swedes did much to make all that I did in later years possible and one, Albert Benson, was not merely the most important man in my entire crew, but there was no spring in which I would not have preferred replacing all my other workmen to going through the summer without Albert. If I could start my business life over again with two dozen of my second-best workmen or with Albert, I would not hesitate. Both sentiment and self-interest would mandate my choosing Albert.

January 2, 1925 was the date set for the launching of my dental career, so January 1 became a day of critical evaluation. I was greatly pleased with 1923 and 1924 at Moss Lake, but the outstanding feature of the appraisal was that even the best of physical education teachers rarely were specialists in any one field, and to take advantage of the opportunity afforded by camp to give the girls a technically accurate social-athletic education, I would need to get people who were at, or near, the top of their respective fields.

It appeared that riding and swimming were going to be our most important and most popular activities, but I knew little of either so consulted my close friend, Philip Farley, who had been the intercollegiate fencing champion and was active in the New York Athletic Club. Also, he had riding experience that I lacked. Without hesitation he recommended John Zimnoch as surely the finest young swimming coach in the country, and said that while perhaps too elderly for camp, Baretto de Sousa was generally recognized as the country's riding authority—not in jumping, but in dressage and children's horsemanship.

It was obvious that my camp career would be greatly advantaged by my developing real proficiency in our major sports, so I arranged to take two days a week from my dental practice and have lessons with John Zimnoch, at his Brooklyn pool, and with Baretto de Sousa at Durland's Riding Academy in New York near Central Park. Both were fine technicians and good salesmen of their sports, and I felt sure I had been correct in selecting riding and swimming for greatest emphasis.

I gained considerable skill from my work with de Sousa. However, I took a minimum of natural talent to the pool and it was fortunate that Eleanor Holm was having lessons at the same time, for I soon realized that her progress would be a much better measure of the Zimnoch teaching ability. She was a near beginner, but an eleven-year-old with a world of talent, and seeing it developed under John's tutelage made me determined to take him to camp. Fortunately, neither he nor de Sousa had special plans for the coming summer and agreed to spend it at Moss Lake.

What these men accomplished that year was so far above our achievements under my physical education teachers during the first two years that I was completely confirmed in my opinion that this was the route Moss Lake must travel. De Sousa stayed with us as long as his health permitted, and Zimnoch spent fifty summers at Moss Lake.

Of almost equal long range significance was the engagement of J. Martinez Castello, the country's recognized authority on fencing. He was a N.Y.A.C. coach and owner of the country's largest fencing supply business—as well as the author of a fencing textbook. However, I was even more impressed through the years by his on-going accomplishments at New York University. As it enrolls few boys from private schools, he had to build his teams from raw material. Although he could allot only two days per week to his coaching, in his twelve years there his teams won the inter-collegiates ten times.

This is a sport that can be either fine or of no interest according to the skill and personality of the instructor. "Papa" Castello had both in most generous measure, and it would be impossible for me to do full credit to his contributions to Moss Lake.

In 1925 we put up a recreation hall and two additional bungalows on the east shore of the lake near the one built there in 1924, and these buildings functioned as a senior camp. There was no dining hall at this location—a half mile from the original camp— and Frank Koster, our very elderly guide and carpenter, built a 24-foot scow with an eight foot beam, complete with seats and canopy in less than two weeks. We equipped it with outboard motors. It was christened the "Ark" and it took the girls back and forth to meals throughout the summer.

In 1926 we built a dining hall and headquarters at Senior Camp—one that included a master suite for the director. Until this time I had been commuting from The Mohawk. The "Ark" had served its purpose and was retired. This year also saw ballet emerge as an important activity. The instructor to give it this stature was Helmy Smirnova, a former member of the Russian Imperial Ballet then teaching in Syracuse.

1927 was a year of universal prosperity and I think Moss Lake could have enrolled two hundred girls with ease, but I decided to settle for an increment of but one cabin of ten girls in the original camp and the start of a third unit giving us a capacity of a hundred and twenty for that summer.

This new building was dining room, craft shop, living room, and bedrooms for twenty-four. It was a substantial house that would have done credit to any residential suburb. I later put up some larger buildings, but this remained the finest. With three camps we had to change our nomenclature—the new one became "Junior Camp," the original unit "Senior Camp," and the old "Senior Camp" became "Lodge."

During the year when we fed the first two camps in one dining room, and in a later year when the oldest camp and the newest one were served by a single kitchen, we took advantage of a local split in time. The Hamilton County line was about a mile from our Herkimer County property. Hamilton County was on standard time—Herkimer, on daylight. Using both times a kitchen could have two 8:00 AM breakfasts, two 12:30 lunches, and two 6:00 PM dinners. This use of time continued throughout the life of the camp and made it possible for our specialists to have two extra hours a day without using any hours that were inconvenient for the campers or the camp schedule.

In 1928 I was convinced that Moss Lake stood in first place among the country's camps and my confidence was unlimited. Our sales campaign went into low gear, but enrollment continued to be more than adequate. Our only new building was a cabin at Lodge and an extra stable.

In 1929 we built another cabin in "Senior" and in 1930 a dormitory for twenty-four more girls in "Junior" and still turned away some desirable youngsters in spite of the depression. At about this time I made tennis a major camp sport by engaging the Davis Cup player, Wallace Johnson, and established strong minors in sailing and archery by adding Harold DeGroat and the nationally known Andrew Brush to our staff of specialists.

This left me confident we had great strength in all departments that should be fitted into a camp schedule, but when the war ended water-skiing became too popular to be ignored. Fortune smiled again and I was able to secure the first giant in this sport,

Bruce Parker, to introduce it at Moss Lake. He was succeeded by Henry Suydam and it ranked as one of the girls' favorite activities until the camp closed.

In 1930 the new Inlet Electric company was taken over by a larger utility. It promptly ran lines from Eagle Bay to Big Moose and as the lines ran through the Moss Lake property they offered me a most attractive contract—large transformers at each camp, no installation charge, and rates so low we could never exceed our $1000 minimum. I believe the base rate was 1¢ per KWH.

We had been cutting our own ice for refrigeration and cooking on large wood burning ranges. After 1925 Albert, and Amos, our teamster, and usually one additional man stayed at camp all winter. There normally were three or four months when they could do little but shovel roofs, put up the ice, and cut and split the wood. Yet since we used over a hundred cords for the camp, delivered some to The Mohawk, and also filled their very large icehouse, it was a busy time of the year.

Men today would be appalled at such an assignment but ice and firewood paid the winter expenses of most natives and both they and the lumberjacks considered it a normal way of life. They usually cut their wood and filled the icehouses in groups of two or three, but the area had two ice jobs that employed many men and used considerable machinery. Both were run by the New York Central which stored enough ice to carry it through the summer. They had gasoline ice saws, machinery to scrape the ice in preparation for the cut, and jackworks to take the ice from the lakes (Raquette and Old Forge) to the cars. Accordingly the coming of electricity had a much greater impact on the residents than upon the vacationists. At Moss Lake we had no jackworks and used an ice plow and needle bar instead of a power saw—supplemented by a hand saw.

Electricity reduced our wood requirements to about forty cords but the transition was expensive as we had to install two walk-in-coolers and a six-door commercial refrigerator, three heavy-duty electric ranges, and a few water heaters; but on balance it was an excellent investment.

In 1931 national gloom did instill some caution and we added no buildings, except an extra stable and some new workmen's quarters. Activities were well grooved and labor rates in the area had been falling sharply, from fifty dollars to sixty dollars a month to an average of fifteen to twenty dollars for waitresses, grooms, and sundry miscellaneous employees. All costs were down and it would be many years before I would achieve as fine a net profit. All of this left me convinced that depressions were for other people, and I went ahead with plans for a large indoor playground—one big enough that the main floor could either be set up for two basketball courts and one badminton court, or as an alternate could serve as a full-size tennis court. In addition there was an archery gallery, a fencing gallery, and a ping-pong area, as well as a large stage, dressing rooms, and a craft shop—the perfect answer to rainy days for all three groups.

We completed that building in time for the 1932 season, but the depression caught up with us and it seemed for a time there might be no 1932 season. Normally our enrollment was completed by June 1st, but in '32 we had less than a dozen on that date and even on the opening day the total was seventy-two rather than the anticipated one hundred and sixty. Nevertheless, it proved to be one of my most rewarding years.

Moss Lake was in my mother's name and she had signed the notes for each year's building. Fortunately, I had reduced the total of those notes by many thousands in '31. However, the Herkimer bankers were worried about their own solvency and when they saw my start-of-the-season deposits were half their normal size, they arranged for a group of the directors and officers to confer with me at camp.

"The Lodge" from the north, 1926

The Lodge from the Lake 1926 built with stone from the property

View from the terrace at Lodge

The beach at Lodge

The Lodge lobby and dining room

Two typical cabins

Junior Headquarters

Lower junior dormitory and playground

Afternoon snacks on Junior porch

Junior Assembly Room

Junior Dining Room

Medical Staff

Junior Infirmary

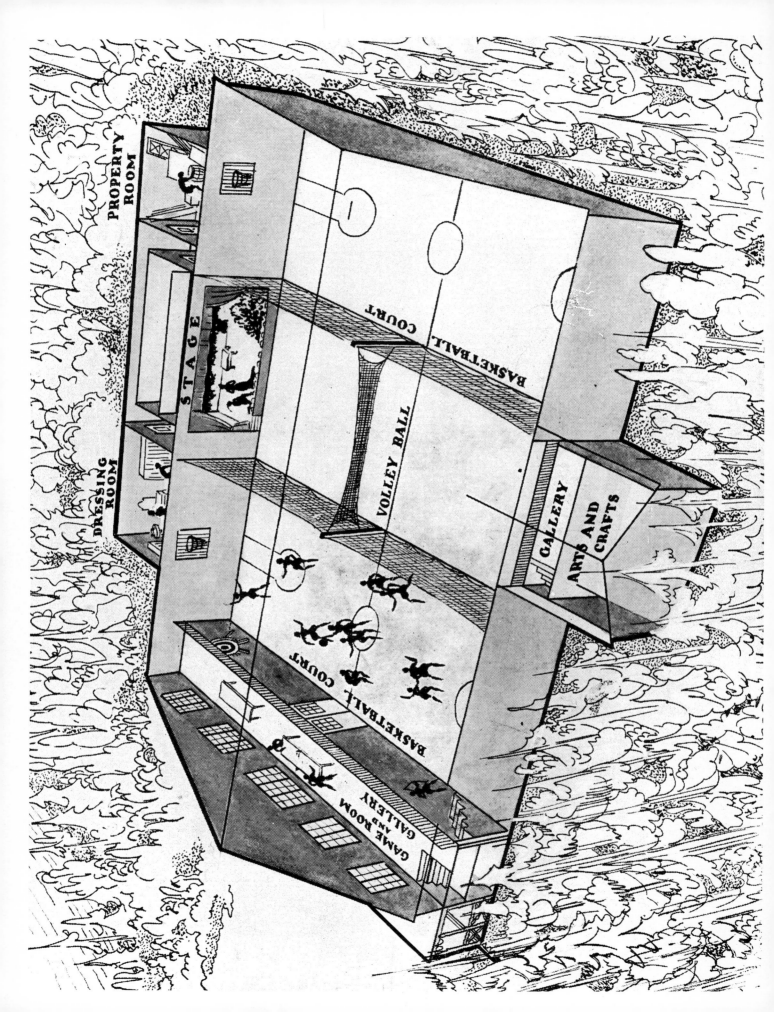

"Madison Square" built in 1932

Inside "Madison Square"

← *Moss Lake solution for rainy days*

Where Lodge Council fires burned

Senior Camp Council Room

← *The Island from Senior*

1927 Staff

The Crew

When paddling your own canoe was more than a phrase

A campfire sing

The 1924 Bridle Path bridge

*The shortest standard gauge railroad
in the country—Marion River Carry*

Felix and friends

A Wilderness trip

Winter house party
at Moss Lake

To make matters worse, local bill paying procedures, while most convenient, seriously compounded my situation. The suppliers expected to be paid but once a year by the hotels. This was usually in late August, but as my money came in by June, I checked it out to them at once, and by being two months ahead of the others I became quite the fair-haired boy.

Fortunately, the bank trustees made their date some days in advance and I had time to discuss long range adjustments. My biggest running expense was my specialists' payroll, so I called them together, explained the situation, and asked if they would be willing to have their future salaries pro-rated on the basis of each year's gross. In the three previous summers it had been about sixty-five thousand, and I asked that they sign 1933 contracts with a ratio clause providing that their pay be adjusted to the ratio which that year's income bore to fifty thousand. This was not planned just for 1933, but was to run through an unlimited number of years so they would gain by the arrangement if and when the business returned to normal. They agreed with no hesitancy and loyalty bonds and my feeling of good fortune swelled with happy overtones.

My next step was to call a meeting of my trade creditors, tell them I would pay my 1932 bills in full, but ask that I be allowed to give each a series of ten-year notes for 1931. They were less than enthusiastic, but all agreed, and I was ready for my directors. They were properly impressed and left with congratulations for the goodwill I had apparently engendered.

It was three years before I built the gross back to the fifty thousand level and then some of the specialists asked that the pro-rata clause be eliminated from future contracts. I, of course, told them I would be agreeable but warned that they quite probably would regret their decision before too long. By 1943 the gross had gone well over one hundred thousand dollars and those who allowed their adjustment clauses to remain reaped a generous reward.

By this time we had taken tremendous strides in a wide range of activities and I was using a sub-title of "The Camp of the Specialists" as an alternate to the original "The Camp in the Wilderness."

Mr. Zimnoch was with the camp for fifty years—Mr. Castello, Colonel Selihoff, and Mr. DeGroat for twenty- twenty-five years—Colonel Shiskin for thirty-five. Two tennis men, Wallace Johnson and Paul Harding, had seven years while four others averaged at least five. On the distaff side, our first dancing specialist, Helmy Smirnova, was with us for about fifteen years and our last, Anneliese von Oettingen, for nearly thirty. Both had war-related histories that almost matched those of my many Russian officers. Personal sketches of these and other important staff members will appear in a later chapter.

The specialists as a group not merely enhanced the value of the camp experience for our girls, but made the operation of the camp a much simpler one. To reap maximum benefits from their presence on staff we had to become a quite formal camp with a fixed number of hours in each activity scheduled for every girl each week. Once this was done the fact that each department was in the hands of a man or woman of unquestioned national stature relieved me of what for most directors had to be a constant concern—the development of camper skills. Thus it left the counsellors and me free to devote most of our attention to personality development and the mechanical operation of the camp. In my case this included the direction of a rather large service crew and the three dining rooms.

Riding was the sport in which Moss Lake accomplishments were easiest to calibrate. In the pre-WW II years we had National Horse shows at Lake Placid and Lake George in which our girls consistently collected a very generous share of the ribbons. However, the best public demonstration of our girls' excellence was provided by the national Good Hands Class. In the twelve years it was sponsored by the Society for the Prevention of Cruelty to Animals, our girls, or winter pupils of our instructors, won the National Blue ribbon ten times. In fact one girl, Edith Anderson, won three years in a row and caused them to change their rules so that a rider securing the national title would no longer be eligible for the competition in future years. Another year a Moss Lake girl won both the national Maclay and the Good Hands. To the best of my knowledge this has been done only twice—the other time by the, later-to-be-internationally known, William Steinkraus. After the war broke out both Lake Placid and Lake George shows were discontinued but we were able to obtain national recognition for our local Darts Lake show. Unfortunately, the competition for our girls was nominal, but it did allow a number to qualify for the Maclay and for the National Horse Show's substitute for the old S.P.C.A. Good Hands. John Zimnoch's swimming quite surely made the greatest contribution to the development of our girls, but history gave us only one day of competitive brilliance.

The consistently high calliber of their swimming made attempts to arrange inter-camp competition depressing, but one year some of our girls learned that the New York State Women's competition was to be held at Lake George and asked "Uncle John" if he would put together and enter a team. He relayed that request to me and, as the event was only a few days away, I judged there would be no overemphasis and approved. He trained our four best free style swimmers as a relay team but did little else except to select a few extra competitors, chiefly for the under-twelve classes. The children's events were held in the morning and at noon he called me to say his girls had been winning so easily that he was afraid they would suffer from undesirable cranial enlargement and asked if he might enter some in the afternoon Women's events. I approved his putting in the relay team and entering three girls in the free style.

That year the New York Women's Swimming Association had the finest relay team in the country, but was not planning to compete at Lake George. This left the Troy Women's Swimming Association as the favorite for they were generally recognized as the second best. To everyone's surprise our girls touched them out, and took second and third places in the free style. John was most elated, however, his elation quickly changed to irritation when the committee announced that the country's two top backstroke amateurs, the Krempa sisters, were there and obviously too fast for the competition. They were going to withdraw from the backstroke event and merely swim an exhibition. This annoyed John because he knew that they had achieved their top national rating only because his pupil, Eleanor Holm, had been disbarred from the Olympics for some questionable irregularity. His reaction was to enter a thirteen-year old girl whose backstroke had been developing very rapidly during the previous month. She not merely took first place, but made better time than the Krempa sisters and validated both his high regard for Eleanor Holm and his faith in his teaching ability.

At about the same time Andrew Brush, our well-known archery coach, took a team of four girls to the New York State Tournament held for four summers in mid-July at Letchworth Park. Each year one of our campers won either the Girls or Intermediate Championship. In one or two years we had both. None of our girls shot at home and in this tournament they had to compete with girls for whom archery was a year-round project—surely fine evidence of what truly expert instruction can accomplish.

Later evidence of this potential came when my elder daughter, Sue Carol, with only camp water skiing behind her won the Eastern States Championship in New Hampshire.

The knowledge of this efficacy kept me dedicated to the philosophy formulated in the twenties. It was reinforced by the consistency with which my second generation campers outperformed the first generation group through the fourth and fifth decades of the camp existence—both as athletes and as citizens. Recently I have been deriving equal satisfaction from alumnae letters written in response to reunion invitations. Girl after girl has volunteered that their camp-acquired skills have affected their lives in a most pleasant fashion. Many in their sixties and seventies still are swimming, riding, and playing tennis. Of course, their letters have left me more confident than ever that I have made a much greater contribution to the development of our country's youth than I would have been able to as an orthodontist.

OUR CAMP PHILOSOPHY

We feel that a summer at Moss Lake must be a real investment in future as well as current happiness. Our lives allow varying amounts of leisure, but its utilization cannot wisely be left to chance, and we earnestly believe that from four to six years in a proper camp represent the most valuable form of "middle-age insurance." We further hold that preparation for middle age, while it receives much less attention than provision for old age, is no less important. It is granted to a larger number and during it one is more acutely happy or unhappy than in later years.

Our basic conviction is the trite one that whatever is worth doing is worth doing well. It is the creed of each of our specialists, is faithfully reflected in the attitude of their assistants, quickly imbues each group of campers, and does much to make every Moss Lake summer one of thoroughly worthwhile accomplishment.

OUR HONOR GIRL CREED

An Honor Girl is in every sense a model camper. She enters wholeheartedly into all activities and is conspicuous for her fine spirit and attitude. In everything which she undertakes she is outstanding because of her effort and earnestness. She includes everyone in her circle of friends and is at all times congenial with all with whom she has contact. She is always a good sport, a graceful winner and a cheerful loser. Her personality is one which permeates the entire group and serves as a model, aiding more passive personalities to develop individually. She is not the center of her own world, but rather often disregards her personal wishes in an effort to make others happy. She accepts things as they come without criticism and tries by her own example to encourage optimism and cheerfulness. She is thoughtful and constantly on the alert for ways in which she may be helpful to others. Her attitude toward the counsellor staff is one of obedience and respect. She is ever willing to do her utmost for her team and her enthusiasm and spirit send forth an enlivening spark that kindles the flame of friendship and good will among her companions.

Evelyn MacDonald
1929

Evelyn was one of three Honor recipients that year whom I asked to reduce to paper our Honor Girl standards as they conceived them. My intention was to use the resulting material to help me phrase an official Honor Code but when I read this version I decided that any changes would yield a less perfect result.

CHAPTER III

Goals and Organization

The feature which did most to distinguish Moss Lake from other camps was our effort to provide technically accurate instruction for each girl in the activities we felt would add most to her future as well as to her current happiness. We accordingly devoted most of our time to activities that could be continued in adult life, rather than to the group athletics stressed throughout the school year, and established a staff of nationally known experts for their direction. Each was a man whose life work was the specialty he coached at Moss Lake, and each had a background of many hundreds of previous pupils. The average Moss Lake service record for these men exceeded fourteen years, and their presence in camp was assurance of an excellence of technique that remained uniform from season to season—a uniformity difficult to maintain in any other way.

To implement these goals and to encourage and monitor individual development, we decided that three completely separate age units would be quite essential—"Junior Camp," "Senior Camp," and "Lodge." Each occupied a separate location on the lake and was physically independent of the others. Each had its own dining room, recreation hall, infirmary, tennis courts, counsellor staff, and waterfront. The large rainy day building was used by all, and while we had three stables and three riding rings, they were centrally located and the division was—Beginners, Jumpers, and Advanced Equitation pupils. In the late fifties we also set up an outside course some distance from the main complex.

Equally essential was a quite highly structured schedule. All families were acquainted with this feature before their enrollments were accepted so that they might plan on a less structured camp if they were not interested in this broad development. As a result, few of our girls were lazy or unmotivated.

In Lodge and Senior Camp a weekly schedule would call for twelve hours of swimming (11 AM and 5 PM), six hours of tennis, six hours of riding (plus road rides), three hours each of archery, fencing, dancing and "Arts and Crafts." Also, one hour a day was set aside for "canoeing or sailing" with the wind conditions of the hour usually the determining factor.

In Lodge riflery replaced crafts and a girl might adjust one hour per day of her schedule by dropping a sport in which she was competent, or one which she and the staff agreed would not be important to her, to put the extra time on one with especial appeal.

In Junior camp an "Idle Hour" was inserted in the middle of the afternoon. This reduced the number of activity hours scheduled from seven to six. To accomplish this, Junior camp had no fencing and tennis was reduced from six hours to three.

In the early fifties crafts and riflery were dropped from our schedule to make room for water skiing.

John Zimnoch had 10:30 and 4:15 swims at Senior camp, 11:30 and 5:15 at Lodge, and Junior camp was on standard instead of daylight so used 11:30 and 5:15 for its swims. This staggering meant the Juniors could have the horses and the rings to themselves after the older camps had finished their morning and afternoon sessions. Also, it made scheduling six hours of instruction possible for all instructors, except the fencing coach. In practice this meant that except for canoeing and sailing, and tennis on alternate days in Senior and Lodge, the department heads could teach all classes. Thus each girl was given maximal exposure to the instruction of the experts and to their enthusiasm for their activities. Incidentally, this enthusiasm was an always-present factor in the success of our specialists—in their own development and in their camp instruction.

For the schedules to operate effectively the timing of the bells in the three camps had to be accurately coordinated, so this was done mechanically.

Through all the years there were two important differences between our Moss Lake and other camps. First, all activities were open to all girls in equal measure—except that basic swimming requirements might temporarily curtail some waterfront activities—a hurdle that soon disappeared under Zimnoch tutelage.

Second, our "No extras" policy had no exceptions. Riding, trips, the attention of camp nurses and physicians, and of tutors were all covered by the basic tuition. This was a major convenience for parents, but in my mind its most important advantage was the complete social equality it engendered. We had families who found meeting the Moss Lake fees difficult and others who could have taken them in stride were they many times as large, but with this approach there were no distinctions.

When first built, the physical plant was unique and even in the last days of the camp I considered it to be far ahead of the competitors that came to my attention. The picturesque private lake was a matter of good fortune and the substantial bungalows with their two- and three-girl rooms and generous bathrooms also fell into the fortuitous category. Although I was both enthusiastic and optimistic about my camp project I realized that I knew little of the new business and decided that my best safeguard would be to put up cabins that would lend themselves to easy conversion into hotel cottages. This also was one of the three factors that caused me to choose a girls' camp rather than one for boys. I was sure such cabins would be more appreciated by the girls and confident they would provoke no unfavorable comments as female accommodations. The other two factors were that my 1922 discussions with the New Jersey physical education teacher (almost my only source of information since I had never even seen a camp) had been confined to a girls' operation and that having a younger sister I was sure of at least one camper.

The substantial cabins drew so many favorable comments the first year that I let them set the pattern for future buildings. In fact, the general appreciation of our unusual structures caused me to favor even more substantial ones as I developed the other two camps. The recreation hall prepared for the first year was a model for the one at Lodge, while the main buildings at both Lodge and Junior were designed to be larger and more impressive than the one with which we started the first unit. "Madison Square," our rainy-day building, went far beyond anything of the kind ever conceived for camp use and proved to be the perfect answer for nearly all bad weather problems.

The bungalow pattern set in the early years was an excellent one but financial considerations might have profitably made the largest one a uniform choice. There was a recessed porch on one side, an open porch on the other, a three-girl room on each corner, and three two-girl rooms in the central portion, one of which was used for counsellors. There were two separate toilet and lavatory combinations, plus a shower room with a couple of extra lavatories. The size was 26 feet x 50 feet. When it was built in 1925, staff efficiency was less important and no others were quite so large as "Wa-Wa." It faced the lake to the south and tennis courts to the north. This was the reason for the two porches. Had the recessed porch been omitted there would have been room for an eighth bedroom.

Each cabin had two counsellors who took alternate night duty and retired with the girls. Off-duty counsellors were free until eleven but not allowed to leave campus during the week. There were two counsellor houses with fireplaces for their use. Each "shift" of counsellors was free to leave camp on four Sundays and on the Monday evenings of the alternate weeks. We supplied them with camp cars and the usual pattern was for Sundays to be used for sightseeing, Mondays for local shopping and snacking. This was a less liberal policy than that followed in many camps (the spread between the most liberal and the strictest was very wide) but ensured against our finding we had counsellors with little interest in younger girls and expecting the summer to develop into a paid vacation—a quite common experience in the more liberal camps.

For many years I engaged only teachers as counsellors but later accepted college girls scheduled to be Juniors or Seniors the following year and former campers with impressive records one or two years earlier. The two-year variance was approved only for former Honor Girls and, as you can tell from the Creed, these standards were very high.

As must be apparent from the text pages our running expenses and investment were much greater than elsewhere, but as the tuition figure was always literally all-inclusive the difference usually was less than first appeared. In 1923 the tuition was $350 and did not exceed $1000 until the late sixties.

Within a few days after her arrival at camp each girl was evaluated by a committee of her peers and assigned either to the "Blue Team" or the "Gray Team." These teams and their officers were a vital part of the life of the camp and once a girl became a member of a team that was her loyalty through all her camping years. All athletic events were on a team basis and although most competition was individual, the system worked smoothly. The individual earned points and those became team points that determined the winner of the meet and in the aggregate the winner of the much prized "Team Cup" at the end of the year.

The fact that our formal instruction was left so completely in the competent hands of our specialists freed director and head counsellors to concentrate on the camp's other main objective—the development of personality and character. This started with the selection of counsellors. Most of them needed to be competent to assist on the waterfront, and tennis ability was mandatory for a few, but in general they could be selected on the basis of their moral values, refinement, and dedication. This so they could be both examples and mentors in these important areas.

Camp expectations were high and to realize them counsellor meetings were scheduled each day for the portion of the staff not on rest-hour duty. Normally the head counsellor presided but since the hours were fixed I could attend as occasion arose—always frequently enough to keep my mental pictures of the individual girls up-to-date.

At the end of each month we scheduled a series of meetings in each camp with all counsellors attending. This was made possible by having the off-duty counsellors from one camp cover the bungalows of another through the evenings in question. As a preliminary for these meetings we asked the specialists to prepare written reports on each girl and from a discussion of these reports we moved to a resume of their individual characteristics and behavior. Frequently much time went into exploring the many facets considered in making our Honor Girl awards. They were highly prized by the girls and their families and as they constituted almost unqualified approval, we guarded our standards jealously.

Detailed reports were sent to all families with accuracy rather than diplomacy as the chief criterion. I always considered this opportunity for parents to view their children through the collective eyes of the adults in contact with them and their peers on a twenty-four hour basis to be invaluable—and a service to which they were entitled.

Most were properly appreciative but occasionally one would be disappointed to the point of resentment. As these usually were our neediest cases, I could not countenance the reports being less than frank. A by-product of the system was that it focused the attention of the counsellors on the importance of their counselling and the uniform enforcement of regulations.

In a typical year our riding staff consisted of four men, two young women as assistants, four grooms and a blacksmith. There were three riding rings, each with its own barn, partially for convenience and partially to minimize the fire hazard. Each had its own string of horses selected to fit the lessons to be given there. Most were "aged" but of high quality. In fact, I seldom bought any horse under eight, and many started with us at twelve to fourteen. There were two reasons for this. The most important was that such horses had their educations and personalities well established, making them easier to evaluate and less likely to be spoiled by the large number of riders to which we would expose them. The other reason was that I could get two twelve-year-olds at the cost of a single six-year-old of similar calibre. This fact enabled us to acquire many with good show backgrounds as well as equable dispositions. They were far safer for my girls and much better assistant "tutors."

In the late thirties a tendency developed throughout the East for Junior Riders to concentrate on jumping. We approved of this, but only so far as the interest could be developed without depriving the girls of a sound grounding in the principles of equitation, sensitive hands, and real familiarity with the "saddle" or "park" seat. We deplored the widespread impression that, instead of being supplementary fields, work in one retarded progress in the other. Our position here was strenghtened when one of our girls won the national "Good Hands" and Maclay jumping awards in the same year.

An integral part of my thinking was that the short stirrup, which came in with the "Forward" and "Italian" seats, was much less secure than the longer stirrup, which we used for our general riding in camp, and I stipulated that when a girl switched to jumping, her stirrups should be shortened but one hole. For a long time it was a minority position but during this period a competing riding camp in New England closed its doors and I was given its mailing list. As I interviewed these families, I learned that theirs had been forward-seat riding and was appalled at the number of fractures that had occurred during the past season. I think the number was five with a stable half the size of ours. The Moss Lake record was less than one for each decade of its operation.

If I had had any doubts as to the wisdom of my stipulation this surely would have dispelled them, but the best was yet to come. Gordon Wright had been the best-known of the country's ardent advocates of the forward seat, and the first intimation I had that he had changed his outlook came when he was appointed coach of our International Team and I noted that they were quite erect between jumps and that their stirrups were much longer than the forward seat norm. After a successful season he wrote a book to which each member of the team added a chapter. It outlined an approach to jumping that seemed no longer to conflict with our Moss Lake teaching, and I was especially delighted when I found that it contained a flat statement that longer stirrups yielded a more secure seat. In fact, I think the wording was "the longer the stirrup the more secure the seat." You can imagine how grateful I was that my instructors had been willing to accept my taboo of the short stirrup and of a pronounced forward position for our jumping. We still had our fracture record of less than one per decade with a stable of approximately forty horses.

Since after the first few years of camp we offered both equitation and jumping, clear guidelines for balancing our assignments were important. Of course, equitation always came first and no girl was allowed to jump until she was competent in this area. If a girl had no desire to jump she could spend all of her riding time in these rings. If she wished to jump she had to satisfy her instructor that she was ready and then she had to ride for me—not because I considered myself a better judge but because I knew I was sufficiently hard-hearted to say no to the most ardent aspirant if I felt she was not ready and because as the years went on I felt this extra hurdle was partially responsible for our enviable accident record. The next step was securing parental permission. Once a girl's jumping was approved we balanced the division of her time carefully. An important guideline was whether it seemed likely her later years would be spent in hunting country or in one affording bridle paths, but lacking the open fields owned by interested and cooperative farmers essential to the establishment of a hunt.

Our judgments also took into consideration the factor that the passage of years makes jumping unduly hazardous for the occasional rider, even though she be competent enough to profit generously, both in terms of health and pleasure, from her hours in the saddle.

With this appraisal of the sport, we deemed it wise to offer adequate instruction and practice in both fields. To achieve this we divided our department into four sections, each with its own mounts and instructor. Beginners started in an elementary ring, where all horses were safe and predictable to the nth equinine degree. From here the girls progressed to the advanced equitation ring, where nearly all the mounts were registered saddlebreds and where many were spirited enough to require real skill from their riders. When the instructor in this ring felt a camper was sufficiently secure in her saddle, she might, with parental permission, elect to spend most of her time in the jumping ring, where the horses were thoroughbreds and part-thoroughbreds. Later when he was satisfied with her accomplishments in his department, she might even devote all of her riding time to jumping. The fourth instructor and the fourth string of horses supplied trail rides for the pupils of all three rings. The accompanying reprint records a time sector of the department's success story.

Another point on which I took issue with the usual camp was the matter of allowing girls to function in the stables. A girl who has, or anticipates having, a horse of her own should know how to take care of it and many organizations elaborated this into programs that had their riders grooming and tacking which left the stable hands with only feeding and the cleaning of the stalls—thus sharply reducing their number and the stable payroll. Two accidents served to confirm my outlook. A friend had a camp in New England with almost as many horses as my own. Before the war his ideas were rather similar to mine and his grooms did most of the work, but when the war came he let his campers take over. I was perturbed but said nothing for I was painfully aware of the manpower dearth. At its end I urged him to return to his pre-war program but he said that his current arrangements were working so smoothly that he intended to retain them. A few weeks later one of his daughters was kicked in the face. Her jaw was broken, some teeth were lost, and considerable plastic surgery was required. Of course, I was happy I had not relaxed our "no girls in the stables" rule.

Some months later Colonel Guenichta and several of our horses spent the winter with a girls' school in Salisbury, Md. The school's procedure was to pair the girls who intended to ride and give each pair a horse for the school year. They shared it as a mount and took care of it as a pet. I always felt subjecting a horse to handling by varying and thus strange amateurs was the big danger in the common approach and judged this to be a reasonable compromise between the minimal risk of a girl's steadily taking care of her own and the group attention procedure, but I soon learned that even this approach could be dangerous.

Colonel Guenichta had selected horses with particularly good stable manners and

HORSEMANSHIP AT LAKE PLACID AND SAGAMORE SHOWS

THE A.S.P.C.A. Good Hands Classes at both the Sagamore and Lake Placid shows were swept by young riders from Moss Lake Camp. There was plenty of outside competition, yet the ribbons all went to youngsters with little show ring experience.

A.S.P.C.A. GOOD HANDS CLASSES

Sagamore		Lake Placid
Miss J. Bausher	Blue	Miss M. McKissick
Miss J. McNulty	Red	Miss E. Feigenspan
Miss M. McKissick	Yellow	Miss J. McNulty
Miss N. Douglas	White	

These young riders may have had other instruction, but the technique that produced this enviable performance comes from teaching methods which have changed little in the past seventeen summers. Riding fads have rocked the foundations of equitation, but Moss Lakers have sat firmly through the same system during all the upheavals. Wherever one of these well trained campers rides, from the National at Madison Square to local home-town shows, the ribbons are apt to go his or her way.

Baretto De Souza, dean of the country's horsemen, started Moss Lake girls on their championship stride in 1926, when he began his ten year reign over the camp's riding program. The camp has grown from a small group requiring one ring and a limited stable, to an organization offering two practice rings, a jumping circle, and about forty mounts.

Col. Alexis Selihoff, formerly instructor in the Russian Officers Cavalry School in St. Petersburg, and a member of the Russian Army Olympic team in 1912, heads the present Moss Lake riding staff. Since 1931 he has extended and emphasized the fundamentals laid down by De Souza. Col. Nicholas Shiskin, graduate of the Russian Cavalry School at Twer, and a commander of the Sixth Hussar Regiment, with Capt. Baldyreff and Capt. Von Bretzel complete the department.

The "good hands," which so uniformly took the judges' eyes at these two large Adirondack shows, comes from a school of riding which requires the extended leg in a fairly long stirrup, slightly inclined forward posture rather than a forward seat, reins held in both hands with the knuckles facing each other in a vertical position, hand flexions and legs controlling the horse.

The above article is reprinted from an early copy of "Rider and Driver.' It appears here because it so accurately captures the atmosphere of the department under Mr. de Souza and Colonel Selihoff and summarizes the traditions that have been carried on so capably by Mr. Carroll and our current staff.

Baretto de Souza with an early class

A warm day

Bridle path at Moss Lake

Trail rides are always popular

anticipated no trouble. One belonged to my elder daughter and was an especial pet, yet that was the one responsible for a comparable, but fortunately less serious, facial accident. Again I congratulated myself for maintaining my camp rule in spite of repeated requests that it be dropped.

As our riding program expanded, we wished to add variety to our road rides and here again our luck was fine. There was a foot trail from our lake to "Bubb's Lake" which the State allowed me to widen for horse travel. This served to lengthen the time required to circle the lake to a comfortable hour.

Much more importantly J. P. Morgan had constructed a fine wagon road from his Camp Uncas to the Big Moose Station which was abandoned a few years later when the Raquette Lake Railroad was built. From the station to the Cascade turn-off it followed the Eagle Bay-Big Moose Road, but took an independent route from that point to the most direct, still unpaved, and seldom used Eagle Bay-Raquette Lake road. Then the two roads merged for a mile and a half but became independent again with the abandoned Uncas Road running to Uncas via Eighth Lake. The supervising ranger, a Mr. Blue, very kindly went over the unused sections with me and recommended that I be allowed to open them. The permit included the privilege of cutting a trail that would parallel the Big Moose Road from Moss Lake to the Cascade junction. This became a second major project for Albert and his fine lumberjacks and it was accomplished in a few months.

Since it crossed the Cascade and the Eagle Bay-Raquette Lake roads, and the Seventh Lake-Eighth Lake carry enroute, it gave us a wonderful and varied twenty-five miles. When the Raquette Lake Railroad was abandoned, the Town of Webb acquired the property and converted it into a cinder bridle path from Eagle Bay to Carter—another ten miles. No camp could wish for a better or a more varied system of trails.

Swimming called for little special equipment. At each camp we built two cribs with turning boards twenty-five yards from each other, plus diving boards and low towers. Our gradually sloping beaches gave Mr. Zimnoch a safe and confidence-inspiring foundation, and except for a supply of kick-boards he never requested any additional equipment.

None of our tennis instructors seemed to have a real interest in auxiliary equipment, and were quite happy with the camp's seven tennis courts. Our one ball machine was used but sparingly.

Together sailing and canoeing constituted our fourth major sport and had the largest staff of the various departments. Mr. DeGroat was head of the sailing department and spread his time between the three camps, but as more than two were never scheduled to sail at the same time he needed only one fully competent assistant and drew on the canoeing staff for extras when that department was not in action. We had no sailing until about 1933 when we started Junior with two steel cats. Two years later we brought two Comets over from Cedar Isles when that camp switched to Snipes. A bit later the Comets went to Cascade and were replaced with four Snipes for Lodge. Senior was given four Turnabouts and we purchased four Prams for Junior. When Sailfish first appeared on the market we acquired six for Lodge and six for Senior.

In contrast with the above, canoeing got off to a flying start and we always had a goodly number of boats in each camp. By 1929 each had two war canoes, Junior a half dozen Old Town sponsons, Senior and Lodge eight Charles River models each and two or three of their fifty-pound trip canoes. After the war, Lodge and Senior had their totals doubled by the enthusiasm I developed for two of the Grumman aluminum models—the thirteen and seventeen footers. I still consider them to be the finest for multiple use.

We never found a canoeing instructor whose methods I completely approved so I kept this as my own department. Since I could not give a proper amount of time to it, I ran a June seminar each year to develop old campers, plus a few other counsellors, into instructors inculcated with my own ideas. A resume of these techniques will be found elsewhere in this book.

Both Lodge and Senior had archery ranges and Juniors traveled about three hundred yards to use the Senior range, which was always idle at the hours they were scheduled.

Dancing classes were held in Madison Square except when rainy days made it a too noisy place. This was not a problem for each camp had its own dance floor and piano to serve on such occasions.

Each camp also had a craft shop but these were idled, except for occasional rainy day use, when we introduced water skiing. The ski instructor lived on the island and kept his boats there.

The cottage on the island was a little gem even a century after its construction in the eighteen fifties. It was built by Bill Dart as a hunting and fishing lodge for Dr. Lawrence who was the first vacationer to put up a fine camp on Fourth Lake. There was no road to the property at that time so he transported lumber, bricks, and cement the three miles from Fourth Lake over a small mountain and across Bubb's Lake before reaching the Moss Lake shores. Reportedly he used a handsled, but as at that time he did have a working bull I am sure he would have employed it, unless it was a winter when the ice was not safe for so heavy an animal. The lodge had a sizeable living room with an excellent fireplace, plus an adjoining dining room and a kitchen downstairs. Upstairs there were two bedrooms, each with a closet. The outside was "board and batten" while the inside was ceiled with Georgia pine. The lodge was burned by, believe it or not, a band of marauding indians from Canada in 1975!!!— more of that later.

We had a jump and a slalom course and as my typically fine personnel luck extended to this department, we were able to attain consistently fine results through the remaining years of the camp.

This organization chapter has been inserted less for its general interest than on the chance it may be read by some capable and well-financed individual who would like to start a similar camp. I feel the need to be even greater in these rudderless times and will gladly advise anyone with concurring ideas and the potential to develop them.

Early Mass Transportation

Swimming Meet at Lodge

Canoe Meet at Senior Camp

Gunwhaling

The Island Ski Center

The newest sport but
a great favorite

Always a happy hour

A Welcome Wind

Moss Lake had a fleet of twenty sailboats

Tennis became a major sport with the arrival of Wallace Johnson and never lost its popularity.

'Papa" Castello
taught both
fencing and riflery.

Dancing added much to the athletic and cultural values of Moss Lake summers

Moss Lake had a forty-horse stable and each girl rode from six to twelve hours a week. The advanced ring is on the left, the jumping oval in the center, and the elementary ring on the right.

Archery like most of the other Moss Lake sports can be continued into and beyond the middle years.

CHAPTER IV

The Depression

CEDAR ISLES

The early depression years were a time of serious deflation, but the pain of that deflation was tempered by the response of my specialists, my tradespeople, and my bank directors, and I soon realized that for me it was indeed a cloud with a silver lining.

A choice island property that I had known for years was foreclosed. The property consisted of three islands, which because of their mid-lake location were never bothered by black flies or "Punkies." It had been managed for some time by Archie Delmarsh, Sr., as a hotel, and then sold to a Mr. Berg from New York, who built a dozen sleeping cabins on the middle-size island and converted the property into a girls' camp. He operated successfully for several years, but sold it when he moved to a larger property on Raquette Lake. The new owners continued to operate it as a Jewish girls' camp, but ran into trouble early in the depression. The mortgage was held by Moses Cohen who offered it to me in 1933 for an irresistible twelve thousand dollars, and I opened it as a boys' camp the next summer.

The location in the middle of Fourth Lake was most picturesque in itself and was enhanced by a magnificent stand of pines. Of course, the absence of flies meant quite as much to the boys as to adults. Its three islands comprised a total of about five acres. I also purchased a half acre of land on the nearest mainland point for stables and a riding ring, and to serve as a land base.

Through, and before, the Delmarsh and Berg years the camp was known by its geographical name, Cedar Island, but the last owners had rechristened it Ten-Rab. I, of course, wished to return to its natural name, but to avoid possible confusion with the Berg operation, I changed it to Cedar Isles.

For years many of my Moss Lake parents had been asking me to start a camp for their boys, and this was the opportunity. We opened with almost exactly the same number of campers as we had had at Moss Lake in 1923, and were able to give them a fine summer in spite of an August fire which destroyed nearly all of the buildings of the original hotel. In fact, only two buildings remained on the big island—a gymnasium and a craft shop. Fortunately, the boys were all living in the cabins on the second island and we completed the year quite happily with a motorboat taking them down to The Mohawk for their meals in a hastily arranged separate dining room.

Getting the property ready for the 1935 season seemed an almost impossible task. While only the two buildings remained on the big island, there was much concrete and stonework, as well as iron equipment to be cleared away. In re-designing the campus I felt a ball field to be important and the only place it could be located was on the high point of the land. That was solid rock, and much of it had to be lowered six or eight feet to secure the needed plateau, and then covered with sand drawn from Eagle Bay and top soil from Moss Lake.

With no heavy equipment, my wonderful foreman, Albert Benson, accomplished most of this during the few Fall weeks. He did the blasting and rough grading, and as soon as the lake had ice thick enough to support a team, he started taking off the debris and bringing on sand from a pile he had prepared on the land base for this purpose. In the process he quarried the stone we needed to make an all-stone recreation hall. He also drew a pile of top soil from Moss Lake and left it to be spread on the ball field after the grading was completed in the spring.

When the ice went out I gave him as many men as he could use for this work, but even so the task of building a kitchen, dining room, office, and infirmary left to be done in the spring was stupendous.

There could be no more striking evidence of Albert's engineering ability and his efficiency in handling a crew than our being ready on the opening day. While the ball field was green, it was not yet playable, but we had a much more suitable camp than the one destroyed by fire.

Had I taken official title in the first year and given Cohen a mortgage, the fire insurance payment would have more than covered the cost of the island and its reconstruction, but he was one of the most honest men I have ever known and we had effected the transfer with little more than a memo covering our intentions so, of course, the insurance money was his.

The enrollment increased steadily during the next three years and held at its revised capacity of sixty until I sold the camp in 1950.

My original expectation was that, as at Moss Lake, riding would be our most popular activity, but in that first year I learned that the average boy has much less interest in riding than does the average girl. The boys enjoyed it but thought of the ring work only as preparation for cross-country rides, and I soon realized it could not be their major sport.

Fortunately, the location was ideal for sailing, but I had not seen a sailboat on the Fulton Chain in the thirty years I could remember. The explanation of this was that there had been a fatal sailing accident on Fourth Lake in about 1905, and the locals had blown up that accident to a point that the lake was considered a death trap for sailboats and the few then-existing craft were either sold or allowed to rot. I had spent so much time on the lake that I knew this notion to be nonsense and purchased two eighteen foot Comets for our first season. They were an immediate success, and I realized that sailing should be the camp's number one sport. With this in mind, I engaged an extremely fine sailing instructor, Mark Worthen, from the Western Reserve Academy, purchased six Dunphy Snipes, and took the Comets to Moss Lake. The Snipes were fitted with bronze hardware and came complete with sails, yet in that year their cost was only one hundred and sixty-five dollars per boat.

Mark was so enthusiastic and capable, and the sport had such great natural appeal, that by the end of his third year the lake had an active Snipe Racing Association of thirty-six boats which held semi-weekly races. The enthusiasm for the sport lasted long after my selling of the camp, and although Snipes are now in the minority the total number of boats is much greater and the now-weekly races have even more entrants. This is a fine example of how superstition can be contagious even in affluent circles. The lake was ideal for sailing, but the death-trap fantasy had prevented its being used for over thirty years.

Riding was retained but lessons were scheduled for only three times a week instead of daily as at Moss Lake. Swimming and tennis were important, and we took many canoe trips. These were our major sports. Wrestling, fencing, archery, and riflery were the minors.

On a per capita basis Cedar Isles was much more profitable than Moss Lake because the original investment was so much lower and the property much less expensive to maintain. Further, sailing was less costly than riding, and as Moss Lake was so much larger its brothers and cousins supplied nearly enough boys to fill the Cedar Isles quota and eliminated most of the normal expense of enrollment from its budget.

We matched our Moss Lake specialists only in sailing, riding, and canoe trips at Cedar Isles, but the other sports were in competent hands and we had a major budgetary advantage in that these men were not super-imposed upon a full counsellor staff, but also served as counsellors.

Cedar Isles sailboats with Eagle-Cliff and the Eagle Bay Hotel boathouse in the background

Cedar Isles was a sailing and swimming camp

Riding and Reveille

Tennis and Riflery were second only to sailing and swimming

Cedar Isles Stone Recreation Hall
The only one of the many Longstaff camp buildings still standing

EAGLE COVE

My next Depression property also had been a hotel, "Grand View," owned by one of our early guides, Ed Rarick. It was about a half mile from Cedar Isles on the south shore of the lake and had also been used as a girls' camp under the name of Lo-Na-Wo. It held some sixty acres of land and most of its buildings were quite new. It was acquired about 1918 by Jewish interests who did extensive building and soon had it operating as a camp of approximately one hundred and twenty-five girls. Apparently the financing was shaky and its clientele seemed to dissolve even more rapidly than those of the Christian camps when the Depression hit. It failed, was soon insolvent and recaptured by the mortgagee, the same Moses Cohen who had held the mortgage on Cedar Isles. He suggested I also take this property off his hands and set an irresistibly low figure of twenty thousand—much less than the construction cost of the new dining room and recreation hall.

The Depression years had changed the enrollment picture; and I was campaigning rather heavily for Moss Lake campers and finding that the majority of my contacts could not afford the Moss Lake fees. Since most of the country's camps were much less expensive I thought we should be able to solve the problem by offering these prospects a well-equipped but competitively priced camp in the same area and decided to follow this path. I named the camp "Eagle Cove" and turned its actual operation over to Ellen Hayes who had been my "Lodge" head counsellor for a number of years, and to Helmy Smirnova, who had been our first dance specialist. Both were from Syracuse with substantial contacts in that city. Our contract was an operating partnership and I was confident that between us we would be able to secure enough enrollments to get the new camp off to a flying start. The ladies produced about twenty campers but my contribution was a meager seven, and I did no better the second year.

I decided that my "sales pitch" for the run-of-the-mill Eagle Cove, was not delivered with sufficient enthusiasm and required the family's admission that they were not really sending their daughters to the camp of their choice.

The second year was so disappointing to all of us that when a former assistant of my mother at The Mohawk, Walter Peck, who had been working with an adult camp on Long Island, contacted me and expressed an interest in Eagle Cove, I told him he could take over the sales contract. This was done with Cohen's approval, and Walter did rather well the first year. However, he was drafted the next fall and let the property go back to Mr. Cohen.

CASCADE LAKE

My third Depression property was almost comparable with the Moss Lake Tract. It appears about two miles east of Moss Lake on the map of the Longstaff properties reproduced on the inside cover. The lake was a mile and a quarter long with seven hundred acres and was most picturesque.

Charles Snyder, its long-time owner, had been the attorney for Seward Webb who at one point held title to nearly all of our Township Eight and other extensive sections of the Adirondacks. Webb also built the Adirondack Railroad and opened the territory for general resort use. Some of his extensive holdings are still in the hands of his family, others he sold, but most were transferred to the State with a special deed limiting their use to purposes he considered proper for a State Park.

Snyder drew these deeds and their "Forever Wild" clause still guides the policy makers and administrators of the extensive Adirondack State Park. His fee included his choice of several lakes, and Cascade was his selection. His camp, while rather less pretentious than most, was built in the Durant-Webb pattern and could easily have been considered one of the "Great Camps."

Snyder had a handsome retainer from the New York Central Railroad and did most of their upstate work—yet as the years went by he found the expense of maintaining the Cascade property keeping a year round caretaker, paying the family guest bills, and meeting the high Hamilton County taxes—a heavy burden. About 1930 he offered it for sale at what he considered a bargain price of Two Hundred Thousand. There were no takers, but he was so certain the figure would be attractive to the right party that he nearly bankrupted himself in an attempt to sell it at that price.

It eventually was taken over by the First National Bank of Herkimer, whose management tried to dispose of it at a much lower price—a price which fell so low in 1938 that Mr. Snyder's son-in-law, Roy Valance, decided to purchase it. The Herkimer directors arranged a fall weekend party which he was to attend to complete the transaction. Most of the family dishes had been removed and when the bank president mentioned this to me I offered to lend them the necessary replacements from Moss Lake stock.

When I arrived at Cascade with the dishes, the bank people were starting to assemble, but had received a wire from Valance informing them that he was withdrawing his offer. The president told me this was quite deflating and asked if I would not make a substitute offer. My reply was to tell him that he knew I was already quite extended and I did not think I could justify a figure over a quite ridiculous twenty-five thousand, and even if they accepted that, fifteen thousand would have to be on a mortgage. I don't think either of us took that conversation seriously, but the next day he telephoned me to say that when the group assembled and received the Valance news they decided to accept my offer.

I considered Moss Lake the more picturesque of the two, but the similarities were so great that through the years I frequently met people who preferred Cascade. The property was larger and the lake, while narrower, was a half mile longer. It obviously was a tract that deserved substantial development, but I had to go slowly and decided to split the Cedar Isles clientele, bringing the boys with a keen interest in riding to Cascade and leaving the "sailors" at Cedar Isles. The start was disappointing as we opened with but seven boys, yet the summer went so smoothly that all seven re-enrolled and were joined by twenty new members the next year.

I converted a large barn into a quite suitable gymnasium, built a tennis court, stables and riding ring, and one large sleeping cabin (there were rooms for several boys in the main house). When World War II came I was still determined to make it a boys' counterpart of Moss Lake.

The profit potential of Cedar Isles and its ideal location as a sailing camp prevented me from merging it with Cascade. This, of course, slowed the Cascade growth. I operated it chiefly as a riding camp but retained sailing as the first activity at Cedar Isles.

The World War, which proved to be most kind to Moss Lake, made staffing boys' camps of comparable caliber extremely difficult. Most of my Cedar Isles staff accepted army and navy commissions before the first war summer, and replacing them with men of similar stature seemed almost impossible. So rather than let the quality slip I re-combined the remnants of the Cedar Isles and Cascade staffs and operated Cascade as a camp for younger children—coeducational ages three to ten. This was an interesting experience.

Mature men counselors were hard to find, but women with good qualifications were still available, and I staffed this nursery camp with one married couple and several young ladies. It was immediately successful, but meanwhile I had married, had my first child, and desired to get away from the eighteen-hour days that the multiple operations were demanding. Accordingly, when I had a lease offer from Fritz Kleeman, the riding teacher at the Penn Hall School, I was receptive.

He brought a fair number of girls from that school and a string of extremely fine horses that did much to enliven our Darts Lake Show. A couple of years later he married and for some seasons Cascade appeared to be operating successfully. I never knew the details of its collapse, but having acquired the larger Darts Lake property, I was reluctant to resume the operation of Cascade; however, I was preparing to do so when I had a reasonably attractive offer for its purchase.

Cascade had the characteristics of the "Great Camps"

Charles Snyder was given the choice of several lakes as his client, Seward Webb, was disposing of this Town of Webb holdings. Cascade was his selection.

Riding is a fine appetizer

The Cascade team after winning second place at the Lake George show.

Cascade, first a boy's camp, then coeducational

DARTS LAKE

Darts Lake was my last Depression acquisition. It was much larger than either Moss Lake or Cascade, and to my mind it almost matched Moss Lake in beauty.

Bill Dart had been one of our early guides, had acquired his first title to the property as a squatter, and then reinforced it by purchasing a deed from Seward Webb. He developed it into one of the Adirondack's finest and most completely rustic resorts and built an extremely loyal clientele of about two hundred people.

Bill had a very unique and workable plan for maintaining that loyalty. He originally allowed guests to occupy rooms in his main house or one of his larger cottages, then built cottages of their own design for them on mutually pleasing sites. They paid for the construction and Bill allowed them free use of the cottage for five years but charged them for their meals.

This was the resort and Bill was the man I had contacted early in 1919 with the purchase of the property in mind. It was he who told me the price was too high and suggested that I take advantage of a family dispute among the owners of Moss Lake to try to acquire that property.

In the interim Bill had retired and given the property to his daughter and son-in-law. They operated it for nearly twenty years but lacked Bill's magic touch. Looking across the mountain with apparent envy of Moss Lake they started first a boys' camp and then a girls' camp on the same property. Neither was a success and by 1938 had been abandoned. The girls' camp had only one building and that collapsed under an especially heavy snow load a few years later. The small cabins of the boys' camp converted rather nicely into hotel cottages. However, its main building was a large kitchen, dining room, and recreation hall complex which they decided to use instead of the much older adult headquarters.

By 1941 it had been in the hands of a Utica bank long enough for them to be extremely anxious to sell it, and when I had a report of a price of eighteen or twenty thousand I consulted my old friend and attorney, Phil Farley, who was so enthusiastic that he suggested our buying it together. Phil's practice had been largely international with German interests as his major clients, and this left him with a few years of unusually light professional obligations and we decided he would be the active operator. As long as Phil could give his summers to it, the operation ran quite smoothly.

We decided that Darts should become a club to give us maximal clientele control. Phil's office prepared the necessary papers and we began operating the hotel as the "Darts Lake Club."

Of course, we wished to make the project self-supporting as soon as possible and as there was a good deal of timber that could be harvested without damage to the property, Phil turned his attention to the legal aspects of the matter. The State Conservation Department was construing Charles Snyder's deed restrictions as allowing them to prohibit all lumbering and there had been none in the area for several years. I remembered that Snyder in talking about his early plans for Cascade had told me that this position did not worry him, for he knew that was not Seward Webb's intention and that he could force them to alter their position—or beat them in the courts. I told this to Phil. He studied the deeds, was sure he saw daylight, and arranged a meeting with the Conservation Commissioners. They decided that instead of risking a legal showdown they would approve our lumbering if we would accept softwood and hardwood size minimums. Their eight- and fourteen-inch figures seemed quite reasonable and Phil agreed. This decision opened the gates for other land owners in the area and conservative lumbering has been regularly approved in the area ever since.

Our net on this lumbering exceeded the price we paid for the property and with

A mile and a half lake with a thousand acres of woodland

Darts rustic but active

Darts Lake headquarters buildings, old and new

this auspicious start the Farley years were good ones. However, they came to an end when the war stopped and his practice returned to normal and required his full attention. At this point we leased the property to Vernon Bowes with an option to purchase it at eighty thousand. The operation continued to run quite smoothly under his aegis, but instead of exercising his option he decided to try for a lower price and this action ended the lease.

I then found myself with an operating problem. This I solved by securing the services of the Thomas family, who had owned and operated the Minnow Brook hotel for some years (sold at auction the previous summer), on a profit-sharing basis. Their clientele failed to follow them to Darts, while some of the Darts clientele followed Bowes to the nearby Covewood he purchased. As a result the profits were not adequate to warrant a second year for the Thomases.

By this time I had sold Cedar Isles and I put its many-years director, Nelson Hopkins, and his wife in charge of Darts Lake. They were not hotel people and did not make the transition from camp to hotel effectively, so once again I had Darts Lake on my hands. In semi-desperation I was planning to be much more active myself but had what I thought, and still think, was a fine idea for its development. Since Phil had set it up as a club and since there were four miles of shoreline quite suitable for cottage development, I decided to sell lots with the owners becoming club members. Unfortunately, the initial impetus was less than I expected. During the period when I was trying to secure the dozen offers I considered necessary to ensure against the sale of a few lots destroying the sanctity of the property, I received a two hundred and twenty-five thousand dollar offer from the Boy Scouts of Rochester. I accepted, partially because the club real estate project was taking shape so slowly and partially because I had been eager for some years to start a boarding school in Florida and this sale would make it possible both financially and in terms of my available time. At this point I am sure the decision cost me in the neighborhood of a million dollars, but at the time it seemed the right answer.

Even now I do not regret the sale for my twenty school years that followed were both challenging and rewarding.

CHAPTER V

Temptations

Cedar Isles, Eagle Cove, Cascade, and Darts were all first class temptations to which I succumbed. There were others that I resisted more from financial necessity than by will power. After all these years they still look like wonderful opportunities.

EAGLE BAY HOTEL

The first was not based on an actual offering but merely on reported availability. It was a well-located waterfront hotel with more than a hundred acres of back land, idle and in poor condition, but an incredible value at the reported seven thousand dollars. A New Yorker bought it, reportedly took out a seventy-thousand-dollar-insurance policy, and had a fire the second year that totally destroyed the main building.

The next morning the proprietor of a neighboring hotel that had taken in a number of the stranded guests after the fire visited the site, found a man surveying the ruins who introduced himself as the owner and extended an invitation to visit his personal cottage. It had escaped the fire and the purpose of the invitation appeared to be to give him an opportunity to exhibit plans for a resort complex of Florida-style buildings to replace the ones destroyed.

I do not know whether this came to the attention of the insuring company or whether they decided independently that the fire was a suspicious one, but I heard that when the owner presented his claim he was invited to bring suit. The guests were largely refugees from Hitler's purge who had been required to pay in advance. The report was that after the fire someone noticed the owner's pockets were stuffed with bills and his explanation was that he did not think the hotel safe to be a secure one.

All of this, of course, supplied excellent grist for the local rumor mill.

LAWRENCE POINT

Another major temptation was on Fourth Lake. Doctor Lawrence had been one of the region's first wealthy settlers and in 1828 had selected what I have always thought to be the choicest sector of the north shore—a large point from which practically the whole six miles of Fourth Lake could be viewed. It had approximately a half mile of shore front and many acres of land—the front twenty having a topography that would lend itself nicely for resort use of any kind. There he built a charming summer home that now is the area's only important survivor of the period.

In mid-depression my acquisition of Cedar Isles and Eagle Cove caught the attention of his son-in-law, who with his wife had held the deed for a good many years, and he came over to offer me the place for twenty thousand dollars.

I am sure that when it was later sold off as cottage lots, it yielded many times this amount. This possibility I foresaw, but I had already "stretched myself" quite thin and

I forced my tongue to tell him that I did not feel this was an occasion on which I could afford to yield to temptation.

CHILDWOOD PARK

The Masaweepie Tract was some thousands of acres with seven lakes, one about the size of First Lake and two the size of Cascade. The old Childwood Park Hotel was standing, but probably beyond repair. Several cottages were still habitable. Mr. Sykes, the then-elderly owner, told me I could have it for seventy thousand dollars, but my final decision was that I would be running a serious risk of losing Moss Lake. I believe it later went to the Girl Scouts of Rochester for sixty thousand dollars.

UNCAS

This estate, unquestionably more feasible because of its proximity to Moss Lake and price, thirty thousand dollars, was equally tempting—at least it was before I inspected it. It had been built by W. W. Durant and later owned by J. P. Morgan. The buildings were great and still in good repair, but I could not understand why Durant with all his holdings to choose from, or Morgan with all his money, had settled for such a small lake, especially as the location of the camp made it seem even smaller than it was. It still was tempting, but I decided that it would siphon off too much interest and energy from my established projects.

CHAPTER VI

The Later Camp Days

While camp was my main interest in the twenties and thirties, my Jamaica dental winters played an important supportive role. My father and I, before opening our Jamaica office, had acquired a highly skilled secretary, Ruth Hager, who was completely devoted to our interests, including those of the camp. She married and moved from Brooklyn to Manhasset about the time the Jamaica office was opened and remained active until cancer intervened in 1949. She came to camp with me one year and vacationed there twice. She was conversant with all my interests and did much to make them jell. I was a dentist from nine to five about four days a week, spending the other three days interviewing or dictating, and between us our camp enrollment grew well.

This program left me a fair number of free evenings and, as in those days ten dollars would cover dinner and theatre for two, I never felt my nose held too closely to the grindstone—especially since my father kept two fine riding horses in town. He would ride many mornings before going to the office, and if I was in town on the weekend his Sunday routine would be to ride with his "horsey" friends before breakfast, with me in the morning, and with my mother in the afternoon. I am quite convinced that this interest and the exercise that went with it did much to make possible his seventy-five years of dental practice. He stayed in the saddle to within months of his death at the age of ninety-three.

Of course, dentistry would have been impossible for me were it not for practicing with my father. Figuring that my seasonal income lacked stability, he paid me twenty-five hundred dollars a year—not a large portion of the office take but much more than I deserved.

I should explain here that I never had any desire to be a dentist but chose dentistry when my father insisted that I enter a profession which could replace my normal income if that should be lost. I think I might have enjoyed the work if I had been blessed with fine manual dexterity, but mine was certainly no better than average and frequently robbed me of the satisfaction of a job well done. Further, most of my dental time was devoted to repair work and that contrasted sharply with Moss Lake, where everything was done with the future in mind. Had there been no Adirondacks, I am sure I would have specialized in orthodontia so that children and their future could be my main concern.

These winters in New York City were helpful as well as pleasant. Many good residential areas lay within easy driving distance and prospects, and counsellors from farther away usually visited New York from time to time, so interviews could easily be arranged in Manhattan hotels. Moreover, my very good friend, Philip Farley, was by now a well-established and able attorney with an office in mid-Manhattan. This made communication simple and his advice, both general and legal, was so important that I might have submerged without it.

Low-keyed attachments popped up from time to time, but faded as I compared the individuals with the Chicago girl of my last Michigan days.

The year 1937 brought two crushing blows. My mother, who had been my constant advisor and supporter, had leased The Mohawk and was starting to enjoy the rewards of her long labors, but died suddenly from an embolism in August. I finished the season and made plans for 1938, but shortly after I returned to Jamaica, Henry Simmons, my closest friend through school, college, and early business years was decapitated as he was driving from Little Falls to Herkimer with his wife. Both died instantly. The car, a Cord Convertible, had plowed into the rear of a flat-bed truck.

Either loss alone would have been a devastating one. My mother's death coming in mid-August was blunted by the demanding routine of those weeks. At the end of the season I rushed the closing of the camps as it had never been rushed before and returned to Jamaica. My father was continuing there but I was learning how heavy such a strain could be and thought my presence would be helpful.

I believe it was for two weeks, but then the news of Henry's death greeted me on the front page of the New York Evening Sun and I left for Herkimer the next day. When I returned, it was my father who was the supportive one and I made a decision that in retrospect appears to have been a selfish one. I judged that a long southern cruise would stand the best chance of relieving the tension and tried to persuade my father to plan one with me. He refused to leave his practice and Ruth Hager judged his office routine to be the most effective therapy possible and persuaded me to go without him.

I picked an island-hopping Canadian Line ship and "the cure" worked like a charm. To make the cost minimal I had reserved an upper berth in a three-man room and had the good fortune to find myself the only occupant of a stateroom larger than my bedroom at home. No one else was assigned to it until we reached Bermuda on the return trip. It stopped at all sizable British Islands except the Bahamas and turned around at Demerara. We were in a hotel there for two days but for the other twenty-eight the boat was our home.

I had been raised on the lavish meals of the early Adirondack resorts but the ship's table was even more varied and generous. The first class salons were spacious and our deck circled the whole boat so, except when loading or unloading, there was nothing to make us realize that Cruise Ship was not its only role in life. There was no Cabin Class and the Steerage segregation was so complete that I remember being reprimanded by an officer for sitting for a few minutes on the steps which connected the two decks and chatting with a handsome and well-dressed girl from the lower one. Later he told me that her grandfather was one of the wealthiest men on Trinidad but that she could not travel First Class because she had been "touched by the tar brush." This I was unable to understand for Canada had never been a slave country and all the Caribbean Islands appeared to consider all races acceptable. He answered my surprised query merely by saying it was a regulation of the Line.

I returned to Jamaica ready to start a new year and found my father in equally good spirits. Apparently Ruth Hager had been right and my misgivings unfounded. The cost of my "convalescence" had been little more than the six dollars a day I paid to the Canadian Line for my upper berth reservation.

The next three years were pleasantly uneventful. A maid trained by my mother kept house for us and as always my father adjusted beautifully—spending more hours with his horses and, when I was not at home, setting an earlier bed hour for himself.

Except for Cascade no camp growth was desired and its minor building schedule went smoothly. We put up one large bungalow, converted a barn to a gymnasium, and added a stable in a more distant location.

However, the war years brought many changes, especially to the boys' camps. My satisfaction as a director came chiefly from the accomplishments of the campers. At Moss Lake they continued to flow smoothly since the staff suffered little from the war as my specialists were in their fifties and only one, DeGroat, volunteered. He had always been athletically active but his age was against him and he soon was given a medical discharge and returned to camp. Counsellors, cooks, waiters, and waitresses were no problem, but by the second year of the war men were getting harder and harder to find. Fortunately, I had forseen this problem and kept several workmen in the fall of the first war year to do as much as possible of the spring work. This decision paid off handsomely for in June of 1943 I had only two men to open camp, plus Mr. De and myself.

The next year the picture was rather better and we adjusted to a male-short operation. The low payroll, restricted mileage, and war shortages combined with capacity enrollments did much to make these the most profitable years in the camp's history.

When my mother died, Moss Lake was still in her name. She willed the Moss Lake property to me and The Mohawk to my sister. I expected the inheritance tax to be crushing, for I was carrying a building capitalization of over two hundred thousand dollars on my books for depreciation purposes. Fortunately, the IRS was less hard-boiled than today and only the land and the few buildings existing when the property was purchased were deemed taxable, as I had engineered and paid for the others.

Shortly after this was settled, my sister decided to sell The Mohawk to the man who had been leasing it. The price was ridiculously low, as were most others in the area at that time. As executor I might have been able to block the deal, but this would have generated some family friction so I approved, consoling myself with the knowledge that Darts Lake could probably be acquired at an even more ridiculous figure.

The next real estate development was an opportunity to purchase a fine riding ring on the upper east side of Manhattan with stables for forty horses. I had heard that Durland's, the largest such establishment in town and the only one near Central Park, except for the Columbia Riding Academy whose ring was made extremely dangerous by many iron posts, was to close. I snapped up Boots & Saddles, and with the closing of Durland's it became the only safe riding ring in Manhattan. It promised to be a gold mine in itself and to save me the heavy expense of wintering my camp horses as well as simplifying our camper campaign by the many contacts with riding oriented families. Certainly I had no idea it was going to present me with my most difficult business decision, but before I was to face that dilemma I had another decision to make.

Memories of the Chicago girl had protected me through the years when men are most vulnerable, but I still thought of marriage as the proper norm and on my fortieth birthday was reminded that my time was getting short. To complicate matters a most promising girl made it clear that she was eligible and to make the picture more attractive she had had ten years at Moss Lake as camper, intern, and counsellor. We were married, and Pearl Harbor arrived following our first child by about six weeks. Then the major Longstaff decision—I was told Darts Lake was indeed for sale.

At the same time I had an offer for Boots & Saddles that would net a long-term profit of ten thousand. I consulted Philip Farley who not only approved but said he would like to go in with me on the Darts Lake venture. Fine as these investments appeared to be, I did not feel I should try to swing both as I did not yet know how difficult or profitable the war years were going to be for camps. Accordingly, I sold Boots & Saddles and decided to purchase Darts—an even greater bargain than Cascade.

Later two things happened that left me wishing I had kept Boots & Saddles and gone ahead with the Darts Lake purchase at the same time. Mr. Kleeman defaulted on his Cascade lease and I received an acceptable offer for its purchase so that book was closed. A while later I sold Cedar Isles and could then have nicely carried Boots & Saddles, both in terms of finances and of the time involved.

Darts Lake
Dr. H. H. Longstaff, age 90,
on Magic Moment

Moss Lake
Caroline Longstaff
Nelson, on Goldie

CHAPTER VII

The Demise of Moss Lake

Moss Lake gave me my most rewarding years largely because it's enrollment evolved into a composition pattern that was thirty to forty percent daughters of old campers. They came to Moss Lake with their mothers' enthusiasm and with many Moss Lake techniques acquired in their pre-camp years. This resulted in their being so consistently outstanding, both in personality and in athletic ability, that they yearly won an average of about a seventy-five percent of our athletic awards. They did equally well in qualifying as "Honor Girls"—an award given on the basis of conformance to the "Honor Creed" reproduced on page 50.

There is much less to say about this period than about the developing seasons, but my satisfactions grew each year. The mothers would find that even after a ten-to-twenty-year interval they knew most of the specialists and that our goals and behavioral expectations were unchanged. The parents marveled at the latter and with teen-age attitudes shifting so rapidly, they found it doubly gratifying. I endeavored to maintain the same standards at school, but in doing so I frequently had some girls who did not conform. This, of course, was a sign of the times, but I think there was another reason. Camp directors campaigned quite openly for enrollments while most schools had their students come in for their interviews. Academically the latter is preferable, but in terms of appraising personalities, family backgrounds, and behavioral patterns I found it less effective. At camp I had met nearly all my girls in their homes—the interviews usually lasting two to three hours and including motion pictures of the camp activities. In a home setting I found it possible to make a much more accurate appraisal of a girl and of both past and future family contributions to her development. Showing the pictures also was a big help for it let the girl prepare herself for the summer or express her doubts either to me or the family if the life pictured was not one which she thought she could enter into wholeheartedly.

It took me twenty years to recover from my Chicago attachment and nearly thirty more before I was willing to attempt a second marriage. For me this "second time around" has been full of delightful surprises, and I am sure that when my time to leave arrives my central thought will be similar to those of Dorothy's first husband, who said at their last meeting, "I am prepared to die, but leaving you is a much more difficult hurdle." Dorothy came to camp with me in '69 contributing much and enjoying it greatly, but the field work that seemed to be an essential part of running camp bothered her very much and I came up with what I felt sure would be a perfect solution.

One of my old camp families, the Robert Riders, had asked me to let them know when and if I considered retirement. The wife, Jane, had been a Moss Lake camper and counsellor for many years—a counsellor in Senior Camp and the Head Counsellor of Lodge during my last summer there. The four daughters had had a total of fifteen Moss Lake years. Jane's personality was documented by her success in each role and Bob was a successful businessman. I conferred with them when he visited camp in mid-summer and we quickly "struck a deal"—a five-year-lease with a purchase option. My over-riding desire was to secure the future of Moss Lake and I had every reason to believe that this also was one of the Riders' objectives. Accordingly I was elated to have so easily found a family who would carry on the work and traditions of the camp.

After running the camp for three years the Riders exercised their option and we made plans to transfer the property. The closing was held in Phil Farley's Park Avenue office. At that time Phil submitted his granddaughter's registration for the coming season, and it was accepted with suitable enthusiasm.

Within two weeks letters went out to all parents announcing that the property had been sold; the buyer was the Conservancy, and hence the state. For me the shock was delayed until I returned from a European trip and had occasion to call Jane from the airport. She cried as she told me of the sale. Of course, I was stunned, for it was the major work of my lifetime being swept under the table, but there was nothing to do but to concentrate my interest on Adirondack-Southern. Dorothy gave of hers in equal measure and things went well, but in a lower key than in Moss Lake's developing years.

In the fall of the year of the sale a group of about thirty Indians came down from Canada and occupied the property. A half-dozen troopers arrived promptly to dispossess them, but word from the governor cancelled the project before they actually entered the property. This decision I imagine the governor made because he had but recently been installed in the office when Rockefeller resigned to accept the vice-presidency, and because he wished to avoid an incident like Wounded Knee which then was still fresh in all minds.

Reinforcements arrived and the Indians claimed the land as part of their tribal heritage, named it "Ganienkeh," and "protected" it so aggressively that they tried to discourage traffic on the highway that separated some northern acreage from the main part of the tract. To do this they used guns. During the second year two people were shot, and one girl was critical for some time. Again the troopers came in—not to dispossess but to find and arrest the culprits. The Indians refused them access saying that Moss Lake was their country, not part of New York State or of the United States. The governor, by that time a democrat, decided to let the matter drop and the Indians remained two additional years; then they agreed to swap Moss Lake for acreage about five times as large as the Moss Lake tract nearer the Canadian border. As part of the settlement they were allowed to take everything they wanted from Moss Lake and the state then came in and completely razed all the buildings in accordance with its "Forever Wild" Adirondack Park policy.

A ridiculous facet of the state's response to the occupation was the establishment of two State Trooper Posts—one at Eagle Bay—the other on what had been my Darts Lake property. They required vehicles to wait to go through in groups. In the first months they were accompanied by a State Trooper, later they relied on telephone assurance from the other station that the car or cars had negotiated the run successfully.

This, of course, sharply depreciated the value of all the land on Big Moose Lake and Twitchel Lake as they could be reached by no other paved roads. It also entailed a heavy state expense—one that at its peak was figured at thirty thousand dollars a month for the chaperoning troopers. In addition the state—not the Indians—paid the family of the wounded girl over $150,000. Further, the legal expenses of aroused citizens, of the Indians, and of the state over this period probably far exceeded the value of the property. The occupation lasted for four years, was highlighted by the shootings, was most inconvenient for tourists, and was serious for property owners. An interesting reaction of the state was the closing of several hundred additional acres surrounding the adjacent Bubb's Lake and West Pond. Big Moose residents organized a concerned citizens group, raised money, and attempted to secure legal redress through the courts, but this was no more effective than the spontaneous and shocked protests that preceeded it.

To make the state's abdication of responsibility more disheartening, I probably should report that the Indians were in the area for several days before the seizure and apparently made little attempt to conceal the purpose of their presence. They frequented a restaurant in the area and discussed their plans quite brazenly. Apparently they were trying to decide whether Moss or Darts would be the more suitable. The family that owned the restaurant reported it to a state senator but that produced no reaction and he later advised them that he could find no one in the executive branch who would believe him when he relayed the story.

It would have been interesting to watch developments if they had selected Darts. The local representative of the Rochester Boy Scouts was on vacation so they would have had no more initial opposition than at Moss Lake, but I think the organization and its friends might have been able to apply more effective pressure, either on the incumbent Republican governor or upon the Democrat who succeeded him.

This disgraceful episode was a logical sequel to "Wounded Knee" while the Indians legal campaign in Maine, which left a cloud on nearly half the land titles in the state, was aided by both. It is the most far-reaching of the three. Together they stand as powerful evidence that we must elect representatives on whom we can count to be guided by proper principles rather than expediency.

My camps made enough money to nicely take care of family expenses—with the help of some conservative lumbering. However, for the first forty years my cash position was never as good as it would have been had I confined my efforts to dentistry. Yet this never disturbed me, nor did I ever envy any of my friends their often-high-riding prosperity. I don't think I was a workaholic but the satisfactions I derived from the accomplishments of my Moss Lake staff and the many months the work left me submerged in my beloved Adirondacks was more than adequate compensation for missing the handsome financial rewards reaped by my friends and even for the contrast with the tremendous affluence of our Moss Lake parents. My only disappointment was that my son never threw himself wholeheartedly into the work, yet in retrospect I must admit that his choice of banking probably was a wise one.

Moss Lake, my first love, was the gem of them all and the one that held my heart through the years, and I mourn it almost as I do my parents. With its sale I was left but one acre of Adirondack land—the riding ring and land base of Cedar Isles. I could not bear to cut my Adirondack ties completely so as soon as Moss Lake was gone I started building a cottage on the north shore of Fourth Lake—almost literally where I had started. After the foundations were laid and the rafters raised we did the work ourselves. Consequently we could not move in until the second year and did not really finish it until the end of the third.

It is on Eagle Point Road, less than a half-mile from the postoffice, and we plan to be in residence from mid-June to mid-October each year. If any of my campers or students who read this find themselves near, I hope they will stop for a visit. Of the dozens I have built in the area this house and the stone recreation hall at Cedar Isles are the only ones still standing. For this credit must be given to the unreasonable "Forever Wild" policy of the Adirondack Park Agency. Many of the "Great Camps" have already been lost and most of the others seem to be doomed.

CHAPTER VIII

A Lake, Mountains, and Peace

(Written by a twelve-year-old camper in the early Fifties)

God has created millions of beautiful places. One special location is a lake nestled in the mountains of northern New York state.

This lake isn't big, neither is it small. It's size is in proportion to the gentle hills that are reflected in its natural mirror. It is supplied only by a few scattered inlets and many hidden springs of clear icy-cold water. No ugly swamps taint its edge, only low-hanging sapplings. Much of the way along the shore has a definite level below which no leaves remain on the branches. This shows that the wild deer have been feeding well. Sandy beaches border the water in different places, reaching out to form the bottom of the lake for many yards until it has become quite deep. It is said that in the depths which are quite deep for so small a lake, good-sized fish live that are so well fed they are rarely caught by fishermen.

In the middle of this lagoon, rises a small island, seemingly from out of nowhere. From here there is a perfect view of the whole lake. Three main coves interrupt the irregular circle; one has a fair-sized inlet, another the principal outlet, and the third is just a sheltered bay. From the northern end of the lake a mountain rises abruptly from the shore to about five hundred feet. No hills begin to climb for a mile or two at the southern end, and when they do, they are only slight mounds. The hills to the east are even farther than those to the south. The mountains on the west ascend almost immediately from the shore, completing the separation of the wilderness reservoir from the civilized world. Few, if any, sounds reach this scene except those coming from the one road which connects it to the nearest towns, one three miles away, and the other five miles. As might be expected, hardly any people come here except those associated with the girls' camp which owns this beautiful lake and location. The idea that a camp would mutilate the peace and serenity here is mistaken. The feeling of friendship and fun that is shared by all the campers makes up for anything that is done to destroy its quiet beauty. Nowhere could there be a happier combination of man and nature.

The low hills, the peaceful waters of the lake, and the joyful companionship definitely show the harmony between humans and God, as expressed in the Bible:

> *"Yet thou hast made him little less than God.*
> *And dost crown him with glory and honor:*
> *Thou has given him dominion over the works*
> *of thy hands."*
>
> *Psalms 8:5–6*

Susie Nelson

CHAPTER IX

The Camp Connection:
After 2000

By Gladys Funk Yost

Leaning heavily on scholars of the future I present that Moss Lake Camp will be connected with the next century. My theme's not the-memory-lingers. Nor is it circular. It holds George Longstaff camp concepts are too vital to just fade or repeat.

This accepts, with Arnold Toynbee, that history spirals. With Alvin Toffler I believe we are now starting a spiral into a new civilization. Regard for guest space limits me to two, of the many, ways Longstaff concepts merit spiraling. Philip Slater explains we can spiral or "It is quite possible humanity may prove a dead end, too big (with technological extensions) and too stupid (with relational insensitivity) to participate feliciously in the dance of life." These aspects which may do us in are my examples of Moss Lake strength.

Of technological extensions Christopher Alexander writes, "when you build a thing you cannot build that thing in isolation, but must repair the world around it, and within it, so that the larger world at that one place becomes coherent and more whole; and the thing you make takes its place in the web of nature."

As the Industrial Age ravaged our world George Longstaff created his camp's physical plant with exquisite understanding of this future principle. Most "good private camps" I've seen abuse their surroundings. Areas are formalized where painted buildings stand starkly, often with a rigid flag pole centering the coherent scene. But at Moss, even Lodge punctuating the shore line, flowed with the terrain: from its main building of logs and stones, and its terraces of mountain boulders cascading to the lake. The natural wood cabins were congenial to the trees which touched them. Vast Madison Square had the forest reaching around with an embrace. Nowhere was there a sight of intrusion on the wilderness. The luxury of electricity and plumbing was added to the wilds but the necessary technological extensions did not subtract from the pristine whole. The Longstaff genius for environmental consideration and architectural coherence must be part of the future if we survive.

Of the Industrial Age George Land says, "Nothing about it was so bad: it served its purpose by raising the standards of living, research and education to such a high level people began asking higher level questions. Then it began to use up its environment, going into disharmony—two signs its time is ending."

The peak higher level question found is, "How can we gain a better quality of life?" Since the quantity of industrialism has had us near disaster, this must be based on more humane emotional sensitivity toward nations, races and each other. It's been women, the traditional caretakers of emotional sensitivity, in America who lead this advance. In this I by-pass radical feminism which even how has in organized membership only a few thousand, though their characteristics have been essential to shock society to attention. Instead I turn to those with Moss Lake Camp's womanly concepts.

The Longstaff Honor Girl Creed, above all else, encourages acute sensitivity to the welfare of others. Exceptional staff and program pushed sports' competence, strong character and social skills seeded self-esteem. The campers selected tended to be those of private schools heading for colleges, promising high potential. The intended end result of these superior qualities is stated in Adirondack-Southern literature: "We assume the most important role in each girl's life will be that of wife and mother in a cultured home."

Obviously this ultimate goal for the Moss Lake woman has been badly battered. It started when the home-centered, stable communitied, together agricultural family was forced to change structure to serve the gigantic industrial challenge. Its members scattered to city factories and offices. Further mobility became rampant, especially for executives climbing whatever their work pyramid. The isolated, fragmented nuclear family soon dominated the country. Its shape—largely absent husband and father, home and child centered wife and mother—was destined for a short life. It is already dead: more and more wives are employed, and a million divorces occur annually.

Herbert Hendin is among the scholars who sum this up. When family life is designed to serve an economic system (instead of vice versa) to the industrial extreme it is humanly impossible to give the excessive emotional support the other needs. A few may find wise balance. More remain intact but unglued. Many others blow. But in the explosion the Moss Lake kind of woman will not be in the debris.

I suggest her record and where she's headed. She was among the advantaged Smith graduates who first alerted Betty Freidan to the "problem which has no name." She was the mother and wife in a cultured home who, by the tens of thousands, confirmed the Feminine Mystique. With her excellent education, self-esteem and strong character, she was the first to seek its potential through a career rather than just a fill-in job. And with her unusual sensitivity and good direction she's now taking her family back home—spiraling beyond the together farm family.

The thrust toward the Stay-at-Home-Society is sufficiently strong to attract scholarly attention. The heart of the farm home, the hearth, now changes to the computer. Here the family increasingly gathers to play, shop, go to the grocery store or movies and be employed together at joint or separate careers handled by telecommuting. Older children can learn and help. Pregnant women pursue their careers in the shelter of home. Jack Niles, Director of Future Studies, says there are 10,000 persons right now who could do their jobs by telecommuting. He expects the numbers doing so to double yearly.

The Moss Lake type woman also pioneers (as do my daughters-in-law) for an economy to serve the family by initiating for non-telecommuters such job aides to provide parental time at home as flex time, joint jobs, parents' leaves, wider spread sabbaticals. Further such innovations seem sure to come.

Scholars do not see a mass return to the kitchen nor do they advise it. They write of increasing gains for the family and society as the feminine approach blends with the masculine in the market place, government and other work worlds. However they accept that a portion of women will still choose to stay at home but with far more status than the "just a housewife and mother" of the industrial era. To Betty Friedan's credit she admits her earlier error about the family and now pushes for gains for the woman at home.

Perhaps the most outstanding of present advance, urged by the keen sensitivity of women alert to the needs of others, is that of helping men learn the supreme satisfaction of genuinely nurturing their offspring. The rewards go much further than only, as I observe with joy in my own sons, their expanding personhood. Genuine child involvement by both parents promises much better mental health for the young so blessed. Recent research by Sue Manfield indicates it can even mitigate the war drive in sons.

George Longstaff's own radical young life adds inspiration for the camp connection after 2000. Increasingly diminishing his traditional status of dentist he turned to the wilds to do his own thing. Spiraling beyond the earlier pioneers, who also did not have a map, he too found his own way to hew his new vision—a superlative private girls' camp.

So the Longstaff camp concepts endure. He put the spring in their spiral.

Gladys Yost was a Moss Lake camper in the twenties, a counsellor in the thirties, a head counsellor in the seventies, and replaced me for some months at the head of

Adirondack-Southern. She received her bachelor's degree in English and journalism from Syracuse University, served on the staff of the Philadelphia Enquirer, directed the judging department for the first contest conducted by Connelly Advertising, and served as a public relations counsellor. Marriage and the raising of a family then became a full-time interest, but in recent years she has been a free-lance journalist.

Of the three Lakes I owned and the many I visited, Moss Lake always seemed the gem.

CHAPTER X

Personalities with Special Adirondack Impact

JOHN ZIMNOCH

The Dean Of Our Staff For Over Forty Years

The country has had many fine competitive swimming coaches, but I am quite certain that none of these, unless it was Matt Mann, could equal John Zimnoch in the development of raw material. When it was time for my son to attend camp, I sent him to the Mann Camp, but only the advanced swimmers received instruction from Matt, and when Geof returned to Moss Lake (his camp had closed more than two weeks earlier) John had to work with him for several hours to readjust his timing.

My first contact with John was as a would-be swimmer wanting winter instruction. I received it on Clinton Street in Brooklyn in the world's most frigid pool. Fortunately, I judged him not by my progress but by that of soon-to-be-world-famous Eleanor Holm, who started at the same time but who was developing into an impressive swimmer before the holidays.

John was a large and initially forbidding man, but after a couple of weeks the "Mr. Z" cry was the happiest on the waterfront. John missed the first two years of camp, but stayed on with its lessees for two seasons after my departure. In addition, he coached ten years at my Adirondack-Southern school in St. Petersburg, Florida but became terminally ill just before we opened the new school pool he had helped me plan.

Recently I had occasion to talk with an early alumna in connection with a camp reunion we were planning, and was surprised to hear that she had recently crossed Uncle John's trail in Ft. Lauderdale. John had been dead for a few years but one of his pupils, the famous Johnny Weismuller, was at pool side and sought her out when she left the water. He told her that in his long career he had met but one coach who could develop such a stroke. Of course, it was John Zimnoch. To properly evaluate the significance of this one must take into consideration that the lady in question had had no contact with Zimnoch for over forty years. When she first came to Moss Lake the Red Cross manual which was the bible of nearly all camps based its approach on the breaststroke and the sidestroke. As they are so much less efficient than the crawl we were quite accustomed to having our families enthuse about the sharp contrast between their daughters' swimming and that of the other girls in their schools and clubs, but having a report like this one from Johnny Weismuller is a pleasure I wish John were here to share.

John Zimnoch

Harold DeGroat

Andrew Brush

J. Martinez Castello

Henry Suydam

Barretto DeSouza

Colonel Alexis Selihoff

Frank Carroll

Hugh Castello

Colonel Nicholas Shiskin

Prince Wolkonski

Mary Elizabeth McCaddon

George Delahay

Carl Thompson

Captain Theodore Selihoff

Anneliese von Oettingen

Edward Luchia

Selwyn Orcutt

Lillian Martin

Stewart McDonald

Colonel Boris Guenichta

Captain Basel Von Bretzel

BARRETTO DE SOUZA

Barretto de Souza came to Moss Lake at the same time as John Zimnoch. Together they laid the foundation for the staff of specialists that made Moss Lake summers a unique and invaluable experience. Spanish by blood lines, he was a Portuguese count with no jumping background, but he had no peer as instructor in equitation and dressage. In fact, I still refer to his books when I wish to check a question of technique.

COLONEL GEORGE OTAROFF

Otaroff was the first of a long line of Russian army officers to serve at Moss Lake. He died early but not until he had convinced me that the Imperial Cavalry officers could be a real asset to our riding department and had introduced me to Colonel Selihoff.

COLONEL ALEXIS SELIHOFF

Selihoff had been in this country no longer than our other Russian officers, but his English was very good by the time he came to camp. The Imperial Officers Cavalry School in Petrograd was most commonly known as the Fillis School. James Fillis, an Englishman, who with the Bouchers, father and son, in France, were generally recognized as the current world authorities, was under contract there. However, since it was an officer's school, the commandant had to be a military man. Selihoff, who had been a successful Olympic representative for Russia, was selected for the post, which he held until the war broke out.

When he came to us he was doing most of his teaching at the Brooklyn Riding Club and already had had a pupil win the national Good Hands. De Souza's health soon forced his retirement and Colonel Selihoff took over. He remained with us for many years until his death, and under his tutelage our girls gathered an impressive list of ribbons in the Lake George and Lake Placid shows and continued to be a factor in the National Good Hands until the ASPCA discontinued the class.

COLONEL SIMON ACOUTIN

Acoutin was a riding instructor at the Knox School in Cooperstown. All of our Russian Army officers were gentlemen with a capital "G". If I had not been completely convinced of this by the time Acoutin reached camp, I would have been before he left. He was a warm person with an interest in the camp and its campers that far exceded any reasonable expectations. Of course, he also was an excellent horseman.

COLONEL NICHOLAS SHISKIN

Shiskin was a complete horseman dedicated to excellence, and in terms of Moss Lake the most durable of them all. Except for a two-year temperment-vacation he was with us continuously for thirty years. Through most of these he taught our jumping, and during his last seasons he headed the riding department.

CAPTAIN BASIL BOLDYREFF

Boldyreff was not a Cavalry officer, but he was a good rider and Selihoff suggested that I engage him for our daily road rides (we had a separate string of horses for this giving us a total of four strings—one for the beginners, one for the Jumpers, and one for the advanced equitation girls). He served the camp well in this capacity for several years.

MURRAY WILDER

Wilder of Richfield Springs was a chance contact, but the fact that he had been associated with de Souza in New York City and had a similar approach to his horses was most reassuring. I offered him a post which he accepted and which he filled most adequately as long as his health permitted. We had three or four male instructors through all but the first few years of the camp, but de Souza, Wilder, and Carroll were the only ones who were not former Russian Army officers, so, of course, the Fillis influence was strong.

FRANK CARROLL

When Colonel Selihoff died I knew of only one man who could fully fill his shoes. It was Frank Carroll who had climbed to the top of the horsemanship world a few years earlier, but as he reached the top had suffered a serious accident that invalided him for over two years. I heard that he was starting to resume work, established contact, and found that Moss Lake fitted into his recovery program.

The girls instantly realized he was a master technician and an inspiring individual, and the severe Selihoff loss quickly became a purely personal one.

The pupils that made and sustained Frank's reputation were quite equally divided between the equitation and jumping fields, but if there had been no reputation his acceptance at camp would have been instantaneous. He was with us for several excellent years.

COLONEL BORIS GUENICHTA

Guenichta was a late addition to our staff but a fine one. His European refuge had been France and Egypt, but America entered the picture when King Farouk sent his wife and daughters to California and wished horses and an instructor to follow. Guenichta was selected and soon gravitated to New York where he was picked up by my men. He was with us for about fifteen years at camp and five at Adirondack-Southern. An all-around horseman of high quality.

Through most of his Moss Lake years he accompanied contingents of our horses to various schools for their winter season—Knox, Avon-Old Farms, Gunston, and Mt. Ida Jr. College.

PRINCE WOLKONSKI

Wolkonski was as polished as the title would indicate and with an excellent reputation as a riding instructor. He was at camp but one year. After that initial summer I made arrangements for some of our horses to serve at a girl's school in Warrenton, Va. that was an extension of the Grier School in Tyrone, Pa. and put him in charge. He married the school secretary and as we could give him no family quarters, I could not offer him a new contract.

CAPTAIN BASIL VON BRETZEL

All of our Russians served with Kerensky during the White Revolution until his effort to save the country collapsed. Most then came out through the Crimea, but Von Bretzel brought his family out through Japan, zigzagging across the Chinese-Siberian border as they went. Mrs. Von Bretzel was royalty and this would have ensured execution, even of the children, had they been captured. In spite of the trip, she was still petite and handsome during the years I knew her. Von Bretzel was the instructor at the Watertown Hunt Club during his first year or two in camp, but later transferred to a girl's school in the Washington area.

CAPTAIN THEODORE SELIHOFF

Theodore had all of his brother's polish, diplomacy, and interest in his pupils, but he was younger and had not had the advanced training and teaching experience that made Alexis invaluable. However, he was a perfect tutor for the girls in the lower ring and filled that post most competently and happily through the few years he was with us.

CAPTAIN MICHAEL TEPLAKOW

His is perhaps the most unusual story of all. Apparently he was a highly regarded officer in the Czar's army and later with Kerensky. He was captured by the Reds and given his choice of a commission in their forces or execution—an option inspired by their desperate need for commanders. He elected to live, rose to the rank of General, and defected through Poland when an opportunity at last presented itself. The Former Russian Officer's Association absolved him and my men recommended that I offer him a position. He served us well but then died unexpectedly. While instructing at Moss Lake Camp during the summer, he taught engineering at Harvard in the winter months.

COLONEL SERGEY POLKOVNIKOFF

Polkovnikoff was a fine horseman with the patience so important to beginners, yet perfectly at home with our jumpers or our best equitation girls. With us fewer years than we would have liked.

WALLACE JOHNSON

In my days of watching tennis most closely, Wallace Johnson was runner-up to Tilden in the national tournament and a Davis Cup player. I wanted some such person to put our tennis department "on the map" and as I had heard nothing of him for some years I thought the chances good that he might be interested and looked him up. He was coaching the University of Pennsylvania team and available. He stayed with us for seven years and established his sphere in the camp as a worthy companion of our riding and swimming departments. Tennis joined them as a "Major", scheduled as a daily activity for Senior and Lodge, and three times a week for Junior.

FRANK ANDERSON

For three years Frank Anderson was the national indoor champion of the country and an excellent technician. When I had to replace Wallace Johnson I felt a keen obligation to uphold the tennis standards he had established. Frank was the first to step into his shoes and he filled them competently.

CHARLES WOOD

Wood was a Palm Beach pro and president of the National Professional Association. He was with us for only one year and, of course, our tennis standards did not suffer during that time.

ELMER GRIFFIN

Griffin ranked in the first ten for some years, was National Doubles Champion playing with his older brother, and a member of our Davis Cup team. His two years at Moss Lake were pleasing ones.

SELWYN ORCUTT

Orcutt was strictly a teaching pro, but a good one, who headed the tennis department for us through three seasons.

PAUL HARDING

Paul was never a top player, although he did win the District of Columbia championship for five or six years, but Tilden thought so highly of him that he made him the teaching pro at his Park Avenue court. He was with us for seven years until his death and these may have been the best years of Moss Lake tennis—in good part because he had the best assistant of them all.

LILLIAN MARTIN

Lillian had many years to demonstrate her teaching ability as Harding's assistant, and when he died I decided I should go with her proven quality rather than look for a bigger name. I never had occasion to regret the decision. She was a teaching pro in Englewood and secretary of the National Professional Association. She remained with us until she died in the late Sixties.

J. MARTINEZ CASTELLO

My contact with "Papa" (a title by which he apparently was known from one end of the Fencing world to the other), like that with Zimnoch and de Souza, was established by Philip Farley and it was as fortunate as the others.

Fencing does not have the popular appeal of swimming and riding, but Papa's personality and enthusiasm captured the girls' interest at once and his teaching ability made it certain that any girl who did average work for him was sure of a place on her college team if the school she selected had one.

He was with us for about fifteen years and the department continued under his N.Y.U. assistants and other instructors he suggested until 1960. They included James Murray of Columbia, George Cherney, his N.Y.U. assistant, Eddie Luchia of C.C.N.Y., Andre of Annapolis, and his own son, Hugo, who replaced him at N.Y.U. and took over his equipment business.

Nobody appreciated the personalities and teaching abilities of our Moss Lake specialists more than Papa and his enthusiasm did much to enhance the camp image. The substitutes he suggested carried us forward, but when we came to the end of that string I made a desperate attempt to have him return. He was well into his eighties but fit as a fiddle. However, his wife was not and he could not leave her alone in Florida. Some years later I had an application for a fencing post at Adirondack-Southern from a Tampa man, and when I mentioned knowing Papa, his mouth fell open and he told me he had crossed foils with him the previous day and been disarmed in seconds. Papa died in 1976 at the age of ninety.

ANDREW BRUSH

"Uncle Andy" was the country's foremost archery instructor with a personality that instantly made his specialty an extremely popular one, even though it is a sport with little inherent appeal—at least when compared with riding, swimming, tennis, and water skiing. While at Moss Lake he took a camp group to the New York State Tournament for four years, and each time some girl came back with the first place award in her age bracket—this in spite of archery being a camp minor scheduled for only three hours per week.

"Uncle Andy" was with us through two severe heart attacks, but after the third told me he did not think he should try to return and suggested Carl Thompson as a replacement. In his description he said that if Carl had concentrated on teaching instead of starting his own archery equipment manufacturing operation in North Carolina his pupils might have been the best of all. I was not able to secure his services at the time, but did engage a recent national champion:

GEORGE DELAHAY

"Uncle George" was a former national champion and as he was also a fine teacher the department flourished during his years with us. He later came to Adirondack-Southern to teach both archery and golf—I remembered that he had once told me that as a young man he had been a better golfer than archer.

CARL THOMPSON

This was another case of my good luck holding. By the time I had to replace Uncle George, Thompson had sold his archery concern and was available for camp. He was all that Uncle Andy had judged him to be, and the department continued to flourish. My opinion of him as an individual was so high that he was my first choice to ensure the safe return of our Adirondack-Southern girls from Mexico when Scotty died of appendicitis in Monterey. He also taught Archery for us at the school.

JAMES HOSFORD

Jim was 6'6" and a typical Texan. He brought more equipment to camp and to school than all his predecessors combined and found use for all of it in his teaching and in maintaining our equipment. He probably was the most exacting coach we ever had in any sport and his efficacy was best demonstrated at Adirondack-Southern. In his second or third year there he entered his girls in a national youth tournament. It was conducted by mail but all scores and tournament conditions had to be attested to by a member of the National Professional Association. Competing against the whole country the girls from our little school took first place in all three age divisions. His wife taught with him so the instruction was doubly intensive and detailed.

HAROLD DEGROAT

"Mr. De" was head of athletics at Springfield College and a sailing enthusiast. The mother of an early camper gave me a description of his work and personality so glowing that I lost no time in contacting him and was able to sign him to a Moss Lake contract. He had taught the sport at Camp Mystic and this was his primary assignment at Moss Lake. Most of his time was spent in Junior Camp and no one man or woman did more to keep it on an enthusiastic but stable course. His children should have been ten girls instead of two boys.

He left to take a military assignment as soon as the war started, but his health broke and he was back in camp the next year. His return coincided with our lowest manpower ebb. Albert Benson had to open Cedar Isles on his own and Mr. De, Martin Swanson, and I had to do all the physical preparation of Moss Lake until the last week in June, with the Colonels looking after their own horses. The redeeming factor was that as soon as schools closed, young workmen and waitresses were plentiful.

Mr. De was with us for about thirty years and his presence helped write a most pleasant chapter of Moss Lake history.

HELMY SMIRNOVA

Helmy was an Esthonian countess who came to this country with the last Russian Imperial Ballet. Her uncle was the Russian consul in New York. When World War I broke out, he gave her three thousand dollars and told her he would be back in a few weeks—as soon as the war ended. That was her last word from him so she was left on her own at eighteen. She started teaching ballet in Syracuse and was extremely successful. Technically she must have been one of the country's finest for she was later offered a post that would have involved the choreography and coaching for the ballet group in Radio City. For ten years she gave us another department that could not be matched elsewhere. Helmy was succeeded by three American dance teachers.

EDITH DONNELL

Edith taught in a New Jersey private school during the winter. Her instruction was adequate but Helmy's shoes were hard to fill.

ALICE SLATER

Alice was not a celebrity in her own right, but she was teaching for the famous Ruth St. Denis during the winter and had a fine approach to the girls. She was popular and most competent but was married and lost to camp after two years.

PEGGY PIERCE

Peggy was even younger than Alice and less experienced but her personality and work were extraordinarily fine, and I was much disappointed when she took a husband even more quickly.

ROSA PARRAGA

I cannot remember how I established contact with Rosa but it was an extremely lucky day for Moss Lake. She was an unusually fine dance teacher and was even more valuable as a person. She and her sister ran the most prestigious of Havana's girls' schools, and after her first year at Moss Lake she started recommending the camp to her pupils.

These Cubans were a grand group of girls, and at her suggestion I adopted a practice of never putting two of them in the same cabin. As a result they became as fluent in conversation in a single season as did our school girls in a full semester at Adirondack-Southern—even though there they had three class hours devoted to English each day. The reasons for this are something of a puzzle, but I think the key lies primarily in the campers being separated in cabins, at table, and to a large extent in the activities with only one Spanish speaking girl assigned to each group. This was more effective in forcing them to abandon Spanish and both talk and think in English than the formal school taboos. Also in camp they were quite constantly doing things that interested them and this engendered a desire to understand and speak the new language. Our camp singing also was a great help.

This stream from Havana to Moss Lake became so strong that even with Rosa's careful screening of applications, it usually exceeded our quota, and I could effect only a partial solution by considering Cubans who had been with us two years as American. Her standards were so high that she advised me to turn down the first two Batista registrations we received, but when the third came told me that this son had married into a proper family and his daughter should be accepted.

When Castro took over, I tried, by letter and through a niece living in New Jersey who also felt she should leave Havana, to persuade her to come to us, but she decided to stay and that decision was Adirondack-Southern's loss. I heard recently that she is now living in Miami.

ANNELIESE VON OETTINGEN

Anneliese was a German dancer whose life was changed not by World War I but by World War II. Her family's situation was made painfully dramatic by Hitler's anti-Jewish program. She had studied in England through the courtesy of a young lady friend who had inherited money there. She was reluctant to repatriate these funds and told Anneliese she could finance the expenses of her British education from them.

Later this lady was classified as non-Aryan because a great grandfather had been Jewish, and when Anneliese returned the favor of helping her leave the country, this was discovered and she and her family were scheduled for one of the terminal camps. Fortunately, Anneliese lived in a rather small city and the Burgermeister and his wife had been in service to her family for many years before he was elected to office. This impelled him to warn them in time to effect their escape. For this, he was taken away and never heard from again.

Anneliese had a sister who had married a Procter & Gamble executive in Cincinnati so she started life anew in that city. I made contact with her shortly after that and Eagle Bay became her summer residence. She continued spending her summers there after the demise of Moss Lake, and now conducts an Adirondack ballet school during June, July, and August. In the interim she developed a tremendous following in Cincinnati that enabled her to build a large physical plant of her own, which she did not sell until the late Seventies. By that time her reputation was established and in one year I saw three feature articles about her accomplishments in national magazines—one of them, strangely, "Sports Illustrated."

A tremendous plus was that Anneliese made every class minute count. There were no displays of temperment when trips or other camp events interfered with her schedule. Were she not more valuable as a dance teacher, she would be a fine camp executive.

In addition to her work in the Adirondacks and in Cincinnati, Anneliese has for some years spent several weeks each winter with our Adirondack-Southern girls. Although she has only had about fifteen hours with each girl she has managed to put on consistently pleasing performances year after year. If we count these school years Anneliese joins John Zimnoch, Harold De Groat, Albert Benson, Nicholas Shiskin and me as members of the "30 Plus Group."

At this point she is carrying a somewhat more extensive schedule for the new owners of Adirondack-Southern, and coaching two ballet companies recruited from her Cincinnati girls that perform each year at churches, colleges, schools, and art centers. One, her Kinder-ballet, composed of girls from eight to twelve, is an extension of a similar company she created for the famous Kurferstendum Theatre in Berlin.

All of the foregoing has been accomplished by a lady who landed in this country without funds and with two young children and two aged parents to support.

BRUCE PARKER

There was no such thing as water skiing when our other sports were being established at Moss Lake, nor was the competition as keen as today when Bruce competed. As a result Bruce acquired more national and international titles than will ever be possible for anyone in the future. In about 1940 he turned pro and operating from Nassau and Long Island built an enviable reputation. Indeed, his reputation was so impressive that Dick Pope offered him a third interest in the then-embryonic *Cypress Gardens* in central Florida for five thousand dollars. Bruce was a friend of one of our camp parents and when I happened to mention an interest in skiing, he suggested him and established the contact. The arrangement we worked out called for his giving lessons on his own account at Darts and our girls going there for instructions. It was a good introduction to skiing for the girls and my elder daughter, Sue Carol, found it especially rewarding. She apparently had a real flair for the sport and, on the strength of her work with Bruce and a few pre-tournament hours with Stewart McDonald, won the Eastern States championship in her age bracket.

The second year Bruce had a very capable assistant, Evy Wofford who came to camp so that all of our strong swimmers could have skiing. We bought a ski boat and the department was launched.

HENRY SUYDAM

Henry was the most remarkable athlete I have ever known. A chemistry laboratory accident cost him his left hand and wrist during his senior year in high school; yet in college he captained the tennis team and was undefeated as a member of the wrestling team.

At forty he took up water skiing and two years later was the country's all-around champion. A year or two later he dropped out of competition and his son (pupil of the father, of course) promptly took the title his father had held.

The Suydams lived on the island, which by the time of their arrival had become our ski center. Mrs. Suydam not merely helped prepare the beginners for their take-offs, but made the island a most cheerful place for the girls to visit.

STEWART MCDONALD

"Stew" was skiing's best salesman and a fine instructor. He filled in some of the years missed by Henry Suydam and also coached at Adirondack-Southern.

HILLYER—FATHER AND SON

Between them the Hillyers covered the other years that Henry Suydam missed. The father was the Rollins College coach and his son's instructor. Roland was the country's all-around champion while he was with us. In short I had as good reason to be proud of the quality of our skiing over the full span of the department's existence as that of any of the other sports.

CAROLINE LONGSTAFF NELSON

My sister, Caroline, is eight years my junior which meant she was fifteen and still camper age in 1923. This was a major consideration in my decision to have a girls' rather than a boys' camp. It paid off nicely from the start. When camp opened she was the only one who knew the immediate territory, except the camp guide and care-taker, and the only one who had even met the director before the first of the year. More importantly I knew I had one camper who was looking forward to the year and who could be counted on to contribute more than her quota of positive thinking, and to bring to my attention any points of camp procedure that might be bothering the girls.

My policy was to take no "young" counsellors but other camps did, so when she was 19 I "farmed her out" to a New England camp to acquire an adult perspective. This proved to be a very wise procedure and when she returned she immediately became a valuable counsellor.

Later she took on part of the interviewing of both campers and counsellors. Her value continued to increase until she married in 1936. Fortunately her husband was a school man teaching in the Detroit, and later, the Toledo area. Both were good camp fields so her contributions continued on a long-distance-reduced-time basis. Most of her summers were spent in the area of camp and she served as consultant and emergency executive fill-in. Thank you, Caroline.

HELEN FROST

Miss Frost was head of the physical education department at Teachers College in New York, director of its summer training camp, "Saneo", a dance authority with a book on the subject to her credit, and an extremely attractive lady in the bargain. She was our 1923 Director and established many lasting camp patterns. Her marriage to an Australian the next winter was a heavy blow to my plans.

ADELE KAUFMAN

"Pokey" was head of the physical education department at Miss Porter's School in Connecticut, but as completely feminine a girl as I have ever known. She headed our 1924 staff, but with the title of head counsellor. I became my own director at this point and between us we gave the camp an excellent year, due in large part to Pokey's tact and unfailing good nature.

EDITH POTTER

Edith was in charge of physical education at the Berkeley Preparatory School in Brooklyn. She was less athletic than most physical education teachers, but her perspective was excellent and for several years she was my most important confidant—yet would never accept a Head Counsellor post. Brooklyn still had many fine families at this time and as Edith was popular with the girls and highly respected by their parents they followed her to Moss Lake in the largest numbers in these early, or any future, camp years. One summer her girls totaled nearly thirty. She married rather soon and her time at camp dwindled, but she and her husband remained personal friends until their deaths.

ELLEN HAYES

"Jim" was the first head counsellor of Lodge. She was so obviously the executive type that I rather discounted her fine background, but even the discounted version was most impressive and I engaged her. Her ability and leadership soon justified the decision. She was with us for several years and made many valuable contributions, but I never crowded my luck by making a similar exception. She served as a WAC colonel during World War II.

HENRIETTA PETERSON

"Henri" was vice-principal of a girls' school on Riverside Drive in New York City when I met her. She was so handsome and so extremely feminine that I could not quite imagine her in a camp setting, but as we talked she told me she had had a year at an Adirondack camp (Ahmo) and loved it. That persuaded me my usual good luck was holding and I engaged her, as a canoeing counsellor I believe, but she served as head counsellor of Senior Camp for several years. While she was with us she entered an osteopathic college in Philadelphia and her graduation ended her camp years. Two of the other ladies whose names appear in this supplement, Elizabeth Lockwood and Elsie Barton, came to camp at her suggestion so her indirect influence ran on into the sixties.

ELIZABETH LOCKE

As the years went on my staff included fewer and fewer physical education teachers for most physical education schools took the position that teacher performance was not important—that one needed only to master the theories. This meant that they were seldom qualified to teach, or even assist, at Moss Lake. This was less the case at the Boston School and, in our earliest years at Sargent, so I kept the door open for their girls after they were closed to others. In general their lack of knowledge was complicated by their having supreme confidence in their book techniques and being critical of our specialists.

Fortunately, my contact with "Libby" was made while the door was still ajar. She proved to be an excellent canoeing counsellor and I was so impressed with her inspirational leadership that I asked her to replace the about-to-depart Ellen Hayes as Lodge head counsellor the following summer. She was with us for years and made a very fine and long lasting impression on Lodge.

ELIZABETH LOCKWOOD

"Lockie" was head counsellor of Junior Camp through most of its early years. She had a soft approach but commanded the respect of both girls and counsellors. She looked the part of a head counsellor and never stepped out of character. She was with us for several years and badly missed when she left.

MARY ELIZABETH MC CADDON

"Scotty" came to Moss Lake in 1934 as a girl of thirteen, seasoned by some years in a New England camp. She rode well, was good both on and in the water, loved trips, and was an outstandingly enthusiastic camper. She won her Honor Mention and Honor award and I would have very much liked to have had her on staff during her college years. However, she chose to take a Johns Hopkins course that would entitle her to a bachelor's degree and a nursing certificate and this involved her summers.

When she was graduated she returned to camp as our Lodge nurse. At the end of her first month I lost a canoeing counsellor and asked if she would prefer my securing a girl for that post or engaging another nurse. She had been viewing the camp activities with envy and elected to take the canoeing post. This position automatically made her

John Zimnoch's assistant during the two swimming hours at Lodge and these widened contacts let her personality and detailed knowledge of camp and camp customs soon make her my most influential counsellor. When a head counsellor vacancy arose she was the logical choice. Fortunately it was Lodge and from that point on it was as much her camp as mine.

When I planned a Florida-Adirondack boarding school she was enthusiastic and agreed to be its dean. She had spent her recent winters as nurse and science teacher in a small Florida boarding school and that background was most useful. The school started happily under the name of Adirondack-Southern in quarters I had rented in a St. Petersburg hotel and some weeks later I purchased a fine property on the same waterfront street and planned to have it ready for occupancy when the girls returned from a ten-week semester scheduled to start in January. Scotty looked forward to that day as eagerly as I did.

She undertook the Mexican project on her own so I could prepare the new estate for the March homecoming. Scotty died at the age of 39 in a Monterey hospital a few days after the girls assembled in that city. The blow to both camp and school was devastating and they carried the scars until they moved out of my orbit.

ELSIE BARTON

Elsie first came to camp as a friend of Henrietta Peterson to be housemother in Junior. Before her Moss Lake career ended she had been head counsellor of Junior Camp, head counsellor of Senior, and assistant director of Moss Lake. In all four positions she was outstanding and my only regret is that her final decision was against joining the Adirondack-Southern staff. All of my early school planning had been done with the expectation that Elsie and Scotty would be part of it, but a few weeks before school was to start she told me she would not be with us.

That summer we had prospects in the New York to Virginia area. I could not well leave camp myself yet felt immediate contact important. She took a week from camp and came back with eight enrollments for Adirondack-Southern, a school that, except for the Moss Lake facility, existed only on paper. This, of course, highlighted the severity of the blow implicit in her resignation. However, I still had Scotty and with so many commitments outstanding, I went ahead.

MARY JOST

Many men are sure they have, or have had, the perfect secretary, but I am certain none could have filled Mary's shoes at Moss Lake. Her husband, Charles, had been one of our Mohawk bachelors for several years while I was a teenager, but I had had no contact with him until he telephoned me to say that he had two daughters of camp age and would like to have our Moss Lake literature.

He enrolled the girls and they were with us for several seasons. I had always avoided having the daughters of staff members as campers but I was very much impressed with Mary, thought I detected a discreet hint in the course of our interview for the children, and offered her a post. I knew that in most camps the practice was to take a family camper in lieu of salary, but I thought the relationship would be a better one if Charlie paid the full tuition and I gave Mary a normal secretarial salary. By the time the girls' camping careers ended Mary was so much a part of camp that she continued without them.

She had been one of the founders of the Berkeley secretarial school in Manhattan, had an educational background and professional preciseness that precluded mistakes in her correspondence, could take dictation at any speed, contributed many constructive ideas, and seemed able to take all emergencies in stride. In addition she had a Social Register background that clearly was part of her personality and she never stepped out of character. Of course this helped to make her an ideal person for contacts with both parents and girls.

EVELYN MACDONALD

Since Moss Lake was an extremely athletic camp, even labeled a "Sports College" by some of its competitors, most girls to be listed here will be outstanding athletes. But "Ev" with minimal skills in sports can quite properly head the list. She was given an "Honor Mention" at the end of her first summer, voted her "Full Honors" the next year, given an internship as soon as her age permitted, and then a full counsellorship. At each level she exhibited an extraordinarily inspirational type of leadership that left a most delightful imprint upon the year and finally upon the camp.

Her marriage was fatal to her counsellor career but provided us with two daughters, one of whom will appear on this list. Further she started, and for fifteen years was the editor of, our Alumnae News.

PEGGY KILBON

Peggy richly deserves to share the same page with Ev. She was a solid citizen and perhaps the finest all-around athlete in the history of the camp. They were contemporaries as campers, as interns, and as counsellors. Peggy captained the Gray Team, Ev the Blues. Between them they could make any year a banner one for both campers and counsellors.

EDITH ANDERSON

Edith was from Berkely Institute in Brooklyn and an extremely nice young lady. She probably was a less-than-average athlete, but was the best of them all when she sat on a horse. This was Mr. de Souza's appraisal, and she did such a good job of proving him right by taking the National Good Hands Championship three consecutive years that the A.S.P.C.A. had to change their rules and disqualify from the National any girl who had won previously. This was recognition that I prized and gave riding an even more important place on our Moss Lake schedule.

BETTY DOIG

Betty was from Berkeley and an excellent rider, and equally fine in all the other camp sports. She not merely was the Blue Team captain, but a good measure of her ability was that she won twice as many team points as any other Blue for a three-year period.

ONNOLEE LOCKLEY, PEGGY SMITH, EMILIE LEONARD AND MIMI MERKLE

They all moved from Senior Camp to Lodge in the same summer. From the first it was clear that they were going to be the "big guns" the following year, although at that time the average age of Lodge was at least sixteen, and they were thirteen and fourteen.

Emilie came to us when she was seven yet never disappointed any instructor or counsellor. Peggy Smith, while the same age as Emilie, did not reach Moss Lake until she was ready for Senior Camp, but quickly established herself and they ran "neck and neck" throughout the Lodge years. As an alumna, Emilie did a better job than Peggy. She produced four girls capable of following in her footsteps. Peggy gave us only three, and while all tried none fell in love with Moss Lake. However, a younger sister, Betsy, took up the family shield and became an extremely valuable counsellor— in her last years the least replaceable on the entire counsellor staff. In fact, she did such a fine job of filling Scotty's head counsellor shoes that I tried for some years to have her desert Harvard and try on Scotty's Adirondack-Southern shoes. Mimi gave us four good years and brought one younger sister to camp, while Onnolee contributed seven brilliant summers and brought two sisters. Without these families the history of all three camps would have been a less memorable one.

LYNN WILKIE

Much later Lynn, the daughter of Evelyn MacDonald, appeared on the camp scene. She combined her mother's dynamic charm with her father's outstanding athletic ability—a combination hard to beat. Of course, I hoped her counsellor years might be many, but she married as soon as she finished college and while she now has a daughter of camp age there is no Moss Lake so the line must end.

NELSON HOPKINS

"Hoppy" headed Cedar Isles for all but two of its Longstaff years. He was an experienced and even-handed administrator who, within my general guidelines, set the pace and determined the atmosphere of the camp. I am sure that most boys from this period asked to name the dominant personality in the camp would say Hoppy, although some with an especially keen sailing interest might pick Mark Worthen.

MARK WORTHEN

I have never known a finer technician in his field than Mark and he exuded a highly contagious enthusiasm for the sport that quickly infected the entire camp and later the whole lake. He should be gratified to know that the seeds he planted are still growing and that sailing is by far the most popular local sport—even though skiing has many enthusiasts in the area. Mark was with us for several years, but we wished we might have had several more. He made Cedar Isles a "sailing camp."

COLONEL VALERIAN KORITSKY

When I started Cedar Isles we took the boys to Moss Lake for their riding instructions for the first two years, but then built a ring and stables on our land base and engaged Koritsky who had a riding school in lower Manhattan. A couple of women patients had given me a happy account of riding there, and when I asked some of my colonels, they endorsed him warmly. I was pleased as I watched his Cedar Isles program, but he could not get the same response from the boys that the other men always had from the girls. The boys' idea of riding seemed to be to learn to stay on a horse and then ride cross-country. Had I not had full confidence in Koritsky, I probably would have persisted in duplicating the Moss Lake pattern. We were both discouraged after a couple of years and I engaged a less technically competent man whose practice favored much road time. Apparently it was the right decision for when I started serious ring instructions and daily riding at Cascade and gave the Cedar Isles boys the option of transferring, only two changed.

CHARLES SPEIDEL

"Charlie" was the nationally known wrestling coach at Penn State for many years, but he had previously taught boxing and swimming and these were his sports at Cedar Isles. Through all his years at Cedar Isles he was "Hoppy's" right-hand man and the most pervasively inspirational.

HENRY SIMMONS

For many years "Hank" was my most important personal contact. We were in school together for a year at about the fifth or sixth grade level. He then moved to Holland Patent but returned when it was time for high school, and we soon found our mutual interests drawing us together. We played on the same basketball team and through our three years in high school were either the number 3 or number 2 tennis pair.

Hank frequently came to The Mohawk as my guest during the years he was at Andover and Yale and I was at Hamilton and Michigan, and this sealed the friendship.

His grandfather, Henry Munger, was Herkimer's most important and most affluent businessman, and as his only son had established himself in another city the family assumed that Hank would go in with his grandfather as soon as he finished Yale. However, "H.G." had different ideas and Hank came to New York to take a post in the Foreign Exchange Department of Chase Manhattan. By this time I was in a New York dental school and we had a year of frequent contacts.

Then Hank went back to Herkimer and from then on we saw each other only during the summer months. When he left New York he expected to be moving up rapidly in the Munger Store, but instead of being an executive immediately he spent three years filling lesser jobs in the store. I found sustaining Hank's morale during this time quite difficult and my success was possibly limited to persuading him not to turn his back on his grandfather's empire.

Before long the picture changed sharply and he was head of the department store and of Herkimer's only bank. This made him the most important man in town while still in his thirties. When he married we saw even less of each other, but the friendship endured.

In 1937 my personal world collapsed—my mother died suddenly in August, and Henry and his wife were decapitated in an automobile accident in the Fall. Fortunately, my next closest Herkimer friend, George Sluyter, succeeded him as bank president so even though the personal loss was heavy, my financial advice and support continued to be entirely sound. In fact, since George was many years my senior, the advice probably was accepted more completely than had been the case when Hank was president.

HELEN MACLACHLAN

My personal contacts at The Mohawk centered around the tennis courts, but the most important contribution to my social development was made by a Barnard student, Helen MacLachlan, who with her mother was an all-season guest for several years.

I guess she was the first girl to take an interest in me and the interest continued long enough to help me sketch the format of the camp and contribute to the selection of its staff. Her tutelage started on the dance floor and carried me through the house parties of my freshman year.

I saw her fifty years later and though she was four years my senior, she seemed little changed from the girl I had known at The Mohawk.

PHILIP FARLEY

My friendship with "Phil" started while we were both in high school. His aunt wished company for a long stay she planned at The Mohawk and Phil came with her. The next year she took him to Europe as a graduation present, but the following summer Phil wrote my mother and said he had enjoyed his time at The Mohawk so much that he would like to return on his own and wondered if she had a job he might fill. She had been very favorably impressed with Phil and decided she would like to entrust the clerkship to him. However, she feared he might be keenly disappointed when he discovered the difference between play and work and wrote him in this vein. He came and our friendship ripened through the summer.

The next year, being through in May at Columbia, he came in early saying that he would like some real exercise. If he got more than he bargained for, he never showed it. We had purchased Moss Lake by this time, but had no immediate plans for it except cutting a supply of firewood. I had had a rather large number of dead beech trees felled in the Fall. In the Spring I had them skidded and purchased a drag saw. Atypically, we were without a skilled woodsman that year, so it was up to Phil and me to fuel the fireplaces. I took a future dishwasher to help me with the logs and Phil volunteered to do the splitting—a job that I could not have done well then or at any time in my lumber-filled career. We finished the work by the time it was necessary for Phil to take over the office.

Later during my dental college and dental practice years in New York we saw each other frequently. Moss Lake Camp started about that time and Phil was my attorney and chief advisor until the property was sold and he retired. In spite of his counsel, I made a number of mistakes, but I am sure there would have been many more had I not had his support. Summer contacts were renewed when he entered his daughter in Moss Lake and made closer when we purchased Darts together.

ALBERT BENSON

Albert was one of the three Swedish lumberjacks Oscar Johnson brought to Moss Lake in the fall of 1924 when I decided we should have a bridle path around the lake.

He was the most completely loyal workman any employer ever had. He came from a fine family, his brother was a physician, and while English was obviously not his native tongue, he had talents that extended far beyond lumber camp needs and into our maintenance and building area. I made him my camp foreman and was able to forget most details and much of the planning for the next thirty-five years.

There might have been a successful Moss Lake without Albert but it could have been neither the same nor as good. Yet one of the stiffest tests of his ability came not at Moss Lake, but at Cedar Isles. After the fire there we not merely needed to rebuild, but also to blast out a level plane for a ball field, to break up much of the rock for an all stone recreation hall, and then draw to the Island from Moss Lake enough dirt to convert the rough rocky surface into a level lawn on which grass could logically be planted.

In addition, we had to build a combination dining hall, kitchen, boathouse, and administrative offices—and have them ready by July 5th. This I accomplished by acting as my own Moss Lake foreman, giving Albert a rough sketch of the buildings and the men he thought he needed. Only the last was difficult. The island and its big rock pile earned it the name of Alcatraz. For most it was a light-hearted label, but for others it seemed all too accurate and many replacements were needed. I gave Albert as many of my old men as possible to mix with the new and he made my unreasonable deadline. No other man could have done it and even Albert could have done it only in a severe depression year.

Albert's effectiveness lay not merely in his own knowledge and skill, but in his practice of always using himself as the pacesetter for the group that had the most difficult or most urgent job.

On one sad occasion I nearly lost Albert. We had a maid at Moss one fall who was not the high school or college student that we usually used for our waitress staff, but a girl from a north-country farm. I realized that Albert and Veronica were spending much of their free time together, but thought nothing of it until Albert, who had earlier asked for a week's vacation, said he had used that time to buy a farm and that he and Veronica were going to be married. My disappointment was matched only by my relief when he came back a few months later and told me he had parted company with Veronica and sold the farm.

Albert told me when he turned sixty-five and suggested that I reduce his wages to the amount he could draw without affecting his social security. I told him that this was too generous but he insisted, saying that as he lived at camp and didn't drive a car, he had little use for money. I tried to reciprocate by taking him to Florida with us for the couple of months that were woven into our year's schedule at that time. He would not come but continued to work at his regular fifty-one week pace for the rest of his days. Some years later he put in a normal day's work, played cards for a couple of hours, and was found peacefully dead in his bed the next morning.

A few days earlier he had asked me about drawing a will and I had suggested our local attorney. He saw him and outlined his wishes. His higher appointment came before the second one with the attorney—who later told me that Albert had planned to give five thousand dollars to each of my children! Since he died intestate, everything he had saved went to his brother in Sweden whom he had described to the attorney as already having too much money.

J. HILLIS MILLER

The Reverend Hillis Miller's role in the birth of the very wonderful Big Moose Chapel was second only to that of the master builder, Earl Covey, himself. He started to serve the congregation before the planning for the chapel took definite form, had much to do with its crystalization, assisted in the fund raising, fortified Earl's morale as occasion arose, and served as its first pastor.

While he was doing this he also acted as our camp chaplain and set the Sunday pattern which we maintained as long as the camp was in my hands. Protestant services were held at camp and we took our Catholic girls to mass either at Inlet or Big Moose in the morning. Mr. Zimnoch held our traditional "Island Swim" when they returned. It was a half mile that had to be made at an unbroken crawl and I always thought it a most valid measure of his teaching genius. We seldom had a year in which any camper from either Senior or Lodge failed to complete the swim before the end of the summer, even though each year brought us a number of non-swimmers. Only one island swim was required to qualify for water skiing and canoe trips, but most girls made it nearly every Sunday. The Millers watched the swim, had dinner with us, and then held Protestant services at 3 P.M.

While still on our camp staff Miller left the Riverside Church in New York City to become Dean of Students at Bucknell University and later president of Keuka College. His next step up the ladder was an appointment as Associate Commissioner of the New York State Department of Education. Shortly after this he accepted the president's chair at Florida University in Gainesville. Although approximately my age he was allowed but four or five years in his important post—yet in those years his personality and executive ability made a lasting impression on that university. Had he lived I think he might have stayed in this post indefinitely, and if he had I am sure that campus would have remained orderly and safe. He was not merely a theologian but a leader with high human goals who would have become a mighty crusader had the principles and morals of his school started to crumble in his time.

MOSES COHEN

Several businessmen did me many favors in the early years, but it was to Moses Cohen I always turned for local advice. He had come to the Adirondacks as a Russian immigrant with very limited funds, and started as a peddler. Originally he went between our scattered communities with his wares on his back, then travelled with a horse and a peddler's cart, and later opened a hardware store in Old Forge. By the age of fifty he had made himself quite affluent, and gained the respect of the community.

My credit with Mr. Cohen always seemed unlimited. Apparently, he was equally generous with others. Their defaults, together with a large number of second mortgage investments, required him to start rebuilding his fortune when he was nearly sixty, but I never heard him complain of either his bad luck or of any double-crossing. This and the fact that when, ten Depression years later, he turned his business over to his son his worth was probably greater than before the crash, increased my admiration. He never told me this in so many words, but his reticence in both adversity and recovery greatly heightened my regard.

In my building years, we had a mutually convenient system of his devising. His bills would be allowed to run without limit through the year. He was a director of the local bank and as such was expected to keep in touch with everything. The day after my bank account achieved healthy proportions in the spring, he would drop by my office unannounced, sit on the porch until I was free, then come in with some irrelevant chitchat. I would ask him for my bill, he would hand it to me and thank me for the check. I disappointed him just once. That time although the season was right, the account was much less healthy than usual. He accepted my non-performance most graciously and I rallied more rapidly than most of his local accounts.

Two years later he suggested my buying one of his defaulted properties, and later another. Both were sales contracts, and I do not think that either was reduced to writing; certainly I cannot imagine that being the procedure with anyone except Moses Cohen. I paid for one in full two years later, and when it looked as though the war would keep the other from working out he took it back without protest merely saying that my yearly payments had been a satisfactory rental.

THE CINCINNATI KID

The greatest impetus for, and satisfaction in, our riding department came from men like Baretto de Souza, Alexis Selihoff, and Frank Carroll, but there were some equine personalities whose contributions were extremely important. Without question the outstanding example was the Cincinnati Kid.

Both the horse and my introduction to him were unique. Prior to 1925 we had rented most of our horses, but that spring we had decided we should buy and save the best for future years—a policy we continued throughout the life of the camp. By June we had acquired the needed number and had gone into Kauffman's, a nationally known saddlery on Twenty-Fourth Street in New York City, to secure twenty saddles and bridles. We had purchased some of our horses from a stable directly across the street; the owner spotted us and came up with a most effective way of catching our attention. He had a horse so handsome he could not understand how it had fallen into his hands. He could find no infirmity but felt there must be a serious one, an admission that left me feeling I must have found an honest horse trader. His idea, which he executed promptly, was to lead the horse into the store and between the long rows of glass show cases to the back of the store where we were examining saddles.

The Kid was not a large horse, 15.2 and about 900 pounds, but his princely carriage would have caught our eyes in a crowded paddock. In the store where no horse belonged, our interest in the equipment almost evaporated and we said we would be at his stable in a few minutes. The senior Kauffman who was selling us the saddles was obviously annoyed at the intrusion but admitted that just looking at the horse was a rare treat.

We had to complete our tack purchases so our "few minutes" stretched to the better part of an hour and that probably had a salutary effect on the asking price. It was so low that we thought his suspected infirmity must be a reality but paid for him on an "as is" basis and left with our fingers crossed. The dealer's estimate of his age was twelve years. When it was made official it was fourteen, but by then he was the hit of the stable and even if he had been twenty-four we would have considered him the bargain of the year.

He proved to be the bargain of the century. His personality made him a standout as soon as he entered a show ring and his training always appeared to be as good as his rider. We continued to show him in both horse and equitation classes at Lake George (The Sagamore) and Lake Placid until the year of his death at the age of thirty.

The man who sold him to me did not know his record, merely that he was from the Handley show stables, but no horse enthusiast who had had the privilege of watching him could fail to recognize him as he moved around a show ring and several looked me up during the ensuing years to tell me where they had seen him previously,

My father took him to Jamaica each winter so he worked twelve months, yet he never took a lame step, nor made a dangerous move. He liked to dance and would throw in some playful bucks from time to time but if a rider's seat became insecure he sensed it immediately and would calm down instantly. He fell once with my father, but although it was a woodchuck hole he was uninjured and my father had only a badly scratched face and broken glasses.

At he end of his last camp summer I turned him out to pasture at Cascade for a month's vacation before he was to be shipped to Jamaica. About a week before his scheduled departure he became ill and our veterinary gave me a diagnosis of "old age" and said there was nothing he could do. I visited him morning and night for three days and on the fourth day found him in the open stable and unable to rise. I bedded him as well as I could and went over every two or three hours. On my evening visit he was barely able to raise his head and I sat down to hold it in my lap. He gave a tremendous sigh and was gone.

I searched diligently for a replacement but it was spring before I found one that was truly fine in conformation, training, and personality. He also was fourteen and nicely filled the void in my father's days. He was still riding him at the age of 93 but we never thought of Major as being a real member of the family as we had The Kid.

The Cincinnati Kid at Lake Placid Show 1931, Peggy Kilbon up

CHAPTER XI

Adirondack-Southern

The next major event of the fifties was my father's death and a few years later the demise of my dental practice. To the end he had been independent and supportive. No one guessed his age and my own calculations were six years short, as I discovered when I found childhood papers among his effects. He had had three generations of friends, each one younger than its predecessor. Both dentistry and riding contributed generously not only to his longevity but also to his unfailingly good health. Until my secretary phoned me in Florida to say she thought he was too ill to be in the office, he had never seriously curtailed his work load nor reduced his outside interests.

He lived but a few more months and his death brought to life a long-ago-shelved dream of having a southern boarding school with the Moss Lake philosophy and a deeply experienced faculty. I was not yet sixty and with my father's ninety-three active years behind me I felt I had plenty of time, but I did shrink from the financial commitments that would be involved. I did not like the solution that in 1960 presented itself, but the dream was a vivid one, and it would give me a balanced year with four active months in the Adirondacks and eight in Florida. The decision was not an easy one, but I sold Darts Lake and went property hunting. Moss Lake had always been my chief love and major interest, and the split-season school that I envisioned seemed certain to react to the advantage of the camp.

Dreaming and ambition were reenforced by two more realistic considerations. We were doing a greater amount of tutoring at Moss Lake, and it was becoming increasingly important to the development of the girls receiving it. There seemed to be two main reasons for this, the neglect of phonics and the spread of New Math. Further, the English situation was seriously complicated by the growing number of hours being devoted to television. They were mentally stultifying in themselves and replaced many hours that otherwise would have been spent in reading for pleasure. Incredibly meager vocabularies and a sharply lessened feel for the niceties of our language resulted so that our goal of the socially well-equipped young lady became more difficult to achieve.

The potential of the much longer school year seemed full of promise and as I tried to forecast the financial picture I could find no reason for the constant pleas for donations and endowments that seemed to be an almost universal part of the private school picture.

However, the field was new to me; so I telephoned the only man I knew who both owned and operated a girls' boarding school. He was encouraging, told me he was going to be in New York later in the week and offered to bring his income reports for the last two years. I saw him in his hotel and found the picture to be more than reassuring. Moss Lake profits averaged about fifteen percent, but his were approximately thirty.

When I turned my attention to locating a school property, my first thought was St. Petersburg. My mother-in-law had owned a bungalow there and we had spent considerable time with her. As I liked the city and its weather, I started my prospecting by spending two months in the vicinity with my son. We checked properties there, then east to Orlando, south to Ft. Myers, and north to Port Richey, and also drove down to Mexico. My vision was of a migratory school starting its year at Moss Lake, moving to St. Petersburg in mid-October, having a second trimester in Mexico, returning to St. Petersburg in March and to Moss Lake in May. This had real appeal to my girls and fortunately to some families.

I probably should have spent a second year seeking and securing a suitable property, but my preliminary soundings were good and the two most important ladies on my staff seemed eager to become part of the twelve-month venture. I persuaded myself that striking while the iron was hot was my real reason for wishing to go ahead at once—not just wanting to see the dream develop as rapidly as possible.

Moving immediately, of course, meant planning the first year with Moss as our only physical base. Since I expected to spend the first and the last six weeks of the school year there, this consideration did not appear to be a serious hurdle, and I made arrangements to rent part of a St. Petersburg hotel until Christmas and secured a similar set-up in Monterey, Mexico for the second trimester.

I felt certain I could secure a proper Florida base during that interval and have it ready for the girls when they returned from Mexico. When I asked the two ladies I thought would do so much to ensure the success of the school for definite commitments, one, the head counsellor of "Lodge" (our teenage division) agreed; the other, my assistant director, declined because her son and daughter had both settled in California with their children, and she quite understandably wished to be near them. Thus, I lost my very wonderful Elsie Barton but felt confident my Scotty McCaddon would make the operation a viable one.

It was too late for a normal enrollment campaign, but some Moss Lake girls secured their parents' approval and Mrs. Barton developed a few outside contacts. We started with twelve girls and with high hopes—much of the enthusiasm coming from Scotty and her Lodge girls. English, French, mathematics, history, and biology were the only subjects during the six weeks at Moss Lake and that period was a roaring success with the camp facilities at the girls' disposal.

The Florida season ran smoothly but as the first trimester closed Scotty told me she had been having intestinal pains that disturbed her and was anxious to get back to her family physician. When I went to St. Petersburg to see Scotty and the contingent of girls she was scheduled to drive to Monterey, she told me that her physician had decided her ailment was merely a nervous stomach and had given her pills to control the pain. She made the drive to Monterey, talked with me after their arrival, and again the next night to indicate that all was going well. Forty-eight hours later I received a call from her father telling me that Scotty had died in a Monterey hospital just two hours after an operation to remove a ruptured appendix. Today's techniques might have saved her life even at that point, but I surely feel that the Boca Raton physician who prescribed the "pain pills" sponsored her departure, for as a trained nurse Scotty quite surely would have been able to diagnose her own case had the symptoms not been so completely masked.

Carl Thompson, our Archery coach at Moss Lake, whose background included some Latin-American years, was the first replacement to come into my mind. I telephoned him and he reached Monterey the next day to take charge of the group.

In our first months in St. Petersburg we had located an immense castle-like house with generous grounds and two hundred feet of shore front on Boga Ciega Bay. I had purchased it and had told Scotty that we would have it ready for her when she brought her girls back in March. Before making the purchase I had canvassed all but two members of the city council and been assured that a zoning variation would be granted. However Nelson Poynter, the head of the politically dominant St. Petersburg

Times, lived about a half-mile from our Park Street location. Although he had the much larger military school, Admiral Farragut Academy, a few hundred yards to his east, he expressed his objections to my using the property for a small boarding school and exerted so much influence that my request for a variance was supported by only two council members when it actually came before the board.

The girls were due back in about two weeks and I scrambled feverishly to locate a suitable alternate, but time sped away and I had to make arrangements to return to the Jungle Prada for the spring session but this time under the handicap of sharing its facilities with many of the regular guests.

In May we returned to the Adirondacks and I was able to get a few of my camp staff members, including a riding master, to come in early, and these few weeks saved the year and made the school's continuation possible. Each girl had her own horse and riding was scheduled daily. Also, the girls were able to play tennis, water ski, sail, and canoe. To make this possible we had all our classes in the morning and devoted the afternoons to our athletic program—a pattern that was to be maintained throughout the life of the school, both in the north and the south.

The second year's schedule was similar to that of the first except that this time the equally suitable property I had purchased was ready for the girls when they returned from Mexico. The new home was too fine to have only four months use and in '62–'63 we omitted Mexico and all went well, although the group of twelve grew only to a disappointing twenty.

However, my Moss Lake personnel luck seemed to hold and I began to assemble a staff that by 1966 included Dr. Frederic Spaulding, the first president of Tampa University; Tobin Haggerty, who had been a superintendent of schools in Vermont; Dr. Traver Sutton, who had been head of the Science Department at a midwestern university and was the author of many books and technical articles; Commander Doyle Leathers, the former head of the lower school of Admiral Farragut Academy; Dr. Carl Schuster, a former president of the National Math Teachers Association and co-author of a series of textbooks on mathematics, who was as violently opposed to "Modern Math" as I; Alicia Cuesta, who had owned and operated a school of three hundred girls in Cuba, as our Spanish teacher; and, perhaps most important of all, Kathleen Whetro, who had been a journalist in Ohio for several years, then had taught in a private girls' school and for eighteen years in the English department of Dayton University. For the last thirteen she was also Dean of Women. She took early retirement in 1965, came to St. Petersburg, and had been Head of our English Department for fifteen years when I sold the school.

Through the years many of our graduates have not merely thanked me for having Miss Whetro on staff but have volunteered that their work with her had made college courses with which other students were struggling seem quite simple.

By this time I had decided that although the girls loved the school's migratory feature the reactions of these faculty members were an even more important consideration, and when I found that only two were willing to follow us to the Adirondacks, I rescheduled the regular school year to start the second week of October in St. Petersburg and we stayed there until commencement. In other words, we adopted a typical one hundred and seventy class day schedule but did it with thirty six-day weeks divided into trimesters. For some years we also had a September session in the Adirondacks at which we taught only two subjects—English and Mathematics. This was done as an answer to the deteriorating skills induced by the new math and the substitution of word-recognition for phonics. This pattern was maintained for several years, except that we later moved the September session to St. Petersburg. It was optional for girls who did well on their entrance test, but mandatory for border-line cases. As a boarding school we could compensate for the short regular session by having Saturday classes, and in retrospect I am at a loss to properly explain to myself our having dropped this September session during my final years as Headmaster.

These departmental heads served for several years, but by the mid or late seventies all had been replaced except Dr. Sutton and Miss Whetro. Still they averaged nearly ten years of service at Adirondack-Southern. I believe this figure to be substantially better than is usual for the younger teachers commonly selected by other boarding schools.

I am certain that in no other community in the country would I have been able to assemble a comparable staff without a practically unlimited budget, and even with such a budget the staff would have lacked one ingredient of very especial value. All of these people had retired with sufficient means to live comfortably without any supplemental income, and their love of teaching, and perhaps dread of anticipated boredom, was their reason for being with us. This meant that their dedication was uniform and unmatched.

We could reward them with only modest salaries but compensated for this by having all our academic classes in the morning, and by running a "tight ship." Our girls were expected to sit erect and pay close attention in class, to answer questions with "Yes Sir" and "No Ma'am" and in general to follow a behavior pattern that would have been considered the boarding school norm in pre-war years.

Some later teachers also deserve special mention. The first was Patricia Dye who taught forum and vocabulary—forum being a public speaking course that I introduced during the first year and which with vocabulary developed into a very valuable supplement to Miss Whetro's work.

After several years of service Alicia Cuesta was replaced by Elsa Vidal and later by Sylvia Andres, a perfect lady, the finest of Spanish teachers, and much to my surprise the best swimmer of her age I have ever seen. Perhaps I might be able to alter this statement if I could have the privilege of viewing several of Mr. Zimnoch's early Moss Lake pupils in a pool. It is not training that one forgets, but there were few coaches in the twenties of his caliber and Senora Andres was most fortunate to have found one of them in Cuba. She has been invaluable as a liaison with our many Spanish girls and their families. In fact, without her I would have failed miserably in judging the calibre of my Spanish families and their daughters.

In our second decade we added an elementary department devoted chiefly to mastering the "Three-R's." Its success was due largely to its early head, Mary Sweat, and to her successor, Sondra Redfern, both the wives of clergymen—one a Methodist pastor, the other an Episcopal priest.

Our Moss Lake tutoring had left me convinced that few girls received adequate instruction in English and from the start we devoted twelve hours each week to this subject. One hour was conventional—grammar, literature, and composition. The other was divided between public speaking, vocabulary, and speed reading. This pattern was maintained through the years, except that as the vocabularies of new admissions deteriorated we secured the extra time needed in this field by playing down the speed reading. In the seventies our Latin-American contingent became larger, and these girls were given a third hour of English during their first year, which we tried to adapt to individual needs, of course this included much conversation.

Of the remaining three academic hours, one was given to mathematics, one to a foreign language, and the third to either history or science. This was the schedule for the upper school, which included grade VIII. Most of the lower school time was spent on the Three R's and a foreign language which we started in the first grade.

In spite of my consistently fine fortune in engaging staff members, most of the school's twenty years were behind us before I found a truly adequate replacement for our original Dean of Girls. The replacement was Maxine Reeser and I soon discovered that I could compare her with our lost Scotty McCaddon without being depressed. The second year I made her Dean of Girls, and any our Moss Lake girls who knew Scotty as teacher, nurse, camper, canoeing instructor, or head counsellor know that my allowing Mrs. Reeser to have her title was the highest possible praise.

In the later part of the sixties and the first part of the seventies we added two classroom buildings and two dormitories, a pool, a director's residence, and a tennis court. Our program was a combination of camp and school. Indeed I practically transplanted my Moss Lake athletic program to our Adirondack-Southern afternoons. Typically the early fall sports were swimming, sailing, archery, and fencing. After Christmas the swimming would be dropped and much time given to tennis and horseback riding, with ballet being brought into the picture. In the spring we would drift back to our fall schedule.

In athletics I could not quite match our Moss Lake staff of instructors but was able to bring several of them to Adirondack-Southern—unfortunately, none for the full life of the school. Colonel Guenichta took care of the riding for several years. Carl Thompson and George Delahay were with us for about the same period. Norbert Fuhrmann and James Flynn taught the fencing for several years. John Zimnoch took care of our swimming until the year of his death, and Anneliese is still teaching the school's ballet.

In spite of my disappointment at the death of Moss Lake, the next decade proved the wisdom of my decision. Mrs. Longstaff soon made herself both the anchor and sparkplug of the school's ship and our operating pressures dwindled. She and our very wonderful staff ensured a good measure of success for the school, but I saw no chance of giving it the national eminence Moss Lake had enjoyed within the span of my active years.

Our final years at Adirondack-Southern were uneventful and financially pleasing, but I suddenly remembered how elderly I had deemed the only school head I had ever known who had remained active after an eightieth birthday. When mine came and went, a bit of faculty scuttlebutt resulted in an offer from our accountant to purchase the school. Two or three faculty members were also involved, and I again envisioned nominal changes and assurance of survival. This was in 1980 and survival seems assured, but more modern ideas have changed the school's philosophy and operation to a point that I am quite sure that if I ever spent a day there it would be one of many surprises.

COMMENCEMENT ADDRESSES

There were two outstanding commencement addresses in the twenty years that I headed Adirondack-Southern—outstanding in structure and delivery, and because they so accurately caught and reinforced the school's objectives.

The first was delivered by Dr. J. Wallace Hamilton, a local clergyman whom I considered the finest sermon-maker I had ever heard, either in person or on the air. Our protestant girls and I had attended his church for some time but I had never discussed the school's goals or procedures with him; so I was quite surprised when he selected "The Importance of Self Respect" as his theme and developed it in a fashion that perfectly outlined and justified our philosophy.

He talked without notes, but knowing his skill I had asked my secretary to take his address down in shorthand. I should like to reproduce it here; but, perhaps because I referred to it so frequently in the intervening years, I cannot find it.

The context of Gladys Yost's address, delivered nearly ten years later, was similar, but Dr. Hamilton was rather more direct in counselling the girls to apply the standards built around the respect of self. I remember he warned them not to go seeking husbands with only secondhand merchandise to offer, and told them that even in the cases where a man fell in love with and married a girl who was not a virgin his counselling experience indicated that lasting happiness seldom followed. He spoke of the suspicions, often unjustified, that had their roots in earlier years which so frequently scarred, and often ruined, such marriages. He further indicated he was convinced the number of divorces would be much larger were not most worthwhile men prone to judge their prospective brides by much higher standards than the casual companions of their earlier years.

I might add here that while the decline of the family, lack of legal restraints, peer pressures, and school compliance are the factors commonly, and properly, blamed for the moral deterioration of recent years, the dearth of ministers like Dr. Hamilton willing to tackle the evils of the day has been a major contributor. Those who avoid this area for fear of the defection of segments of their congregations should study the prosperous development of the Pasadena Community Church under Dr. Hamilton— the biggest church in town overflowing into a large auxiliary room and into the large church yard Sunday after Sunday.

I have the text of Mrs. Yost's address but as it is quite lengthy to be reproduced in toto here, I have attempted a *Readers Digest* type of condensation.

THE 1970 LADY
by
Gladys Yost

In choosing my subject, THE 1970 LADY, I will only mention the obvious which Adirondack-Southern offers its graduates. Certainly THE 1970 LADY must have a firm academic background; and certainly Adirondack-Southern offers this through an exceptional faculty. Of course, THE 1970 LADY should have ability and knowledge of social sports and social graces; and, of course, Adirondack-Southern has an authentic program in this field. Surely THE 1970 LADY should have social acumen and surely that learning is here.

What I choose to dwell upon this morning is the *plus* quality of ladyship—so very much needed in our times—which is given the Adirondack-Southern graduate. Significantly the school offers no courses in this extra advantage. If such subjects were given they could be called: smoking, doping, and the French bikini. These symbolize a whole gamut of activities which have become fashionable for the 70's—violence, rebellion, delinquency, and crime—to mention a few.

For my generation ladyship came in a neat little package. If you followed the rules of the church, the community, the family, and the school you automatically became a lady. It was something like instant pudding. Education, we were told, was the one key which would unlock a beautiful future—the world was our nut to crack. Things have changed. Ladyship no longer comes gift wrapped—and the world out there is full of nuts waiting to crack you.

It is important to understand something of what has made the change in order to appreciate what it takes to be THE 1970 LADY. Today, according to sociologist Dr.

Hendrick Ruttenbeek there are masses of people who do not feel they belong. They are frustrated, alienated, and without a true sense of identity. Psychiatrist Dr. Rollo May writes of the "Shizoid World": the majority of individuals split from the ability to feel and to love. Anthropologist Dr. Margaret Mead presents that we are in a period of chaos because we are entering a cultural pattern never known before.

This change seems based on three factors: (1) never before in the history of man have all the world's people been able to communicate quickly and easily. Even so-called primitive tribes now have TV antennae on their huts. Fifty years ago such "savages" did not know a land existed beyond their jungle patch. Now some of them know more about the U.S. than we do. (2) Rapid technological advance is the second significant matter causing unprecedented change. The problem of the wheel and the lash—machines' control over man—has been a threat since ancient Babylonian times. But today technological control over man has become a fact. A computer can think better than some of us. (3) Third—formerly man feared war, flood, illness, and famine because they destroyed many human beings. But never before have we had the bomb—oblivion for *all* human beings.

No one now over twenty-five can comprehend a world wherein all societies can communicate—but in which few can understand each other. It is not so much a matter of language barriers as of emotional barriers. Nor can anyone over twenty-five truly grasp the meaning of a life run by machines. Nor can anyone over twenty-five accurately sense a world which can be ended by a bomb. We can intellectually accept these changes, but we cannot *feel* them.

On the other side of the coin, those under twenty-five cannot possibly understand any other world than the frightening one into which they have been born. They can study the past, but they cannot *feel* it—a "small" world of common communications, wherein man and not machine was master.

There is much confusion about self-love and selfishness. Many think they are the same. They are actually quite opposite. The selfish person does not love herself too much, but too little. In fact, she hates herself. Regardless of whatever grandiose pretenses to the contrary, the person who hates herself will show it in much of her behavior. A common argument in the younger generation is "It's my life—I have a right to live it as I choose." It certainly is your life. Never before in the history of mankind has your life been so much your own. If you want to mess it up the responsibility is yours. The older generation did the best they could within the limitations of their knowledge. The knowledge you can gain about yourself through the sociosciences—which did not really exist in our day as they do in yours—gives you no excuse, except the enjoyment of self-hate, for misusing your life.

Never before have the facts of self-hate and self-love been so clear. Never before has behaviour been so well understood in these terms. Self-haters want to dull the pain of not being able to love themselves or anyone else. Thus they shock, they hurt, they wound others—and in the end they destroy themselves. Since self-haters lack respect for themselves they do not require respect from others. They are indiscriminate—do not care—whom they pick for friends, what they choose for activities, how they select a marriage partner. Self-haters, lacking self-knowledge, reflect their low opinion of themselves in how they live.

The Adirondack-Southern 1970 LADY has gained—through lack of courses in smoking, dope, and the bikini—the great value of inner restraints. Today this value is priceless because there are no longer outer restraints. As the A-S 1970 LADY goes out into that world there will be less and less requirements about how to live. The only discipline will be self-discipline—which you have learned here and can carry with you.

The Adirondack-Southern 1970 LADY has gained the value of self-love. She has learned self-respect, so that she need do nothing to keep herself from feeling and from loving. The world out there will do little to make life easier for you. But if you take with you the inner restraints and the self-love learned here—you can do much for that muddled world, and more for yourself.

My farewell words to the Adirondack-Southern Class of 1970 is—never cease to respect yourself.

Maxine Reeser

Tobin Haggerty

R. Kathleen Whetro

Doyle Leathers

Frederic Spaulding

Silvia Andres

Traver C. Sutton

Dorothy G. Longstaff

George H. Longstaff

CHAPTER XII

Potpourri

ON THE EDGE OF THE LAKE

This title will cover two urgently invited accidents with nothing but their locations in common.

My father was the "hero" of the first. Neither he nor my mother ever gave me the details but as a young boy I found an old issue of Utica's weekly paper, the Saturday Globe I think, with a picture of my father in color on the front page. He was on a large limb that projected over the water and was blissfully sawing it at a point between him and the trunk. I can't remember what the title had to say except that it used my father's name. Perhaps I was not yet able to read. The family never denied nor explained the incident but I judged that my father was embarrassed.

The other incident was more serious. All hotels of any size on the lake had gas plants except The Mohawk—which went from kerosene to electricity. One, the Cohasset, on the south side of Fourth Lake had located its gas house on the shore of the lake with the door opening onto the water, probably to facilitate transferring the carbide drums from boat to gas house. The proprietor was Si Wood and he tended the plant himself. On the day in question he apparently forgot that he was smoking a pipe when he went in. His exit was instantaneous and dramatic. He was blown out into the lake, unhurt, and as the water was not too deep waded back to shore. One version I heard reported that he still had his pipe in his mouth. I think that since she valued both my grandfather's life and mine this incident may have been at least partially responsible for my mother's decision to install the area's first gasoline driven electric plant in the new Mohawk.

THE ALONZO WOODS

When I later list the hotels I remember from my youth I will not include the Lon Wood place. It could no longer be considered a hotel when I knew it, yet I think it may have been the first lakeside hostelry in the area. It was a farm, livery stable, boat livery, and produce store, that probably was able to accommodate from 15–20 boarders. Everything they sold they produced—milk, eggs, fowl, fish, and maple syrup. When I knew them they were quite elderly but still active—active enough that they still included making maple syrup in their support cycle though they no longer had horses nor took in boarders.

They had been getting their sap from trees tapped on the present Mohawk property before my mother purchased it and the usual large iron sap kettle was centrally located and protected by a roof. My mother permitted them to continue using the area for this purpose and each spring Lon would come up shortly after we arrived carrying two gallons of syrup and expressing surprisingly effusive thanks for my mother's allowing them to continue. If our best syrup today scales at eleven pounds theirs must have been twelve or thirteen.

Even after they discontinued their syrup making they still had a cow and I can remember carrying a pail down for milk. This was in the early weeks before our guests started to appear, then milk and eggs came by train from Remsen—B.K. Brown— while the provisions we did not buy from the Pickle Boat were shipped in from Boston. Meat, poultry, and fish would be shipped from Batcheledor and Snyder in the evening and reach Skensowane between six and seven the next morning—packed in ice, of course. The milk cans from Remsen were merely jacketed but they spent only two or three hours in transit and seemed ice-cold when they arrived. When I started walking down to the Wood's they no longer had any visible employees, but "Uncle" Ed Arnold was very much in evidence. He was about the same age as the Woods so I assume he was a cousin rather than an uncle. He was one of the very early guides and before my time had supplied fish for the Camp Mohawk table, and was still maintaining three or four fishing buoys and supplying Becker's in whole or in part.

The Wood clearing was the largest on the lake and two steamers were built there, our largest, the Clearwater, and the Adirondack which was moved to Raquette Lake on the railroad. I can remember neither the death of the Woods nor word that they had moved away, but I last saw them when I was eight or nine.

CHESTER GILLETTE

When Chester Gillette started to write "The American Tragedy" for Dreiser with his tennis racket by murdering Grace Brown on Big Moose Lake, I was young enough that my memory probably has blended what happened with family and employee discussions.

After he had disposed of the body, he apparently traveled through the woods from Big Moose to the vicinity of my father's hotel, a half mile from the village of Inlet. I cannot recall why or how it was decided that Chester was in that vicinity, but apparently it was and as the sheriff was a political crony of my father, he awaited reports at Rocky Point. It seems to me Gillette was apprehended between there and Inlet, and whether I was present when he was brought in or whether I merely remember one of the deputies coming in to report his capture, I cannot say.

This was in mid-summer and my next exposure was in my home town of Herkimer, the county seat. It was a year when we were having many of our dinners at the Palmer House, and apparently the jury was frequently chaperoned into the dining room at the same hour. Of course, I was never allowed to attend the trial and never even saw the defendant in town. Nevertheless a murder in our backyard in the Adirondacks and the trial in the immediate proximity of our Herkimer home left an imprint that has remained quite clear through the years, although the impression is chiefly one of the twelve grown men being chaperoned into the hotel dining room.

JOHNNY RANK

Johnny Rank had been the conductor on one of the long distance trains of the New York Central, but an accident resulted in a partial disability that slowed him down to a degree that made it unwise to let him retain that heavy responsibility, so he was assigned to the twenty-mile Raquette Lake Railroad. "Twenty-mile" because longer lines had a much lower fare ceiling. If I have the figures correctly, the actual mileage was twenty-two which at that time would have let a Clearwater to Raquette Lake ticket cost but forty-four cents. As a twenty mile road they were allowed to charge a dollar.

Even without his background Johnny would have been a very special character. As in his Herkimer years my father came up each weekend and while he was in New York or at least alternate weekends, they had a more-than-casual acquaintance. Twice prior to the incident I am about to sketch, he had asked my father to bring forceps and take out a tooth for him en route. This time there had been no warning and the pain was acute so when he saw my father get off the sleeper he asked him if he would come back and meet the train on its down trip. My father did and Johnny stopped the train long enough for the extraction. As it was a noon train with a large daycoach contingent, half a hundred people piled out and watched the operation.

Incidentally, this little Raquette Lake Railroad regularly carried more sleeping cars than you will find on a New York to Florida run today. On the weekends the grade behind Bald Mountain would usually necessitate breaking the train into two sections and taking them up separately—no inconvenience to anyone for even with that delay the first stations would be reached by six or seven o'clock in the morning. The road was built to accommodate a group of "Great Camp" owners in the Raquette Lake region and there would commonly be a couple of private cars waiting on that siding on summer days. Although built for and by this very special group, several were railroad magnates, the road was a major business asset for the Fulton Chain hotels.

It made them more accessible to the main line cities between New York, Cleveland, Boston, and Detroit, than they are today. Indeed it was a short overnight trip from any of the three and even Chicago guests did not need to leave until about four o'clock the previous afternoon.

OUR ITINERANT TRADERS

A group of itinerant traders added much to the color of the early hotel days. The ones I remember most clearly arrived in guideboats. One was an Armenian with the nickname of Rusty, who carried many cases of truly fine linens. 'Truly fine' was my mother's appraisal, and I am sure she would not have allowed him to display his wares in our public areas if she did not approve both the quality and the prices. As I recall we saw him four or five times a year, which with the low turnover of those early years meant nearly everyone saw Rusty at least twice.

Rather more frequent were the visits of the Dennis family with their sweet grass baskets. These Indians lived in the Old Forge area and I believe made their own baskets, but the variety was large and the quality good.

The itinerants were an industrious lot, but it always seemed to me that the hardest workers were the ones who came with the performing bears—two men at different times, one with two bears, the other with one. They walked the bears from hotel to hotel, but I have no recollection of how they got them into the area. They were immense animals and must have weighed eight or nine hundred pounds apiece. Occasionally we saw an organ grinder with a monkey and a cup who hardly could be considered real entertainment, but he did add some color during the few minutes he would spend with us.

The man who most deserves a place in the history of the Adirondacks was much more artist than tradesman. I knew him rather well for a number of years and I do not think anybody loved the Adirondacks more wholeheartedly than Fred Hodges. He would spend much of his year wandering through them with his cameras, would give a good part of his winter to painting and coloring his prints with great skill, and then return in the summer (usually by canoe) to sell them. He was always welcome at The Mohawk and to my delight frequently ate at the family table, so I had much opportunity to talk with him. For some years he used a motor canoe that supplied an extra bond. It was very different from mine—I think it had been purchased as an ordinary canoe and a stuffing box, an engine base, and a rudder added. This made it a much faster but less stable craft than mine with its special sponson construction and one hundred pound keel. They were the only motor canoes on the lake and I don't think we ever decided whether my iron jacketed Ferro or his copper jacketed Waterman was the more reliable motor.

His photographs were of the very finest quality and I should have many of them in my collection but somehow they failed to survive the sale of Moss Lake. I feel that history should place "Adirondack Hodges" alongside Stoddard and "Adirondack Murray." Maybe the day will come when the Blue Mountain Museum will aquire and display his work.

Incidentally, when my sister sold The Mohawk the dining room walls had several 3′ x7′ murals that Fred had developed from his early 35 mm Leica. I recall his explaining the mechanics of the procedure, but I do not remember exactly how he exposed the positives, only that he pinned large sheets of Velox to his darkroom wall. After exposure he developed them in a bathtub by holding an end in each hand and moving them up and down.

THE PICKLE BOAT

The few paragraphs devoted to our steamboats in connection with Mohawk activities could not adequately portray their importance to the area in pre-automobile days. Hotel guests, cottagers, and natives depended upon them in whole or in part for their transportation and supplies. Provisions were the most vital part of the supply picture and this special need was met in a very special way.

Marks and Wilcox had a grocery store in Old Forge and also operated a sizeable steamboat of their own equipped as a floating store through the first four lakes of the Fulton Chain. Howard Marks "kept store" in Old Forge and Charles Wilcox guided the boat from dock to dock from one end of the navigable portion of the chain to the other—up one day and back the next. It whistled its way from camp to camp (both cottages and hotels were called camps in the early years), and if you wished to make a purchase you merely appeared on your dock as it approached. If you were not there but were a regular customer there would be some more whistling before the boat departed.

The storage space within the boat was generous and well-stocked. The prices were competitive with those of the few small stores in the area. Hotels were considered wholesale customers and their prices were extremely reasonable. If they did not have items you needed they would try to bring them on a later trip. As Marks & Wilcox also had the Standard Oil franchise for the area they carried gasoline and kerosene barrels on their stern deck.

When I purchased Cedar Isles the Pickle Boat was still operating and I secured nearly all our provisions from it. However, by this time both sides of the lakes had paved roads, the demand for Pickle Boat services dwindled, and it stopped running.

THE BURROS

My father had new and strong enthusiasms at frequent intervals. I think one of the strangest was his sudden interest in burros. He found that they could be purchased in the West and delivered in carload lots for twenty-five dollars an animal.

He suggested to some people in the area that they take a number and ordered a carload. Where they all went I do not know, but our allotment was four. Three were with us for only a short time but the fourth was a large black well-trained male that worked almost like a mule and did considerable work both around the hotel and camp. We named him "Felix". He brought trunks from the station, carried out the garbage, and even skidded some of our small logs at Moss Lake.

I very much doubt if Felix earned his board but the contrast with the other burros made him look very good, and as he became popular we did not begrudge him his keep for the few years that he remained with us.

MY FLYING CAREER

Some years after I did my Florida flying and received a license, I conceived the idea of buying a plane and using The Mohawk dock as a base for sightseeing flights. At that time the government had not yet made provision for the granting of private licenses, but the American Aeronautical Association did give two, and it was the lower of these grades that I received. Today my flying time would be considered insignificant and my knowledge miniscule but everything seemed simple and it did not occur to me to question my ability. Yet in retrospect I am very glad that my project was aborted before it left New York.

I found a most beautiful flying boat that had been designed by Harry Atwood, one of our most prominent pioneer flyers, and built in mahogany by a Chicago piano factory. It had no military value and Atwood left it in a warehouse when he enlisted. After the war a man who had been employed in an airplane body shop purchased it and advertised it for sale. I noticed the advertisement, saw the plane, and viewed the reconditioning problems through rose-colored glasses. The price was $1500 and I made a $100 deposit.

The owner was in the process of recovering it and said he would call me when he had finished. The call took longer than I expected and I decided to run down to Sheepshead Way where it was housed. I arrived just as it was being launched and he invited me to go along on its test flight. Of course, I accepted.

He had talked glibly using aeronautical terms I knew and others I did not, so it did not occur to me to question his flying ability. He gave me the controls and after we flew around for a few minutes he said we should go down, and asked me to make the landing, admitting he had not held the controls in any plane. I had never been in a flying boat before and realized that putting it down would be very different from landing the Jennys with which I was somewhat familiar. Also, the $1400 balance looked very big, and I insisted that if we were going to crash he keep the controls. He did, and we did.

He hit the water very hard and instead of holding the controls down, he zoomed. We flew just long enough for me to realize that the hull no longer had a bottom. Seeing the water between my feet was a unique and a frightening experience. However, he gave me no time to express my concern, but headed sharply down. We hit and this time it was a nose dive. We kept going down so long I decided we were going to stay under and tried to extricate myself. Just as I was getting out of the cockpit the ship started to rise and I rode it to the surface. A boat picked us up promptly. He was unhurt and except that my lower teeth were sticking through my lip I was fit, and fit to be tied.

I never saw either the boat or its owner or my hundred dollars again and never held the controls of a plane until my son started to take lessons, and then just to see what it felt like and to find out if I remembered anything.

LUMBERING CAN BE PROFITABLE

In 1921 I was becoming conscious of the financial load that my enthusiasm for Moss Lake had imposed upon my family and hit upon a not impractical scheme to change the picture. Pulpwood was far above its usual price, and as Moss Lake had a substantial stand of spruce and balsam I decided to market it. When I found that the price of the Newton Falls Paper Company was $35.00 per cord delivered at the railroad, I asked them to send a representative down to inspect our timber and see if it would qualify. He approved it, but did not stay to cruise it, and we merely estimated that the area I had in mind cutting would produce from five hundred to one thousand cords.

They gave me a contract which generously allowed me to deliver any amount within those limits and set the price at $35.00. This was in the summer, but before I got around to cutting, the bottom fell out of the market and the price became $20.00 to $22.00. I promptly located a man that was cutting but who had no sales contract. I sold my contract for $5.00 a cord, but the Newton Falls people refused to accept his trees.

Of course, I consulted Phil Farley. He corresponded with them and made an appointment for their representative to meet with us at Moss Lake. The representative proved to be their attorney and argued that all lumber was not alike and that they had bargained for our special trees. However, Phil had been briefed on the pulp market and knew that the controling factor in pulp prices was the percentage of spruce.

The new man's land had cut a higher percentage of this than mine would and the freight rate from his station was the same as from Big Moose, so the attorney agreed to pay me $5.00 a cord to cancel the contract. This was enough to pay the taxes on Moss Lake for two years. It was my first venture in lumbering and a most encouraging one. Thanks to Phil I had both my trees and my profit.

THE PICNIC TO END ALL PICNICS

Usually even short trips were planned for one camp at a time or for a fraction of one camp, but on this one midsummer occasion we had engaged the largest motor boat in the area and as it would take Lodge plus Senior Camp we decided to let both go. Incidentally this large launch was designed to navigate the shallow waters it would encounter on its intended runs between Sixth Lake and the Eighth Lake Carry and built by its owner, Gerald Kenwell.

That was the trip we planned for the girls and all went well until the meal was about over, then the girls and some of the younger counsellors started "dropping like flies" with intense stomach pains. Scotty and another nurse were along and had waited until the girls were served before starting to eat. By that time the rising distress was evident and they had more important things than their own eating to think about so were unaffected.

Fortunately the boat had waited for the return trip and Scotty had the girls walk or be carried aboard. Another stroke of good luck was that someone with a small outboard had stopped to talk with Gerald, and was asked to go on ahead and request the Inlet physician, Dr. Cole, to meet the boat at the Sixth Lake Landing. His account was sufficiently vivid that Dr. Cole called for an ambulance and asked an Old Forge physician to join him. By the time the boat reached the landing there were nearly seventy cases as adults started to succumb, but Scotty noticed that the girls stricken first were in less pain so the concern lessened and all were brought back to camp, the sickest to our three infirmaries, the others to their cabins.

The obvious answer was food poisoning but Dr. Cole was familiar with our food preparation and was skeptical. The next morning the mystery was in the hands of the state health department and they agreed, partially on their reading of the symptoms, that food was not the cause. An hour later they came up with the answer after tracing the picnic preparations with me.

I had purchased a large round thermal container and had used it several times with real pleasure. However, this time we used the outside container for five gallons of punch. There were three inner containers that were intended to receive all food but there had been no mention in the directions that although they looked the same as the outer one only they were intended for food. Metalic poisoning was the verdict and it was confirmed by a telephone conversation with the manufacturer. All girls could navigate comfortably by that time but some of the adults who had succumbed slowly required two or three more days.

"THE WILDERNESS"

There is a large area along the Red River and the south branch of the Moose that through most of the camp years was Gould Lumber territory. It was already largely stripped of its soft-wood when I first knew it and now with the lumber operations completed it is State Forest.

Our name for it was "The Wilderness" and my introduction to it was a short hunting trip with Henry Froehlich, a fine German chef who served at The Mohawk from time to time but whose real love was the woods. I must have been twelve or thirteen when my mother, knowing that Henry would be a skillful and careful mentor, approved my first hunt. Since I had no skill with firearms Henry suggested a shotgun and we started off through this territory. The first two days I enjoyed immensely—Henry's cooking in the woods seemed even better than when he used the hotel stoves, but then on a quite rainy morning I found my first deer within range and shot it. It dropped in its tracks with only a startled look. There was no touch of romance, only some meat to pack out a dozen miles. I have not hunted since.

The second or third year of camp we had a girl whose father owned one of the lakes in the area, Beaver Lake. Whether he had purchased it from the Gould Company or whether he held an earlier title I do not recall. It had a nice log cabin and he said our Moss Lake girls would be welcome to use it.

We did and the trip was a notable success. On future trips we used a similar, but somewhat larger, camp on Otter Brook owned by Gerald Kenwell, the man whose boat we used on our disastrous Eighth Lake picnic.

I accompanied the girls on none of them because that would put me too completely out of touch with camp, but one Saturday afternoon I had a horse taken to the start of the trail so I might ride in the next morning. It was fifteen uninhabited miles but I saw little game. However, on the return that afternoon I came upon a bear eating berries about ten feet from the trail. I was practically abreast of him before he saw the motion. Of course, I had often been told through the years of horses' fear of bears and expected a badly frightened mount, but she didn't even break her stride. A little further along a buck jumped across the trail ahead of us and she gave a few not-too-spirited bucks, but within the next mile a partridge flew up practically under her nose and I nearly lost my horse. These Wilderness trips were a happy part of camp tradition for several years.

OF NO IMPORTANCE BUT SOBERING

In one of our earlier years I received an evening phone call from a distraught parent asking me to get her two daughters to New York as quickly as possible. I am not sure of the reason for the urgency but I think the father was in a hospital at the point of death as the result of a severe stroke—whether her father or that of the girls I do not recall. I told her that the sleeper was due to go through Big Moose in about an hour, and she asked me to try for it without baggage.

With the train right on time it was very close and the train was in the station as we approached. Our road crossed the track a few hundred feet from the station but detoured around behind it. I was afraid the engineer might pull out before we arrived and turned down the railroad right-of-way so the engineer would see our lights—it was customary to stop trains at unattended stations with a flashlight. Apparently he started his train before he saw us and not realizing that the right-of-way was wide enough for both of us made an emergency stop which although the train had moved but a few feet jolted passengers and slid some out of their seats. This I did not know—nor did the conductor or trainman who opened the door for us. We bundled the girls on and I returned to camp with no idea that I had created an incident.

Two days later a New York Central representative called on me, told me of the jolt, and added that one of the passengers was Mr. Crowley, the president of the road. My reprimand was polite but apparently heartfelt and he told me that the Central probably would have taken legal action except that we appeared to be their best customer in the area. The "Best Customer" label was probably used because we engaged two or three sleepers each year from New York and Cleveland and at that time were shipping our horses in by freight. My comment was that I could understand their point of view but that since my questionable actions were the only ones that could have coped with the emergency I was pleased that I had acted on impulse—but that I surely would do nothing of the sort again.

HOW TO GET A BIG BANG OUT OF JULY FOURTH

For the first three or four years of camp we opened on July first or second and that meant all the girls expected to see fireworks on the Fourth. I don't think we provided them in 1923 but were ready with a good supply in 1924.

I knew they could be a fire hazard so asked Frank Koster, our guide, to take them out to the middle of the lake in his flatbottom boat. He did but the very first one he set off took all the others along and Frank jumped overboard. Very few of the early guides could swim so Frank hung onto the side of the boat until I arrived in a canoe and engineered his landing. He was quite chagrined and "de-machoed" but everyone else thought it a fine show.

Next year John Zimnoch was living on the island so I decided to play it safe—certainly a young man with an engineering degree and naval experience could have no difficulty. All went well through the first half. There was no second half and on land we did not know the reason. The next morning his arm was bandaged and I drove him to the physician in Inlet. Apparently the burn was quite bad and the arm was not without a bandage until mid-summer.

The following year I did find a way of "playing it safe." I moved the opening to after the Fourth and left it there for the rest of the camp years. Of course, this was done more to protect the girls from blackflies than to avoid a third accident.

BIG MOOSE CAN BE COLD

For many years the Big Moose station which was the highest in New York was an official recording station for the weather bureau and it was in the habit of turning in the lower readings than any other eastern station except Mt. Washington. I paid little attention to them until I was in on a record kill one night. I had visited camp in January and as we had no car in service during the winter I had used a pack-basket instead of a suitcase with the four and a half mile walk from station to camp in mind. The return sleeper went through shortly after midnight. As the camp thermometer read 30 below "and dropping fast," when it was time for me to leave, I dressed heavily. Since donning the extra clothes had taken some time, I walked rapidly with no feeling of chill (in fact, I was perspiring). When I reached the station the agent was just taking his official reading and in spite of the always overheated waiting room I began to shiver. Forty had been my lowest previous reading, but this one was an even sixty.

HERKIMER HAD A PLUMBER WHO WAS A REAL SPEED ARTIST

His name was Albert Ertman and he proved his right to the title three times in one summer. There was a Sunday excursion from Herkimer to Inlet and return that allowed about two hours turn-around time. I imagine the half-mile trip from Rocky Point added about thirty minutes. In that time this man installed a full bathroom for my father, did it again the next week, and again the third. I am quite sure he could not have connected the water in this time, but on the second occasion I saw the bare room before he came, not even a hole in the floor, and when he left it looked complete to my young eyes—fixtures set, faucets in place, the pipes to the floor. I expect that our maintenance man, George Graves, connected them to the water supply the next morning, but in my building years I found a bathroom to surely take a full day and this served to fix the Ertman feat firmly in my mind.

THE SINKING OF THE MORRO CASTLE

I doubt if there was any camp incident that made a deeper impression on John Zimnoch and myself than the wreck of the Morro Castle off the Jersey Coast. The heroine was Loretta Hassel, with us for only two years but a girl who worked most assiduously for John.

The fall of that second year, Lori, her mother, and father were on the Morro Castle when it foundered. They went to a lifeboat and the officer in charge boarded Lori and her mother, but said that no men were to be allowed. Lori protested, told the officer she was confident she could swim the seven miles to shore, and asked that her father be given her place. He seemed skeptical, so she quickly took off her outer clothing, dove overboard, and when her mother and father reached shore, Lori was waiting for them. From our point of view and that of her parents, she certainly deserved a Carnegie medal as surely as any of the many recipients of the award for direct rescues.

I never saw mention of the matter in the newspapers but, of course, all the girls and staff members learned of it the following summer.

TRACTORS DON'T FLOAT

A few years after we purchased the Darts property I had occasion to skid some logs across the lake on the ice. I was a little apprehensive, yet the ice seemed firm and I thought I had made the crossing safely, but as I drew near the shore I crossed the main flow of the water to the outlet and with no warning the tractor went through the ice and down some fifteen feet. I was fearful that it might tip on its side and pin me, so struggled to get loose, but the suction was so great that I could not free myself until it hit bottom.

Fortunately, it was right side up and while I realized that these might be my final seconds I did not have the classic panorama of earlier events passing through my mind. I merely used the interval before touching bottom to decide that my best chance of finding the hole in the ice was to free myself, relax, and just float upward with no swimming strokes.

There were only some fifteen feet of water and my luck was good so I shortly had my head above water and could see Albert Benson running toward me with a long pole in his hand. I grabbed the end and was pulled out in a matter of seconds.

It was a below zero day and none of the Darts Lake buildings were open so I had to drive to Moss Lake as quickly as possible. By that time my clothes were frozen stiff, but I was able to press the latch on our door with my elbow and enter the heated building. There was no one at home, but the next half hour probably was the most luxurious one I ever enjoyed.

I turned on the water, got into the tub with all my clothes and watched it fill, regulating the temperature with an occasional poke. Twenty minutes later I started to take off gloves and shoes and continued the process until I was able to finish with a normal shower.

The next morning we attacked the problem of salvaging the tractor. Fortunately I was pulling the logs with a long and securely attached chain. We unhooked it from the logs, connected it to a long cable from the land, positioned our "stiff-leg" hoist on the shore and started pulling, with two men sawing the ice ahead of the cable as I reeled it in. I do not think the operation took more than two or three hours, and as the day was a much warmer one we were able to get the tractor into a heated garage before serious damage was done.

THE TIRES THAT GRIPPED ICE

The tires that gripped ice like flypaper on wood were the invention of Earl Covey, who was catalogued in my mind as Adirondack's most skillful and energetic artisan and the area's greatest Christian. I believe the development started with his discovery that unvulcanized crepe rubber as used for the soles of shoes had a highly desirable affinity for ice. The idea caught the interest of an executive of the Firestone Company for it held out the promise of their being able to produce tires that would realize this potential safety and pulling power for automobiles in winter use.

Several were manufactured and I believe they out-performed his expectations. Certainly it was hard for me to believe that such traction could be obtained by anything short of steel spikes. Unfortunately for Earl, for Firestone, and for residents of the north in general, they had a rather painful limitation. As long as they were not used on bare pavement, they were quite durable, but a few hundred miles without the protection of snow and ice would destroy them; therefore, production was stopped.

The invention still stands as a fine testimony to the inquiring mind of this most active of men.

BRIDGE

Bridge may seem like a strange camp activity but remember that one of Moss Lake's chief goals was preparing its girls for the social activities of the years to come and at that time bridge was popular at college, in the home, and at the country club.

Philip Farley may have for many years been the country's best player who did not make the game his main occupation. He introduced me to bridge and gave me considerable early guidance. At one point he suggested I enter an individual tournament that was being held in New York. Of course, I was far over my head but I did get three "tops." That could happen to any beginner, but two were made against Phil Hal Sims who was currently considered to be the country's best tournament player and that nudged my ego. In retrospect I am sure my ineptitude was so obvious that he saw an opportunity to make easy tops for himself. Once he tried a psychic that was sufficiently similar to one Phil had discussed with me a few days before that I felt confident a double would pay off. On the other hand I misread an opening and replied with a bid that threw his partner completely off track.

Theory was interesting and I was prepared to like the game very much but I soon discovered that my card memory and hand visualization would never let me compete with the players in Phil's circle. In an attempt to make my bidding sufficiently informative to offset this great handicap I spent a good many hours working out a system of largely artificial bids. I was pleased with the way it worked and printed and copyrighted a small book. The flaw was that so much explaining had to be done for opponents' information that I could feel it lessening their pleasure. From this point I played but little bridge—without the system. However, I do remember reading a resume of the Italian system when their teams were dominating international play and deciding that mine was less artificial than theirs.

The bridge I taught at camp was a combination of Culbertson and "One over One" plus a couple of simple facets of my own system. I hope that some girls may have found their camp start a foundation for later play at home or in college.

Bridge was starting to fade by the time I started Adirondack-Southern, but it was a wet-weather afternoon class for a few of the initial years.

WINTER HOUSE PARTIES

After Junior Camp was built with its all-year design, we had several successful Christmas house parties—successful largely because the weatherman treated us especially well, with equable temperature yet enough snow for skiing and ski-joring. One year we worried about the scarcity of snow, but two days before the girls came the thermometer dropped to 20 below zero and for forty-eight hours did not reach zero even at midday. The result was lakes like mirrors, yet very safe. We skated the full length of Fourth Lake and the girls forgot all about the skiing disappointment.

The next year early conditions were similar, but with the ideal skating weather that had ensued the previous year in mind I did not call off the party. This time our luck turned disastrously bad with three days of rain and that was our last winter house party.

MGM AND COLLIERS

MGM was a big name in the days of silent movies and I was flattered when a "representative" came in and asked if he could take some reels to be used as background for a Jane Withers picture. He assured me that the location would be identified and that the camp would be given credit for the activities shown. We granted him carte blanc for two or three days and he took several hundred feet of film. I never saw the film myself, but some of our girls did. Their report was that only a small fraction of what had been taken was used and that no mention was made of Moss Lake. I later learned that he was a free-lance operator with no authority to promise the credits.

That, of course, was disappointing but shortly thereafter (I think while I was still expecting to see the MGM production on screen) Colliers Magazine asked if they might get pictures for a story on American Camping. I approved and their man came promptly, stayed only a few hours, but produced results far exceeding my expectations. We had the cover and two or three inside pages of colored pictures. The text was general and rather rambling but Moss Lake was given credit. People remembered that issue for years, and I am sure it was helpful with many prospective families. The two pictures reproduced on the dust cover of this book were chosen from the eight which they used.

OUR FIRST ENCOUNTER WITH THE INDIANS

Our Uncle Andy loved a practical joke, and when some counsellor saw smoke coming up from a spot a half mile in from the south shore of the lake and asked him what it could be, he said he didn't know, but had heard that a small party of Indians was camping on Bubb's Lake and assumed it must be one of their campfires. He was pleased with the credulous look on her face but dismissed the incident until some girls asked him about the Indians at Bubb's Lake and if they were dangerous. He told them they need not worry but strung them along with background for a story that was forming in his mind.

This spread like wildfire and one day he asked me if it would be all right if he told the girls that one of our counsellors (of course, picking one with the proper day-off and plans to be out of camp) had been kidnapped and held for ransom. We worked out the details to take advantage of the wildfire grapevine that had developed and arranged a hike through the woods to deliver the ransom.

Uncle Andy told them that if a large party went the Indians would take it as a sign of good faith and harm neither them nor the hostage. The word went out about five o'clock and by six we were on our way. The head counsellors had been briefed and while some of the others later maintained that they were highly skeptical all went along—for real or for fun.

Our destination was an old lumber camp clearing in the area, and when we reached it all of the male staff except Uncle Andy were there and blanketed, with their hostage in the foreground. Uncle Andy went forward to parley and returned to tell the girls that the chief had invited them all to dinner. When they crossed the creek and recognized the Indians they really broke up and had the merriest meal of the season. Mr. Z had prepared his very special schoslick and new eating records were set. The price for Uncle Andy was a high one, for none of his tall stories were believed either that year or the next.

WILLIAM WEST DURANT

As I have mentioned earlier, we probably are part of the Adirondacks largely because of my maternal grandfather's association with Mr. Durant. As a boy of eleven I was aware of that and was excited when I heard he was on The Mohawk grounds.

Had I not had those few minutes of advance knowledge or even known his name I still would have been intrigued and awed. I had never seen anyone in striped pants and tailed coat and my only view of high hats had been in minstrels. So when he walked across the lobby in full attire I am quite sure my mouth dropped open, certainly my mental picture of him there and in the dining room—again walking across an open floor—is very clear and probably quite flattering.

He stayed but a short time after lunch and left with his male secretary, without my even being introduced, yet few of my childhood scenes remain so clear.

Apparently it would be hard for many to recognize the Central Adirondacks of today if there had been no William West Durant.

HOLLYWOOD IN THE ADIRONDACKS

The developer who did the most, and certainly tried the hardest, to shape the growth of our region was the same Joseph W. Young who had developed Hollywood in Florida. He purchased a large tract of land with frontage on First Lake and included, until that time the completely unnoticed, Hell Diver Ponds, which he renamed the Okara Lakes. Of course, the land was plotted and surveyed but that was only the beginning.

He engineered the construction of a much needed and still excellent golf course with the help of Donald Ross, one of the country's famous designers, built a large casino on piles in First Lake, and selected an excellent location for a hotel in the same area. It was made entirely of peeled logs and that was the finish both inside and out. I believe I have seen nearly all of the large lobbies and lounges in the Adirondacks but none could match the grandeur of this large two-story room with its four face fireplace and its immense stone chimney. I considered the design and construction to be nearly ideal except that the bedrooms were small for a hotel of this caliber and for the most part had only a single window.

This inn was part of the big Hollywood development of the Young corporation. Artistic, well located, and expensive, it appeared to have a most promising future, but the promise was never fulfilled. It struggled through the depression years with a few management changes. Each seemed to do less well than its predecessor and in 1959 it was turned over to the auctioneer who had served as coroner for so many of our local hotels.

I attended with intentions that did not run beyond some items of kitchen equipment, but stayed for the final ceremonies. When the main building with grounds that included an excellent waterfront was announced I expected an opening bid of about fifty thousand. The figure was twelve and it climbed but slowly to seventeen. I had difficulty believing my ears and bid twenty. Of course, I realized that I could make no use of it and as the sudden jump seemed to be upsetting to other bidders I had several apprehensive moments before the bidding resumed. It closed in the mid-twenties and went to a couple of brothers for family use—a hotel that should have been able to compete with the best in the region had its bedrooms been larger and its management more capable. The final chapter was written recently by its conversion to condominiums.

Two other facets of Young's promotion were equally difficult for me to understand. The two railroad stations in the area were Clearwater and the even more informatively titled Fulton Chain. He engineered the change of Fulton Chain to Thendara, and since the Clearwater name was changed about the same time he may also have been responsible for that, although I have never heard any explanation for the new name, Carter. I believe Thendara is an Indian name and probably has an appropriate meaning. I am sure that few people in the area know what it may be so the change quite certainly has had a negative value.

The Young organization was able to sell a goodly number of lots around the Hell Diver Ponds and in the Hollywood region, but the prices were lower than expected and the numbers disappointing by his standards. I believe the venture had about a three-year life, but it did result in substantial gains for the community—the cottages in the Hollywood and at Okara, and most important, the very fine golf course. Young's efforts deserved a much richer reward but I do not think either he or his publicity man, Mr. Hutton, took the change from Hollywood conditions to those of the Adirondacks completely in stride.

FLIES DON'T ALWAYS FLY

The scourge of the Adirondacks had always been the black fly with some late-season help from "punkies," the local name for gnats. My reasonably effective answer had been delaying the opening of camp until near the end of the first week in July, but in some years this was not adequate to protect our susceptible girls from a frequently annoying series of bites.

My uncle was head of the Nassau County Mosquito Commission for several years and when his son-in-law finished law school he was offered an appointment as my uncle's assistant and decided to put law on the back burner and practice out of his home evenings and weekends. Shortly after this the war broke out and on the basis of his mosquito commission title and expertise, he was given a commission as Lieutenant Colonel and assigned to a series of camps in the Pacific theater.

At the close of the war he was so impressed with the potential of DDT that he decided to use his knowledge of etymology and his war experience to establish a fly control company. I was one of his first clients and the experiment was incredibly successful. Unfortunately, he was not able to reach camp until we were about ready to open so he could not interfere with that year's breeding of black flies and gnats. But he and his assistant went through the camp with a DDT supply, giving special attention to the kitchens and to the stables.

When he finished his treatment he left me a generous supply of material and told me to spray it when needed. Our first year none was needed and both kitchens and stables remained completely fly-free. He also left some DDT impregnated blocks that looked like plaster of Paris bricks and told me to put them into the streams feeding Moss Lake the following spring as both the gnats and black flies breed in running water. This was equally effective and the next year was even more perfect except that I did have to spray kitchens and stables twice.

The third year immunity became a factor and we found ourselves spraying almost once a week. From that point on DDT, while more effective than anything I had used before, was just another spray. By this time the township was spraying its resorts from an airplane and the general picture remained quite comfortable. After a very few years environmentalists and sportsmen decided that DDT was detrimental to the fish and the birds as well. Its use was discontinued and while there are still some towns spraying with substitutes, they are less effective, but much better than no spraying at all.

BOOTS & SADDLES

During the 1940 season my colonels informed me that "Boots & Saddles," a riding establishment on New York's upper east side with a fine indoor ring and forty stalls, was for sale and that they thought it could be purchased for $25,000. They were right and I bought it. Except for the old Durlands (I forget the then-current name) it was the only riding establishment in the city with a ring that did not have a roof supported by dangerous iron posts. Naturally I was elated and we picked out a string of horses to send down, and Selihoff and Shiskin went into business.

It was all that I hoped it would be but Darts appeared on the horizon and Prince Gagarian who had operated "Boots and Saddles" earlier found a backer and offered me a $10,000 profit. Without Darts in the picture I would not have considered it, but the timing was too perfect and I accepted.

Of course, I should have let judgment rather than expediency control but it did come at the time of my greatest extension and I feared the stable and Darts together might be a real problem.

Durlands was closed at about this time, but in spite of its virtual monopoly on quality riding in Manhattan, "Boots & Saddles" was sold a few years later and converted into a factory. I have not talked with Gagarian since and when I did see his sister at Adirondack-Southern, she did not know why he sold—a too attractive offer probably is the best guess.

THE LOST OPPORTUNITY

After the war the country was much more air-minded than had been the case before and the government had a special interest in having additional air fields in the outlying areas as defense properties. Old Forge was selected as one suitable point and as I recall, their offer involved paying most of the cost of the field and supplying a controller.

At first I assumed that all the residents of the area would be eager to have the extra income and convenience that would ensue, but when I realized there was considerable opposition I wrote my only article for the local newspaper, urging that we accept their offer and giving what I thought were very cogent reasons. Of course, this was in good part self-interest because my clientele was more widely scattered throughout the country than those of the local hotels, but to me it seemed quite certain that everyone would benefit.

The vote was very close, the proposition losing by a margin of two I believe, and I guess most people whether pro or con gave credit to one of the most progressive and agreeable hotel owners in the area. Roy Higby was a second generation hotel man, but was young enough that he had led the way in many operational and promotional procedures, and he certainly was the man from whom I would have least expected opposition. In fact, I would have judged that, with the possible exception of myself, no one in the area had as much to gain from an airport. However, he took a different view, gathered a carload of voters and defeated the measure—one that we never had a later chance to approve.

At the time I did not discuss his action as it seemed merely to offer an opportunity for unnecessary friction, but a few years ago when neither of us was still active in the area I posed the question, preceding it with a statement that until that time I had thought him the most progressive of the hotel men in the region and had been totally unable to fathom his thinking. I did not get a real answer for he merely said that it was a major mistake and he had never been able to explain it to himself.

The loss to the community surely should be appraised at a multi-million figure for the Mohawk Airlines had been interested and indicated that they would either schedule it as a stop on some of their New York-Utica-Watertown flights, or run a shuttle from Utica to Old Forge. This would have given us a real advantage over, or at least parity with, the Lake Placid and Lake George areas. While many hotels had already closed, it would have been in time to ensure the solvency of the others which, of course, were the best of the earlier hotels—notably: Beckers, Darts, Higby's, Holl's Inn, Hollywood, Lakeview Lodge, Minnowbrook, The Mohawk, and Rocky Point.

THE POST OFFICE

One of Bill Dart's patrons held a position which carried considerable political clout and when he left one fall he told Bill he would send him a post office for Christmas.

He was as good as his word and when we purchased the property it came complete with its own post office. This was a matter of some prestige and a financial asset. It developed about a $1500 annual salary during our years which could have been increased substantially by arranging for the office to generate more business.

It was a Fourth Class office and its financing was a fine example of federal logic. There was a minimum but most of the salary was based on the value of the stamps sold. The ratio was most interesting. As I recall the salary went up about $250 for each $100 of sales. Of course, if such an office did too much business it would be upgraded to Third Class and a different set of rules would apply, but the Fourth Class ceiling was high enough that a postmaster running a modest mail order business would have held a substantial advantage in his field. Eisenhower was aware of the expense and of the potential for abuse and abolished all but the most essential offices within weeks after his inauguration.

Mrs. Farley was our first postmistress. She was a college graduate, a school teacher, and a tournament bridge player with a more than ordinarily keen mind, but the report forms were so complicated that she had to request assistance from her husband. Even with his legal training they needed to consult Beryl Roach of the Third Class office in Eagle Bay from time to time. The punch line is that at the end of these forms there was a space for the postmaster's signature followed by the advice that if he was unable to sign his name he should "make his mark."

ASEPSIS

I think the general impression is that we live in a more aseptic world than our ancestors, but the reverse appears to be true if we compare the dental offices and barber shops of today with those of the twenties and thirties.

Pasteur's work was still fresh in the popular mind and these professions had had time to implement his theories, and the better practitioners had done so most conscientiously.

Barbers washed their hands before each customer, opened sealed brushes and combs, and used freshly sterilized shears and clippers. Aprons were always crisp and neat with either a towel or gauze around the neck. The barber's uniform was a spotless white.

Dentists were even more scrupulous. Instrument trays and often headrests were covered with fresh paper. Saliva ejectors, handpiece covers, and most instruments were boiled and the others, including any burs to be reused were autoclaved. Handpieces without covers were sterilized chemically as were the other mouth-entering items that would not tolerate the autoclave. Further many of us prepared nearly all our cavities within rubber-dams which had the effect of taking the operating field out of the mouth and eliminating the chance of either becoming infected. It greatly improved visibility, allowed the use of strong chemicals to sterilize the cavity, and gave a dry field for the insertion and setting of the filling material. Unfortunately it cannot be used with to-day's high-speed water-cooled drills, but could still be employed for the final phases of the operation. I cannot help feeling that not using it is a step backward in both accuracy and asepsis.

Price schedules contrast quite as sharply. Haircuts instead of ranging from fifty cents to two dollars start at the latter figure and rise to ten and fifteen. In the dental field the difference is even greater. When I joined my father in practice his extractions cost from two dollars to five, silver fillings from three to five, hammered gold fillings and inlays from five to twenty, gold crowns ten, porcelain crowns a most pleasing thirty-five (the laboratories charged us seven) bridges from ten to twenty per tooth, and vulcanite plates thirty-five each. When one realizes that with these prices my father netted better than twenty thousand a year you can estimate today's average dental income. Surely expenses are higher and the money is worth less, but the spread still astounds me.

CANOEING

Through the years I was able to secure instructors with real expertise in all the sports I thought should be featured at camp except canoeing. When we started, the Red Cross canoeing was generally accepted by camps and physical education schools, but it was so awkwardly inefficient that I could not endorse it.

My solution was to start teaching myself and to pick well-coordinated young women with no knowledge of the sport and inculcate my techniques. These had developed as a matter of personal practice rather than as the implementation of theories, but the principles were so obvious that it was not difficult to extrapolate and then substantiate the mechanics involved.

The current practice endorsed and promulgated by the Red Cross was to select paddles long enough to reach from floor to eye. This yielded a paddle too long to dip easily and too long to withdraw except by swinging it in a wide arc. It also gave the paddler no opportunity to use the powerful bicep muscle, and indeed the Red Cross system kept both arms straight at all times.

I substituted a stirrup (armpit to finger tip) measurement for the paddle handle and had the girls bend their arms on both the recovery and the powerstroke. This produced an easier and more powerful as well as quicker stroke, and the blade was nearly perpendicular much more of the time water was being pushed—thus spending more energy sending water back, instead of up or down.

The next absurdity was requiring a kneeling position. Some instructors were content with normal kneeling and others went back to the Indian practice of sitting on their heels. This was somewhat reasonable in the soft bark canoes with sides too limber to support seats but ridiculous in a modern canoe. I had the girls use their seats for general paddling but suggested a simple (one knee) kneel for racing or beating into a strong wind. The girls with good balance were also taught to paddle standing for this is the most powerful, though most tiring, position.

Most revolutionary was my almost complete elimination of steering strokes. The half and quarter moon and the "J" are needed for a sharp alteration of course and are also useful in countering quick puffs even in straight ahead paddling and in angle landings. Otherwise they are a waste of time and energy. Even with a single paddler a canoe will go nearly straight ahead if the paddle is dipped near the gunnel with the blade at a right angle to the keel and drawn straight back. A slight tendency to turn toward the passive side will remain, but this is easily counteracted by tilting the boat toward the active side. Balancing these to retain a straight course soon becomes as subconscious as the steering of a car. The still-conventional paddle was eight to nine inches wide at the bottom and tapered into the shaft. I had paddles made with five to six inch blades and with that width maintained all the way to the junction with the shaft. This made it possible to dip the paddle about an inch and a half nearer the gunwale, retained the total area and brought more of it nearer the grip where the leverage is best.

When two girls paddle their canoe in calm weather, the course is controlled merely by varying the distance of blades from gunwales. For windy days no special adjustment is necessary with two paddlers but for one it is important that the canoe be trimmed so that in a passive state it points in the desired direction—or rather just enough to leeward that the power of the stroke the paddler wishes to use will pull it onto course.

The maintaining of a course is done by adjusting the paddler's position and the first part of the first lesson was boxing the compass. Girls were told not to use their paddles but to make their canoes point in the directions indicated by the instructor. S, SW, NW, etc. These basic principles were applied quite easily by most girls and I still do not understand why so many paddlers wherever seen (since there now is no Moss Lake Camp) use such inappropriate equipment and use it so badly. Indeed I have put this material in primarily so that any of my own girls who wish to teach their offspring can make use of this theory review.

My desire to have the paddle turn the canoe as little as possible and to comply with obvious kinetic principles was facilitated by the paddles I designed in our early years and had made first by our local Standard Supply Company and later by Old Town, but we still had difficulty keeping the blade at a right angle to the surface of the water and thus pushing water straight back, not some up and some down as with the usual stroke and paddle. This I accomplished by teaching them the "Double Break". This was effective but sometimes tiring and did not blend in easily when steering strokes were called for. I tried both concerns to see if they could make paddles with the blade at a twenty to thirty degree angle to the shaft. Neither felt they could at that time but recently racers have realized the advantage of this and some are being made in metal and plastic, and a few in laminated wood. For some reason most of their blades are triangular but I recently asked one man with a small shop to turn out one for me with a six inch width from tip to handle. It attains the objective for which it is designed but adapts itself less well to steering strokes than a straight paddle and should be considered an alternate to be used when the type of paddling planned for the occasion makes it suitable, not as a replacement. In the "Double Break" both upper and lower arms bend on the power stroke allowing the paddle to remain at or near the vertical for a longer period. My suggestion was that it be used when extra power was desired and as a restful alternate. The angled blades have the same objective and are especially effective when combined with the double break.

MY LAST LUMBERING

In the late forties or early fifties, a veneer mill opened in the area and the price of birch and maple, which had been worth so little that most lumbering operations would not bother with it, soared to fantastic heights. At this time I spent two winters with my family at Moss Lake, joining my father in New York for only about ten days a month, and decided that Albert and I would do some lumbering on our own. I purchased an old telephone company truck that had a good stiff-leg hoist for loading the logs, and as I had previously acquired a small Caterpillar, we were able to run a profitable two-man operation with the aid of an old but indestructible Mack truck.

This was a matter of only a few thousand dollars and no damage to the property, yet it made me realize that my Cascade hardwood had real value, and I gave a contract for the cutting of all that could be found on the never-used south shore of the Lake. It produced an appreciable and most welcome income.

NEW YORK STATE PRIVATE CAMP DIRECTORS ASSOCIATION

In the early thirties all directors of private camps in the state had a real scare. An assemblyman from the Bronx—I think the name was Newman became aware that the son of a constituent had drowned at a New York summer camp. Apparently the swimming hour supervision was very casual and Newman decided to make it a cause celebre. He drew a voluminous and drastically punitive bill that dealt not merely with waterfront safety but with practically all aspects of camp operation—the amount of bungalow space each child should have, the counselor-camper ratio, the pay of staff members and their working hours (long before even New York had a minimum wage law), kitchen equipment, menus, and the camp plumbing probably plus some other items that I no longer recall.

If passed and enforced it would have made it impossible for most camps to operate and would have skyrocketed expenses for all. The New England dominated National Camp Directors Association seemed quite unconcerned so we organized a New York State Private Camp Directors Association and dug in our toes. The bill passed the assembly but was narrowly defeated in the senate. Newman announced that he would bring back another bill the next year and we continued to run scared. He tried a second and a third time, but while we were a small group we did have a number of individual parents with influence and his first showing was his best.

By then the association had solidified and we thought it would be permanent. In fact, we worked quite effectively on enrollment and some other problems but broke up before the war started. I had suggested one-year tenure for officers and probably on the strength of that I was elected president, and as I was very much the youngster of the group it pleased me greatly.

The Association was not revived after the war but we did have a Camp Director's Round Table comprised of directors living near the metropolitan area. It was highly informal but it provided an excellent chance to explore common problems and exchange views. It was still going strong when I sold Moss Lake.

CHAPTER XIII

Tragedies

THE STOIC HUNTRESS

I suppose five tragedies make a modest list for a long life, but it surely seems to be five too many.

The first happened when I was a boy of about seven. The Mohawk then stayed open for hunting season and one woman rifle expert had been a steady patron—usually getting her deer. Her tragedy occurred the night before the season was to open when a small group of hunters had gathered in the living room of one of the cottages. The talk ran to a comparison of guns and Miss Mills went to her bedroom to get hers. She wore glasses and as she bent over a chair in the dark room (we did not yet have electric light) she drove a knob on the back of a chair through her glasses and into an eye.

Several pieces of glass went with the knob and the damage was extensive. There was a physician at the hotel. He looked at it, applied a protective bandage and said that she must get to an eye surgeon at once. We knew of none in Utica or Syracuse, but she called and made an appointment with one in New York. By the time she finished the call the New York sleeper was due to leave our Skenswane station in about a half hour so she did not go back to her cottage, merely took her money from the safe and walked to the station. Of course, several people (including George) went with her. Although I was but six at the time I somehow appreciated the gravity of the situation and could sense her pain. She paced the tracks until the train came, said goodbye to everyone, and climbed aboard. The next day we had word that the eye had been removed and the picture jelled in my mind to leave a lasting impression of horror and courage.

THE WRONG ASSUMPTION

Some years later there was a drowning in front of The Mohawk that left me with a quite guilty feeling. Guests were starting to arrive by car and one party was scheduled for early evening, but when they failed to appear my mother asked me to wait until they came regardless of the hour. Shortly after midnight, I heard some noise, went out to investigate, and found it was coming from a hotel adjoining our property. I walked over, asked that the party be a quieter one, and returned to The Mohawk living room.

Later what I thought was noise from the same source became even more strident and I prepared to return. As I went down the hill from the main building I saw other people running from the cottages—people who had correctly diagnosed the noise as a distress call. We soon had a flotilla in the water, but one of the three men in the capsized boat had drowned in the interval—an interval that could have been at least ten minutes shorter if I had recognized the calls for what they were.

STANLEY

In about 1926 we had a rather elderly, but still husky Polish teamster. His first name was Stanley, but I never mastered the last. On a crisp autumn morning he was picking up stones along the bridle path of a size suitable to dress up the edges of one of our lawns. As he was loaded and ready to start back, the team bolted. With characteristic loyalty, Stanley tried to stop them, fell under the wagon, and was so badly crushed that his death came before he could be moved to a hospital.

The depth of his loyalty was probably best measured by his only words to me, which were repeated several times—"I tried to stop them. . . . I tried to stop them."

BILL MAX

Tragedy number four was the drowning of a Florida fisherman in Moss Lake. Actually Bill Max was a carpenter, but he had spent the previous winter in Florida as a commercial fisherman so I had no qualms about taking him over to the island and assigning him some post-season repair work. We went back to the shore and he loaded the tools and material into a canoe. Unfortunately, he also loaded a generous supply of nails into the various pockets of his overalls. Just before he reached the island the canoe tipped over and the nails carried Bill to the bottom without his once rising to the surface.

THE DEATH OF SALLIE ROOSEVELT

The fifth tragedy drew worldwide attention. In the late fifties President Roosevelt's thirteen-year old granddaughter, Sallie, was enrolled at Moss Lake. She was popular, capable, attractive, and unspoiled, with a real interest in camp activities.

The Senior Camp afternoon activity on the fateful day was a supper climb up Bald Mountain. Sallie was in the front seat of my car on the way to the mountain and was chattering like a magpie, but by the time I returned to camp the secretary was reaching for the telephone. It was a counsellor telling us that Sallie had walked a few hundred feet toward the base of the mountain with her, passed out, and seemed to be very slow in regaining consciousness. I called an ambulance and started back to the mountain.

The stretcher and I arrived at about the same time. When Sallie was in the ambulance and on her way to a Utica hospital, I called the hospital to alert them and ask them to have the city's best physicians awaiting her arrival. One of my youngest but most capable counsellors, Lynn Wilkie, had stayed with me to see if she could do anything, and I put her in my car and started after the ambulance. Of course, it arrived before us and Sallie was already in the operating room when we arrived. I had telephoned her father, John Roosevelt, before leaving the woods, and he, his wife, and Mrs. Franklin Delano Roosevelt, arrived by chartered plane two or three hours later. By then the doctors had admitted defeat and I had to greet the family with that news. A blood vessel supplying the brain had ruptured and their trepanning had been ineffective.

If this story has a good part it was the family's reaction to their tragedy. There were no critical questions, nor any hint of reproach, Eleanor Roosevelt was most gracious and, in retrospect, sympathetic. I am certain her sympathy caused me more than a little chagrin for I had been one of her husband's most consistent critics through all his years in the White House.

When Lynn and I started home I began to react and Lynn spent most of the trip trying to pull me out of my doldrums—a man in his fifties being consoled by a girl still in college may seem strange, but I was mighty glad she was there.

Of course, the Roosevelt name assured much attention from the press and I had the gateman turn reporters away. However, you do not need to go through the gate to reach the stables, and one of the riding instructors when questioned about Sallie's interests admitted that she was a jumper and had fallen from her horse a few days before. Colonel Shiskin (in charge of the jumping ring) assured the reporters that it had merely been a case of a horse refusing and that Sallie had landed on her feet with the reins in her hands, but they had their angle and I envisioned disastrous publicity for the camp.

Fortunately the Roosevelts belittled the idea and it was soon dropped. Their report to Sallie's school, Miss Hewitts, must have been a reassuring one for our contingent from there doubled the next season. The accident was mentioned by many of the prospects I interviewed that winter, but none seemed apprehensive and most enrolled.

CHAPTER XIV

Local Changes

The years my life has spanned saw the central Adirondacks change from an area of prosperous, but perhaps rather primitive, resort hotels, and a generous number of equally rustic, but often impressive, summer cottages supported by, and supporting, a native community of several hundred, to its present rather amorphous state. Almost without exception these "natives" were honest, hard working men with a wide range of skills. Nearly all were woodsmen and guides, and many were caretakers, carpenters, and icehouse-fillers in the winter. Several built and operated their own hotels. In other words, they were a very special section of early Americans even after the phrase was more commonly applied to antebellum pioneers.

Honesty was taken for granted and few places were really secured, even in the winter time. An owner might return to his camp and find that someone had entered, built fires, cooked food, and perhaps spent the night, but nothing was ever destroyed and seldom would any article be missing, and that would be something that was probably urgently needed at the moment—such as an axe, a pail, or even a bit of rope.

Lumbering projects went on in the surrounding woods, but by the turn of the century few were in the immediate vicinity, and the lumberjacks were a transient segment waiting for a camp to open or coming out in the spring to spend their winter wages. Some were French Canadian, many were Scandinavian, and others were native stock. Several of the best stayed and became valuable members of the local population.

The region opened long before automobiles were invented. In fact, it was quite well developed when my home town of Herkimer got its first automobile—one made in the local machine shop. Essentially, it was a wagon with a motor, and had neither differential nor transmission, and clutching was accomplished by slacking or tightening a drive belt. Before regular cars started to appear in numbers (another ten or fifteen years), ownership was limited to only a few families, and I can remember it being very nice to have friends with a car who would occasionally invite you for a Sunday drive or picnic.

When I started Moss Lake, the roads from Old Forge to Eagle Bay and from Eagle Bay to Big Moose were dirt. A contractor by the name of Doyle was about to put in a macadam road between the last two communities, but after two or three seasons he went broke in the attempt and we operated for several years with roads more difficult than the original wagon trail. The black top was to be constructed on a sub-base of sharp blasted stones, probably averaging ten to twenty pounds. They were laid for rather long stretches, then would be followed with finer stone, then much more time would elapse before that section of the road had a top dressing. The sub-base stage was particularly punishing and the two-and-a-half-mile stretch from Eagle Bay to Moss Lake was largely in this condition for about three years. Tires were quickly cut and we tried to solve the problem by putting hard rubber tires on a couple of Model T's. They would outlast the cars but the repeated shocks allowed the cars' axles only days or weeks to survive, and I decided that replacing tires was the lesser of the two evils.

Actually the Big Moose Road was completed before the road from Old Forge to

Interior Big Moose Chapel

Big Moose Chapel built by Earl Covey

Holl's Inn, South Shore, Fourth Lake

Eagle Bay, and when the latter was finally laid in concrete the hotel business began to collapse—a process that has continued to the present time. Now, of the twenty-five Fulton Chain hotels I remember, only two remain in full operation my father's Rocky Point which seemed so old when he contrasted it with the 1910 Mohawk that he wished to demolish the main building, and the much newer Ara-Ho, now Holl's Inn. Both owe their survival to fine locations and extraordinarily capable and stable management—the Delmarsh family at Rocky Point, the Holl family at Ara-Ho. My mother's successor at The Mohawk, Allen Wilcox, did equally well until his health failed. It is now operating as Mark VII, a catholic camp for the deaf.

The twenty-five hotels of my youth were: the Forge House, the Moosehead, the Forest House, and the Adirondack in the village of Old Forge. First and Second Lakes had none, but the Bald Mountain House on Third Lake was large and flourishing. Fourth Lake had the greatest number—Manhasset, Bay View, Camp Fulton, Camp Minnebrook, Mountain View, Burnap's, Onondaga, Ramona, Cohasset, Beckers (standing but with operation curtailed), The Kenmore, The Mohawk, Camp Monroe, Grandview, Cedar Island, Neodack, the Eagle Bay Hotel, Cliff House, Mohegan Lodge, Hart's Inn, Rocky Point, The Wood (still standing but not operating), New Arrowhead, Ara-Ho and Parquette. The Seventh Lake House was alone on Seventh Lake.

I imagine the summer population is about the same as it was in that time for these early hotels averaged better than a hundred guests, and the motels which were their replacements, while numerous, did not have as many rooms. However, this loss of space is not the important factor. Each of the old resorts was an especial entity with patrons returning year after year, who acquired personality imprints as characteristic as those of the alumni of various colleges. Further, they had ties with the traditions of still earlier years and the atmosphere was consistently wholesome.

Undoubtedly the place least changed in this Fulton Chain area is the Little Moose Lodge of the Adirondack League Club. The Club owns thousands of acres, restricts the location and types of buildings, and has nothing more modern than the wooden tennis courts that were in operation when I first saw the place. Motorboats are taboo and cars are used only for ingress and egress—indeed, roads do not reach many of the camps.

In the Big Moose area the number of hotels was not as great, the most artistic being Camp Cragg built and run by Henry Covey. It was a rustic masterpiece and had an extremely affluent clientele that bowed to the whims of its proprietor. He set his own codes and did not allow women to smoke, wear jewelry, make-up, or anything but the most proper attire of the period.

Higby Camp, farther up the lake, also was built by an old guide and then rebuilt after a fire. It was operated for many years by his son, Roy, as Higby Club. In the seventies the cottages were sold off one at a time and finally the hotel was torn down.

Two hotels built by enterprising natives were not rustic, but large wooden structures. The Glenmore at the head of the lake was destroyed by fire in the thirties. Dwight Sperry, who erected this hotel, surely was one of the most enterprising natives of his generation. He also built the even larger Eagle Bay Hotel which was operated for many years by his nephew, Ben Sperry, and he established a telephone company to serve the area. I can remember his appearing from time to time as his own lineman, and I can recall the admiration my family had for the man's energy and enterprise.

The largest hotel on the lake was Lake View Lodge built by Charles Williams and operated by his son, Fred, until the mid-fifties. Both men had other interests in the area and in Utica. When the hotel reached the end of its days its fate was similar to those who had previously succumbed. It was turned over to an auctioneer and the individual cottages sold along with some empty lots. The hotel itself still stands but by now it is degenerating into an eyesore.

Also on Big Moose Lake was a small rustic hotel, The Waldheim, which has stayed in the Martin family since its inception and still operates successfully. Across the lake there is a small frame building which operated as Burdick's in my early years, but it is currently known as the Big Moose Inn and I would judge it now to be more restaurant than hotel.

Camp Cragg also was destroyed by fire, but by then Henry Covey's son, Earl, was developing into a master builder and constructed and started his own hotel on Twitchel Lake. Later he turned it over to his daughter and son-in-law (it also went by the auction route at a later date), and then built the still prosperous Covewood Lodge now operating under one of our Darts Lake managers. It is situated across the Bay from the former site of Camp Cragg. During these years Earl was constantly building for other people and many of the nicest camps, and almost all of the finest fireplaces, on Big Moose were done by him.

These various buildings were enough to establish him in the minds of many as the greatest artisan the Adirondacks have ever known, and anyone visiting the area should surely attend services at the Big Moose Chapel. This structure he designed, and built much more with his own hands than with the hands of others. He quarried the stone at Darts Lake, drew it to the site, cut and shaped it with a care that I have not found duplicated in any of the "Great Camps" of the area. He went into the woods, selected the trees for its paneling, trusses, and rafters, and even brought in a great birch burl for a pulpit: It sounds rustic and it is, yet each piece is fitted as finely as could be expected of the best cabinet makers, and I believe the end result has a more compelling religious atmosphere than can be found either in the great cathedrals of the world or in any of its country churches. Of course, I have not visited them all and I am sure there are people in other sections familiar with structures they think should challenge that statement, but I have never known anyone who attended service there who could suggest a comparable structure.

Perhaps the greatest testimony to this man's patience ties in with the history of the church. After the laborious work involved in fabricating such a structure he had to witness its destruction by fire on the day of the first service. All the wood had to be replaced and as I recall, he refused to get in a sand-blasting machine but instead scrubbed and re-chiseled the blackened surfaces of the stone walls. By this time he was suffering from arthritis, but was still out-working the men under him.

In short, the scene at Big Moose is somewhat better than on the Fulton Chain with Martin's Waldheim surviving from the early period and Covewood from the thirties.

The start of the collapse of the resort empire was one that established a route that nearly all followed. An auctioneer from the midstate area, Charles Vosburgh, and his satelite attorney would approach a hotel owner he felt to be financially distressed, pay a nominal sum for the property, and then contract to hold an auction of his own design. The usual pattern was selling the contents of the building, then the individual cottages, followed by the idle land cut up into parcels, and finally the main building. Commonly this was accomplished with the sale running only one day. I think the amounts realized were quite realistic and my displeasure relates not to the honesty of the operation, but to the fact that it so completely dismembered the hotels. Once this happened there was no return. When mortgages are foreclosed or a hotel stands idle, there is always a chance of its revival, but these sales were very final and in a single decade quite changed the map of the area.

We now have good roads and a larger summer population due to the number of private cottages that have been built around the carcasses of the hotels or on other plots sandwiched in between them. It is a make-shift countryside, but I believe some of the cottage owners have built a community spirit, yet I have never heard of motel loyalties nor motel personalities, and the community, while still prosperous, no longer fits its early pattern.

In short, the biggest changes in the central Adirondacks took place in the first half of the century—certainly before 1960—and this stands in sharp contrast to the timing of the metamorphosis that has been effected in most of the country during the last twenty-five years. They have been the years of degenerating morals, rising crime, and crumbling educational standards. Incidentally, the Town of Webb Schools seem to have maintained their integrity and are still turning out well-equipped and well-motivated youngsters. Of course, the tax picture has changed as evidenced by the fact that we now pay as much on our small lot and cottage as was levied on Moss Lake through its first three decades. However, the officials are honest and responsive and the community is law-abiding.

Until recent years the Adirondack Park was in the hands of a State Conservation Commission designed to preserve the state lands within the park boundaries, make sure that they were used for the benefit of the public, and to minimize any impingement from the surrounding private lands. This they did tactfully and effectively, but a decade ago much of their authority was transferred to a newly created Adirondack Park Agency which quickly developed into a quite oppressive bureaucracy.

Three groups have suffered most seriously from their ill-devised regulations, the holders of large tracts within the Park who wish to develop them into summer colonies, vacationers who would like to have a summer cottage of their own on a lakeside plot of modest size, and the waterloving itinerant.

The large land-owner must in some cases require his prospects to purchase lots of more than forty acres, which means that he must set prices too high for all but the wealthy. This commonly means that he must sell to the state.

The family wishing a lakeside location for a summer home must, unless they are one of the wealthy, try to secure an unused plot in a developed area. If they succeed in finding one they will be required to get a permit quite as though they had purchased a city lot. Some of the restrictions will be designed with the public health in mind, but they will be apt to run into one that will cause them to drop the project. A frequent hurdle is that they will be required to keep all of their buildings, except their boathouse, fifty feet from the lake. If their neighbors are that far back this will not be a handicap, but if they are near the lake their view can be badly restricted.

The frustration of a family member can be matched by that of the canoe or guideboat enthusiast who in earlier years needed only to know that a piece of state owned shoreline offered an attractive camp site. Now he must either find, and usually share with many others, a public campground, or select a place "at least one hundred and fifty feet from any lake, road, or stream." First finding such a place may mean walking along parallel to the shore but fifty yards back, and probably with no trail, for many hundreds of yards before a suitable place is spotted. Then he must go down to the shore, mark the spot and return to his boat. Then he must move that to the marked spot and carry his gear to the selected site. Once this is done he has no water to drink, to bathe in, or to admire. When he leaves he will need to carry water from the lake or river and if he fails to carry enough a fire may break out after his departure and since the site is hidden in the woods it may have a fine start before anyone sees it. Once discovered there will still be the problem of getting water to fight the fire.

To my mind this is inconsiderate bureaucracy at its worst—a show of muscle at the expense of the people it was created to serve. The Conservation Commission merely tried to preserve the Adirondacks for the pleasure of its inhabitants and the public at large. The camper felt welcome and at home and usually returned from each trip with renewed enthusiasm. The Agency seems to have little interest in either residents or vacationists yet has been able to acquire vast additional tracts by making their private use difficult.

A still more outrageous position is that when they acquire land all buildings must be destroyed regardless of their historical value or their potential for public use. Moss Lake was in excellent condition and could have been used as a Fresh Air camp, a Cancer camp or as a vacation retreat for state employees. Cascade buildings while less elaborate did not merit oblivion, for the earlier ones were fine examples of nineteenth-century Adirondack architecture. I doubt if any of our early greats contributed more to the Adirondacks than did Seward Webb but his tremendous place on Lake Lila is being razed and the equally impressive Santanoni probably will be next. The list is a long one and it seems that each is more senseless than the last. At Cascade and at Lila they have closed the roads two miles short of the camps—apparently to make sure that they give but minimal pleasure to the public. They could not have chosen two camps with histories so well designed to demonstrate their arrogance. It was Dr. Webb who engineered the sale that established the Adirondack Park and it was Mr. Snyder who drafted the basic restrictions and incorporated them in the deeds for the many thousands of acres sold to the state.

Ironically, all of their rules seem to stem from the "Forever Wild" clause in the Webb deeds. Charles Snyder, Dr. Webb's attorney who drew these deeds, was a close personal friend of my family for many years and I discussed the deeds with him and with his son on several occasions. I am sure that the Agency's rulings would cause both him and Dr. Webb to roll in their graves.

Further evidence of their not having the public interest at heart stands out clearly if we contrast their present attitude with that of the earlier officials. In the fifties we had an extensive blow-down in our area. The Conservation Commission made a quick survey and gave natives and lumbermen permission to go in and utilize the fallen trees. Now with an extensive beech kill and a more localized blow-down, plus an expensive fuel situation, this is not being done. Letting residents help themselves to the dead and down trees for firewood would alone help solve their fuel problem and alleviate the local unemployment, but we should go further and give serious consideration to making our state lands at least produce funds for tax equivalency payments.

I have no figures, but the yearly taxes that would be paid by these lands if they were in private hands must be of astronomical size. As it is, the state is making payments of many millions to the towns and counties within the park. Few people love the Adirondacks more than I, but I can see no reason why a carefully monitored conservative lumbering program should not be established. I have done it around all three of my lakes with no damage to any tract. It could be planned so the lumber roads would run in a pattern that would improve access for both vacationists and firefighters. Only selected trees should be cut, and with the help of a firewood harvest we would have a much neater and more interesting forest than the present one.

This could be done on a contract basis, or by establishing a Civilian Conservation Corps and enrolling able-bodied men who are drawing, or wish to draw, unemployment benefits—with loss of those benefits as the penalty for not signing up. Perhaps a combination approach would be best—the CCC contingent swamping the roads and harvesting the dead and down trees ahead of the lumbermen to facilitate their work. They could then come back after the lumber men to scavenge the culls, branches, and tops, being sure that anything too small to be used as firewood is left flat on the ground to expedite its decay and minimize the fire hazard—which surely would be less than before the operation was undertaken. The CCC's should be able to earn their wages at the present price of firewood and the voided and avoided unemployment payments should serve to make their part of the operation most profitable. The money saved by cancelling the benefits of the unwilling men might be surprisingly substantial.

I am now a Florida resident, but that is because the state's equable climate is much better suited to an ageing man, not because I prefer it to my Adirondacks. Unfortunately social decay has infected both states but for the present our neck-of-the-woods stands as a welcome oasis in a confusing world.

PART TWO

CHAPTER XV

Facing Our National Dilemma

As I started writing this book a major purpose was to paint for my generation and others the extent to which our Adirondack area and the country as a whole have changed in the fourscore plus years of this century. I am sure that some of this has been woven into my running account of the years, but I think out of loyalty to my theme I must make some contrasts stand out in bold relief.

First, we have had a great and pleasing development of living amenities. Electric lights and electric power have arrived. Plumbing and central heating are in general use. We went from horses to trains, to automobiles, to airplanes, and are dabbling with missiles. From primitive and unreliable telephones, to wireless, radio, television, telex, and computers. From brooms to vacuum cleaners. From washboards and stove-heated irons to washing machines and wash-and-wear fabrics. From the one-room schoolhouse to the electronic classroom. From the seldom-seen slide rule to the ubiquitous solid-state calculator. From appendectomies, hysterectomies, and mastectomies to pace-makers, open heart surgery, and organ transplants.

Railroads first refined and extended their services, then let them deteriorate to a level that could not have been envisioned by anyone living in their heyday. Competition with trucks, buses, and airplanes became fierce, but the cruelest blows of all came from government. It subsidized the newcomers with airports and our tremendous network of roads while piling high taxes and onerous regulations upon the railroads, and taking away from them a major source of income—U.S. mail.

Now there is a law in the congressional mill that would take from states their right to prohibit tandem trailers and which even has a clause permitting trains of three on some roads. It quite surely is PAC initiated and can have a critical impact on our roads, our railroads, and our oil.

Private automobiles have gnawed away at the vitals of the old giant through almost the whole period and made certain that shambles must be the result, even while the industry remains healthy or is expanded in some other countries. Horse racing and gambling have survived, but the widespread prosperity of the legitimate theatre has been destroyed by movies, and television.

Some of our changes have been marvelous, some good, some of doubtful value, and many pernicious. But, however you appraise them, the ones on the debit side of the ledger stand out in bold relief and threaten to destroy the life we know. I put the crumbling of moral standards at the head of my list. We give lip service to some of the Ten Commandments, but most are ignored by a terribly large segment of the population. A frightening increase in all categories of crime is one facet, and the disintegration of the work ethic and of patriotism are equally serious, but the one that poses the greatest threat is the breakdown of family life and authority, plus the concomitant sexual license extending to the female as never before. The physical effects of this (disease plus the mechanical damage done to the young girls) can curse more than one generation. It will perpetuate the disintegration of the family, reduce the number of children, and make orphans out of many who are born. Cohabitation and the boredom that usually result will make marriage seem inane to many, and our best men are going to be unwilling to give their lives to women who have previously given themselves to others. Even those who do become enamored with individual girls and marry them are apt to live out the days of the marriage in suspicion. I very much doubt if this country or any other can come up with a satisfactory substitute for marriage, home, and family.

Next in terms of potential damage and horror is the burgeoning use of drugs. It is spawning crime at every turn, ruining the lives of millions of users, and damning their children and the children they have been unable to produce.

In short, the "From Heyday to Mayday" title selected with our northern resorts in mind is equally accurate and descriptive when applied to the whole state of the nation. Our educational system, from the lowest grades through college, is in shambles; our immigration policy and our foreign policy seem to no longer be operated with the good of our own country in mind; our welfare, medical, and correctional costs threaten to destroy our economy, and this is hastened by a free trade policy that fails to protect our workmen and our industrial machine, yet which most politicians seem to regard as a sacred cow. Further, our large corporations are allowed to waste their capital by cannibalizing each other—often reducing production and employment in the process—and even worse, to establish plants in countries with low labor costs, thus making their capital expenditure clearly counter-productive by funding foreign payrolls and providing the host countries with plants that can be taken over by them at any time. Drugs, moral disintegration that is destroying the family unit, declining patriotism, a meddlesome foreign policy, a flood of inferior aliens, and rampant crime complete the sorry picture.

During his first eighteen months Reagan moved to correct or alleviate some of these tremendous handicaps, but he moved too slowly on some and apparently felt others to be too politically sensitive. The latter is a valid consideration in a democracy, but without bold action the situation may soon deteriorate to a point that will make an orderly return impossible.

I started rooting for Reagan when he ran for the California governorship, was most enthusiastic when he campaigned against Ford and against Carter, and remained in his corner through his first year and a half in office; but his endorsement of the bill which extends the promise of citizenship to the millions of illegal aliens who entered this country by 1980 will, if the measure passes, do more long-range damage than all his years of creditable public service can possibly balance. His insistence on free trade has already made him a doubtful asset.

I think I can best summarize my thoughts by saying I feel it is time to resurrect such slogans as "America First," "America for Americans," and "Buy American." All other countries have policies designed with their self-interests in mind, and since we have spent four decades implementing the whims of our "do-gooders" with disastrous results for our own country and without inspiring kind thoughts in foreign lands, it must be time for a change of course. This is especially true because we seem to have kindled almost world-wide hatred during these forty years and a general expectation that we stand ready to bail out any mismanaged country that needs our assistance, ignoring the fact that our mismanagement has been the most illogical of all and that our per capita debt is the world's largest. Even our NATO allies regard us merely as a source of funding and protection. Sadly, that is protection only the English-speaking countries would consider returning if we were the land under attack. I feel strongly that the role of Santa Claus is ignoble rather than noble when it is played at the expense of the critical needs of our own people. Unfortunately, these needs are now too serious for the palliatives being offered by our public officials, so I feel impelled to diagnose our ills and to offer comprehensive correctives.

CHAPTER XVI

Industry

Autarky was the goal of this country through the 19th century and the first forty years of the 20th. During World War II it was our decisive advantage. Our industrial machine could outproduce all others in the world and made it possible to win the war. At its end we dominated the globe as no country has in any period of history. This domination was both military and industrial. The Russians promptly started to chisel away at the military dominance and we took vigorous steps to end our commercial supremacy.

In the reconstruction years we continued full production and increased our capacity at a rapid pace to supply both goods and machinery to the nations we had conquered. During this period free trade was fine and we espoused it wholeheartedly, closing our eyes to the inevitable consequences; well equipped and highly intelligent countries whose labor costs were so much lower than ours that we could not compete, especially since we had told Germany and Japan that they need not spend great sums on their military machines for we would protect them.

As was so predictable, we started to lose much of our export trade and soon serious import penetration was underway. At first it was confined to the most labor-intensive products. Textiles and apparel led the list and were soon followed by home electronics. This penetration was so successful that now most of our large buyers procure the major portion of their cloth and clothing from India, Korea, and Taiwan, and we have lost our home electronics market and the quality camera market. Now thirty-percent of our auto market is gone and we are rapidly losing out to oriental microwaves. We thought we were safe in the computer field, but Japan is assaulting there, and if we do not move strongly to protect our other industries only minor remnants will remain. Our 1982 trade deficit is certain to be the highest in history and the prediction for 1983 is of a one hundred billion dollar shortage.

We know that our all-important steel industry is one of those under Japanese attack, but I had not realized until recently that our own government was aiding in the assault. I was in Alaska last spring and the largest bridge I saw was a steel structure fabricated in Japan and erected by Japanese labor. Now a California group is trying to raise five billion dollars to launch a San Diego to San Francisco "Bullet Train" project. They plan to give the Japanese national railroad a contract for its construction with everything to be manufactured in Japan, including the ultrasophisticated computer system that controls the operation. Tampa-Miami now faces similar developments.

A large congressional delegation has taken the time for an inspection trip and expressed their approval. Local governments plan to waive environmental regulations and cede a right-of-way of incalculable value paralleling their expressways. Also the corporation is to be granted some tax concessions.

The Bullet is not being selected because it is the world's most advanced. Both France and Germany have faster trains, and MIT constructed a small prototype in the mid-seventies that was complete and functional in every detail, and which had repelling magnets that lessened the noise and made still higher speeds practical. I am sure that with MIT supplying the technology Budd could have the California line completed within a year or two of the completion date for a Japanese project, and we would then be in the vanguard of land transportation, instead of having something the Japanese expect to render obsolete in the near future. They already have a full size prototype embodying the essential of the MIT design, but which they did not allow our delegation to ride, lest they decide the Bullet was too far from being the last word in its field. Incidentally, Budd's Metroliner which needs only better tracks to equal the speed of the Bullet is a much more comfortable train.

If we do contract for the Japanese installation it will be a clear signal to the world that we have abandoned our industrial leadership and that we lack the willpower and self-interest to resist playing the role of a Japanese satellite. The Japanese have called this trend to the attention of their nationals and the world by two patronizing offers of financial assistance. The first was to our ailing automobile industry, and the latest was a five million grant to the California group for a feasibility study of the Bullet project. What a change the last thirty-five years have made!

In spite of our crumbling economy we still seem to be committed to a Free Trade policy although we have gone far beyond the point where that can sustain our living standards.

Our wages are much higher than those of the nations whose products are idling our factories and are pricing domestic goods out of our own markets at a frightening rate. Further, many of our plants are elderly and in need of heavy capital investments. This capital is hard to find in recession years, and perhaps shortly depression years, and even if available it would take many years to bring our plants up to Japanese, German, and even Taiwanese standards (plants for which we gave them the foundations in the early postwar years while letting our own drift toward obsolescense), and would sharply reduce the number of our industrial jobs.

The Free Traders insist that we must meet foreign competition by updating our plants, but they ignore the time element and fail to realize that our high interest rates and faltering economy make that a solution which must wait for better times, even with our currently high write-offs. Also they fail to acknowledge that our low man-hour production is due almost as much to the weakening of our work ethic and to the rules and regulations imposed by both government and unions as to our inferior plants.

Further, with all these factors corrected we would still have to compensate for the much higher wages in this country. I do not think any of us wish to see them brought down to competitive (oriental) levels and the only workable alternate is a protective tariff. Other countries protect their industries and failing to shield ours is like a sharp unilateral reduction in our military defenses. Incidentally we are still giving our chief competitors a tremendous economic edge by providing military protection that enables them to hold down their national budgets.

A modern Smoot-Hawley probably would work, but I think my VARIABLE TARIFF suggestion would be more effective and would have the added advantage of making it impossible for any nation to feel that they were being discriminated against, or to be able to retaliate effectively.

The suggestion is that we impose a tariff on goods from countries with whom we have an unfavorable trade balance that reflects the degree of the imbalance, probably up to a twenty-five to thirty-percent limit. This would yield immense budget-balancing revenue during the adjustment period and would sharply reduce imports and unemployment. Rates should be based on yearly or quarterly reviews of the statistics and a formula worked out that would make it clear that all nations were being treated alike, and since we would be asking no more than an evenly balanced trade flow from any nation none could either protest logically or retaliate. Indeed it is not protectionism per se, but rather a reciprocal trade arrangement that would increase our foreign sales as countries beamed their purchases in our direction to secure more favorable treatment for their exports.

Such a bill would surely have the support of labor and of most industrialists. Of course, some of the latter have fled our labor market by selling under American brand names items manufactured abroad in toto or in partum, and others have established factories in foreign lands, but most would be glad to return their operations to this country—especially if we cancelled our credits for income taxes paid abroad.

Except for the oil countries the tariff as outlined above would affect only those sending us manufactured items, but as we have seriously considered an oil import tax for revenue and to stimulate the development of alternate energy resources, this might be most salutory.

Obviously getting our plants back into this country and operating at capacity would greatly strengthen our position for the next conventional war. Indeed this surely would be more valuable than having an extra half-million men scattered around the world.

Some economists see no need to fear this disindustrialization, but such optimism could not be more unfounded. If we do not manufacture we will have nothing but our farm products and natural resources to sell and the paucity of the proceeds will depress our living standards beyond recognition. The service industries on which some economists seem to count so heavily cannot sustain us and if we lose our factories we will have little left. As children we learned that we could not pick ourselves up by our bootstraps, yet the service-economy optimists seem to feel that we can sustain each other in this fashion.

Even now the entire results of this disindustrialization are foreboding. The auto workers who have been laid off cannot use their carefully developed skills in other factories so they lose their status and their security, while men laid off in other industries face a similar situation. In short these mills and factories must run again or we will sink to depths we have never plumbed before, and that quite surely would lead either to socialism or dictatorship. In either case the nations who have so prized our support will turn their backs and the return road to a prosperous democracy may be one that we will lack the fortitude and unity to travel.

The reaction of our large corporations to this rapidly deteriorating situation has been very bad. They have turned to foreign lands to build their plants, to the money markets to invest their funds, and to their peers for cannibalistic feasts that lower rather than improve production and employment. The first and the last should be prohibited.

There are some who try to envision a world in which we gain a monopoly in the robot and electronic fields and maneuver ourselves into a position that would give such dominance that the less developed countries would in effect be working for us. There are many reasons why this will not be effective, the most immediate one being that we have no monopoly on brains and that as we come up with new inventions and refinements the Germans and Japanese and Taiwanese will promptly pirate them, and probably improve upon them. Since there are many countries as smart as we, and possessed with the normal supply of self-interest we lack, it behooves us to realize that our real advantage lies in our abundance of natural resources and start developing it for the benefit of our own people. We might sustain ourselves for a while (though not at the high level we have enjoyed through most of the century) by pushing and exporting a robot and electronic development, but the more we automate the more unemployment we invite. Indeed if we follow this route we surely will be depressed as never before as other nations use their equal brains and lower labor costs to take over that market as well. On the other side of the coin a return to autarky would free us to regain the world's highest standard of living and stability.

I have been both pleased and displeased by the growing support for quotas on various products as a response to foreign competition—pleased because it indicates that more people are becoming aware of the danger competition poses, and displeased because the process of putting quotas in place would be a laborious one. First, we would have to select the damage-wreaking items, then undertake negotiations with the countries involved, and finally cope with enforcement problems. All would be expensive and later we would face the task of placating displeased nations. In contrast, the variable tariff could be put into place promptly and unilaterally with no need to distinguish between products. During the initial adjustment period it would yield revenues that would do much to balance the federal budget, and the re-opening of plants which would result would be a great step toward solving our unemployment problem; but there are other measures which would aid in its solution. In addition to stopping the establishment of foreign factories by American firms and using the variable tariff and less favorable tax laws to effect eventual return of existing ones, we should prohibit investments in, and loans to other countries. Both further the development of other countries rather than ours and provide employment for foreign labor at the expense of our own.

Another step should be to outlaw large corporate take-overs. They are a check on our industrial growth. Many of our largest and richest companies are buying existing concerns—frequently against the will of the their directors. They may prove to be good investments but the labor forces of the combined plants usually shrink and the capital involved in the take-overs is not productive. If such mergers were made illegal, the funds for the most part would be invested in new plants, our industrial pace would improve, and more people would be employed. This could be a major factor in stabilizing our economy.

Perhaps most important of all is the deportation of illegal aliens. Recent newspaper accounts of attempts to ferret out jobs being held by these aliens indicate a step in the right direction, yet except for the cases that result in deportation it will not prevent their being a drag on our economy, but will merely transfer them from payrolls to welfare rolls.

For basic, economic, and social reasons, we should revert to our mid-century quotas and make no exceptions! They were designed to moderate the flow and to yield readily assimilable recruits in whom respect for the laws of their new country would be instantaneous and patriotism not long delayed. This is in sharp contrast to the current influx of Hispanics who wish to maintain their language, their culture, and their basic loyalties. It is a situation we have never faced before. Of course, ghettos appeared but this was more from necessity than as a matter of choice. Indeed most inhabitants were anxious to break out as soon as they comfortably could and they encouraged their children to leave the ghettos and become Americans. This is what made our melting pot concept a valid one.

There are two effective steps the president could take immediately under his emergency powers. He could send all recognizable illegals back to their own country—in naval transports if necessary, through Guantanamo in the case of the Cubans. Then he could order the screening of the remaining aliens and the issuing of identification cards with both fingerprints and photos to the legals.

Also, I believe all federal financial aid to aliens could be stopped overnight by presidential edict, but if not, congress should act promptly. I know the Hispanic vote is important to some congressmen, but surely they must be few. If they are not, we are indeed in a bad way for the national health is so critically at risk that even those who stand to lose many constituents should be impelled by patriotism to vote for such a program, instead of resorting to "humanitarian" posturing at the expense of their own country's welfare.

It should be clear to all that we can continue to support large sectors of the world only by impoverishing ourselves, and that impoverishment will soon lead to impotence. Obviously locating and deporting illegal aliens will be a labor-intensive project, but most of the manpower could be supplied by army units with their personnel being subject to immediate recall. Psychologically, army units operating in uniform would be much more effective than immigration officers and county sheriffs in persuading aliens that we do at least mean business.

At ground level we, like all countries, have many people whose labor is marginal, but although the minimum wage laws were enacted for their benefit they have, in most instances, had the opposite effect. This is especially true in times when labor is plentiful, for employers will not pay the established minimum to inexperienced applicants while experienced ones are available at or near the same cost. Nor will they select people whose age or health has caused their production to drop below the norm. This is especially damaging to the young for it makes it difficult for them to acquire the skills necessary for pleasing positions later on and leaves them with much idle time that is seldom put to good use. Errand boys, busboys, bagboys, groundsmen and household servants could find much employment that is now denied them were it not for this artificial barrier. Most importantly, these marginal workers could keep their self-respect and the public would be saved much charitable expense and vandalism.

Except in the Great Depression (the current one may eventually earn the right to that impressive title), unemployment has never been as bad as it now is and even then the resulting load on the working majority was less severe, so for all of us the need to solve this problem has never been greater.

I am confident putting the Variable Tariff in place and deporting the illegal aliens would put most of our people to work, but if many do remain unemployed we should revive the WPA with the repair of roads and sewers as its sole objective. At present there is a tremendous pool of construction workers, miners, lumbermen, farmers, and truck drivers, and even some engineers on our unemployment rolls. All should have skills useful in both fields that would allow the operation to be a truly effective one instread of a boondoggle, and since their ages and occupations are on record the recruiting should take little time. Any able-bodied man refusing the jobs offered should be dropped from unemployment and welfare rolls and refused reinstatement for a two-year period. This and the fact that the ones enrolled (at the minimum wage except in the case of very special qualifications) will no longer be collecting state or federal allowances should practically eliminate the labor item from the operating sheets and make WPA the least expensive and most valuable form of public assistance.

All aliens should be barred from welfare and unemployment and we should invoke the responsibility assumed by the sponsors of those who have come in legally but are not self-supporting. If that sponsorship cannot be enforced these people also should be deported. We should fence and patrol our southern border (with army detachments to minimize the extra expense) and intensify coast guard patrols. If this produces a migrant worker shortage, able-bodied people on unemployment should be required to take their places.

CHAPTER XVII

Affirmative Action

I think most people are conscious of the damage being done to the service business in general and even to industry by the application of our Affirmative Action policy and the number of resulting court cases. It is repeatedly used to secure jobs for which many minority members are unfitted, and once they are employed it becomes a defense against dismissals and an excuse for demanding unmerited promotions. In many cases the effect on their fellow workers is so demoralizing that both production and service suffer.

Certainly we should obsolete the new meaning of minorities by eliminating Affirmative Action and quotas. Employers must be free to put the right man on the right job. When you restrict this privilege you place a burden on other workers and damage the morale of the operation.

Another facet of affirmative action is that it places the capable and earnest members of a minority under the cloud of the disapproval engendered by the vast numbers holding positions their ability and application do not warrant. Indeed many blacks resent affirmative action as heatedly as the general public for they are well aware that the country has many races that immigrated in the 19th and early 20th centuries who have now established themselves on complete financial and social parity and have done it with no pampering and in spite of racial antagonisms. At least three of these groups now have incomes well above the national average—the Jews, the Japanese, and the Chinese. Many blacks would very much like to have that same opportunity but legislators and courts are denying it to them by their racial preference laws and rules.

CHAPTER XVIII

Energy

When 1973 brought us face to face with an oil shortage and skyrocketing prices that reminded us we were driving our cars at the indulgence of the Arab states and supplying whole countries with incomes higher than our own, we were soundly shocked, but the seriousness of the situation soon faded into the background. We did start some nuclear plants, which the environmentalists are now throttling most effectively, and we talked about alcohol and the sun, but we did not take the obvious steps to protect ourselves.

This in spite of the fact that Germany had supported its vast military machine on coal distillates through World War II and that thirty years later South Africa was using a similar process and supplying thirty-percent of its needs—selling the distillate at the same price as petrol. They offered us the details of the process for a token fee as a gesture of goodwill, but we turned it down and appropriated millions of dollars over their figure for experimental development. Of course, by now, our scientists have the technology to build whatever plants are needed—in fact, a pilot plant was to go into production some time ago, but apparently we are content to buy our oil from the Arabs even though that source may be lost at anytime, or require military intervention to save.

To my mind a currently obvious answer is taking advantage of Mexico's dire financial straits to tie up their petroleum resources by TREATY so we can forget the oilpot of the Persian Gulf. This can greatly simplify our diplomatic, commercial, and military planning, and assure us of available oil even if the Mideast erupts. This probably can be done by friendly bargaining for surely we can offer a better price and more uniform flow than countries who must transport their oil by sea, but if pressure is needed it should be applied.

I think time is demonstrating the wisdom of the Monroe Doctrine and I feel we should also take similar steps to tie up Venezuelan oil if our experts' appraisal of the Mexican fields does not indicate that they can develop an adequate supply. In case of war they will be a much less vulnerable source than even our own Alaska with its pipeline vulnerable to a single bomb.

If Secretary Watt's approval of offshore oil leases for Kuwait is a valid expression of administration thinking we are charting a most dangerous course for which there can be no possible justification. It is diametrically opposed to our self-interest and if there is any country that has no need for additional oil it is Kuwait.

CHAPTER XIX

The Budget

Our trillion dollar national debt is one no other nation could conceivably hope to master without very drastic inflation or substantial repudiation. We must turn the deficit tide soon or we will be required to make this painful choice ourselves.

We should approve the proposed constitutional amendment to require a balanced budget now under consideration and start immediately to comply with its spirit. It is a step in the right direction but it should contain a provision barring foreign aid until we have liquidated our national debt. It is unreasonable for the nation with the world's greatest indebtedness to be asked to borrow, or raise by additional taxation, money for either the people or the governments of other countries. This is particularly unconscionable while we have uncounted thousands of homeless and destitute of our own. Certainly these should come ahead of the needy of other lands. I would not advocate maintaining them at the level of those now so securely ensconced in the arms of our welfare system, but minimal shelter and enough food to sustain reasonable health should be provided. Also, it is important both in terms of fairness and of national health that everyone on either welfare or unemployment be required to work at any available job within their physical and mental capacities—with permanent loss of support as the penalty for refusal.

Without waiting for the passage of this amendment we should begin to gradually dismantle much of our bureaucracy and, in the interim, steps should be taken to reduce the government payroll by graduated salary reductions to be reversed only when the budget is balanced. These salaries, with the exception of police, firemen, and career soldiers who are exposed to special dangers should remain at a level slightly lower than those in the private sector to partially offset the security of employment which the government payroll traditionally affords.

Our social security costs currently exceed the entire defense budget and are growing at an alarming rate. The rate itself is indeed frightening but probing the future makes the picture appear even grimmer. We now have about five wage earners to support each retiree but statiticians see this picture being cut in half in the not-too-distant future. So far we have met increasing costs by higher employee and employer assessments and another is about to go into effect, even though the present rate is unfairly high.

The situation can be helped by deferring the age of eligibility and making less generous cost of living adjustments; but in the long view the SS octopus which is now devouring thirty percent of the money we raise and borrow seems to present us with the alternative of diverting much general tax money to its support, increasing our payroll taxes insuperably, or delaying eligibility substantially.

This painful choice I believe should entitle us to substitute for the SS system, plus all government, and possibly private, entitlements a uniform old age pension, not based on previous earnings and inflation, but to be set each year at a level equal to one-half the average national per capita income of the previous year and made subject to any income tax then applying to wages. Adjusting to such a standard would be much fairer than using the present automatic cost of living increase because it would also take into consideration the ability of the rest of the nation to supply this support. In other words, there would be neither a disadvantaged nor a preferred sector of the economy. This fifty-percent may seem like an overly generous figure, but the cost could be reduced in a most salutary fashion by raising the retirement age and abolishing the illogical stipulation that pensioners should not be permitted to work without their stipends being reduced. Of course, a complication to this plan is that the government in effect has a contract with the people paying into and receiving SS. On the other hand, there is no contractual obligation to raise payments to compensate for cost of living increases, but any unadjusted entitlement that proves to be greater than the proposed pension should allow its holder to receive the larger amount. People still working who have made payments into SS should have the total of those payments computed and ten-percent of that computation added to each year's pension payment, or perhaps more simply, one-percent per month.

This suggestion would do two important things. It would make old age payments secure and predictable and it would avoid the vast expense to the government and employers in effecting the various deductions and payments and making the necessary reports.

If substituting the uniform old age pension for SS is deemed a too sweeping adjustment, I would like to see the pension systems at all levels of government merged with SS. The enlarged revenue base would help to meet current payments and the transfer of the funds now in these pension plans would swell the SS reserves.

Current pressure from political action committees is so great that it could well be characterized as the most expensive corruption of our legislative process, one that has reached a point where many major office holders and candidates find it to be their chief source of campaign financing and a favor which they often are pressured to return.

Last fall we had an unprecedented number of legislators retiring voluntarily while still in their prime. One has stated quite frankly that the necessity of "groveling" for campaign contributions and the irate reaction of contributors who later request favors which should not be granted was a major factor in his decision. That, of course, is but the tip of the iceberg and it seems quite safe to assume that other men have their working efficiency reduced by barrages of such requests. Quite surely some of the decisions made under such pressure do not represent that legislator's best judgment.

On balance, the PACs, with their great potential for corruption surely do more harm than good and we should move for their elimination by excluding all but individual campaign contributions carrying a one hundred dollar limit, by placing a ceiling equal to the first year's salary on the candidates own investment, and by requiring the country's TV and radio stations to give free time proportionate to the importance of the office to all candidates qualifying for primaries or winning a party nomination. This time should be granted for two weeks prior to the primary contest and for a similar pre-election period.

In addition to freeing our candidates from the work consumed in our long campaigns it would interfere less with the running of government as incumbents are also campaigners. Further, it would reduce the time invested by the public, yet with the uniform media coverage it would not leave the voters with inadequate information on which to base their choices. Perhaps most importantly it would keep candidates from buying, or attempting to buy, positions of power and prestige. With 1982 producing multi-million dollar bids some barrier surely is needed.

The current income tax situation is horrendous both because of the payments involved and its many inequities—some inherent in the law, others created by loopholes and avoidance. The federal government is most conscious of this and is working on two quite different solutions. One is the much publicized level tax rate with lower percentages and the elimination of many credits. It would be a major simplification and could be adjusted to yield revenue comparable with that of the present system, but in the interest of fairness it probably should be a two or three, rather than a one, level tax and home mortgage interest and taxes should be retained as deductibles.

The other approach while not a new concept has had little publicity. It is a tax on consumption rather than on income. This I feel would not only be a confusing change but would also present many inequities, most notably in the cases that are approaching, or have reached, retirement age with a nest egg sufficiently substantial to make possible comfortable living and many luxuries. This "hoarded" income has, of course, been taxed as it was acquired, and taxing it again as it is spent would be double taxation of the worst kind.

Since present tax structure makes the IRS a very powerful and extremely expensive government arm. A third approach would be to repeal the income tax. This would eliminate most of this expense, but the loss of the revenue would make the budget imbalance much greater than ever before contemplated. In part, we should compensate for this by deep cuts in expenditures, but the remaining billions would have to be offset by federal borrowing or by legitimizing printing press money.

As using bonds would leave us still walking the nationally popular treadmill of escalating interest payments I would like to see us travel the generally discredited printing press route. It has been treacherous for many countries only because it has been unrestrained. Therefore, whatever authorizing legislation is designed should tie the amount of each year's issue to the gross national product of the preceding year.

Currently our income tax yields about 23% of that three trillion figure and it surely should be drastically reduced. Accordingly I would suggest that there be a mandated shrinkage to six hundred billion and that the cap be dropped an additional ten billion in each of the next two years. At that point an adequate but economical percentage should be established with stipulation that a fixed portion of it be used to reduce the national debt.

If a uniform old age pension is substituted for our SS payments the GNP percentage should be increased to cover the extra expense, but the combination would end both payroll taxes and withholding deductions.

Resulting inflation would reduce the purchasing value of all income and services and should be regarded as a tax. Its advantage would be that it would be evenly distributed and would involve no individual, government, or corporate paperwork, and the millions of accountants, bookkeepers and IRS employees necessitated by the present system would be freed for constructive work. This in itself would do much for our economy, since in the long run we cannot live at a higher level than can be supported by the goods and services we produce. Indispensible as many government employees, including the military, are, they must be supported by the workers of the country, and the greater the number of people in the supporting group and the fewer in the supported group the higher the standard of living becomes.

In addition to transferring a vast number of workers to the productive category, abolishing the income tax would have the tremendous advantage of freeing all from direct taxation which would be a major incentive for everyone to work earnestly and to devise productive enterprises.

Eliminating government borrowing would free much capital for private planning and while the certainty of inflation would rule out low gross interest rates, the strict and simple limitation on the money to be printed each year would make calculating them much simpler than in recent years. They should not exceed the highs of those years and the fact that we learned to live with those highs even while carrying our high tax burden should make them seem quite affordable with no income tax payments to meet.

The variable tariff advocated earlier would increase revenues and the work done by a revised WPA should minimize the heavy sewer and road maintenance or reconstruction costs facing most sections of the country. If accounting for the funds spent by our tourists abroad and those of other nationals in our country is too complicated to make their inclusion in variable tariff computations feasible, we should limit the funds our travelers are allowed to take abroad until we have liquidated our national debt.

If the income tax is continued, as it quite certainly will be, most nonprofit institutions should loose their federally granted tax exemptions and preferential postal rates. I would suggest that only long-established churches, the Red Cross, and the Salvation Army be allowed to retain their present tax exemption, and that heart and cancer research groups be evaluated. Hospitals accepting a uniform and reasonably low rate schedule, and colleges with tuitions under $5,000 and with room and board under $2,500, should be allowed a 50% exemption. Present privileges are being badly abused and I am quite sure these changes would net the government between twenty-five and fifty billion.

If we retain the income tax and an old age pension is not substituted for SS payments, those payments and all other entitlements, plus all fringe benefits, should be taxed as ordinary income—even the benefits of our ex-presidents. The cost of their bodyguards should cease being a federal expense after the first twelve months. Like military men they know they run the risk of violence when they take office and should not shrink from the slight residual danger still with them a year later.

In any case, off-budget expenditures should be abolished, probably with the substitution of a presidential discretionary fund limited to a few million dollars. The present system is concealing tremendously costly items from the public view that should be aired for congressional approval. Loans, grants, and military aid to foreign lands should be suspended.

The next step should be to weed out all false claims, punish by imprisonment, and bar from all future welfare considerations. Recipients under sixty should be advised their checks will shrink to a sustenance level by gradual steps during the next year. and they should be given cards permitting them to work below the minimum wage during that period—this to facilitate their attaining a self-supporting status.

It is important that all welfare and unemployment recipients be required to work at any available job within their physical and mental capacities, with a permanent loss of support as a penalty for refusal.

We should eliminate the use of tax-exempt debentures to finance commercial enterprises. It is a most improper distortion of their intended use, unfair to the public, and unfair to competing enterprises that must pay commercial interest rates.

As all realize, our defense expenses are astronomical and present us with an opportunity for the greatest cuts. Reagan is quite right in saying that we cannot risk a unilateral reduction in our nuclear arsenal, but if, as I suggest in the military section, we withdraw our conventional troops from the eastern hemisphere our standing army could be halved and its costs trimmed dramatically with no dimunition of our power to defend ourselves.

None of the suggestions I have made, nor all of them together, should be considered a substitute for a systematic pruning of governmental expenditures. I can remember the first "Billion Dollar Congress" and the nation-wide criticism it engendered, even though it occurred as World War I was approaching. Of course, we cannot limit either our services or our expenditures to those of that day, but they might be used as a basis of comparison to decide which are dispensable and which have too seriously outpaced inflation. With an 800/1 ratio and our depressed quality of life substantial deletions and economies should surely be possible.

CHAPTER XX

Foreign Policy

Our foreign policy seems to enthusiastically embrace the guiding principles of our trade policy and abjures any thoughts that appear to be tainted by self-interest. After World War II we made it clear to our former enemies that we would protect them from the Russian Bear and that it would not be necessary, or even permissible, for them to maintain an expensive military force. As a result "defense" expenditures are still the biggest item in our budget—so large that our national debt has now passed the trillion mark. This debt by far the world's largest—even if figured on a per capita basis—is a load so heavy we may be forced to consider partial repudiation either by letting the value of the dollar fall drastically or by cancelling interest and gradually returning principal.

Unfortunately this situation seems to make little impression on Washington and we spend more and more each year—both at home and abroad. Taxes bring back part of the home spending, but the billions that go abroad are lost forever. If we were on a cash basis popular protests would make continuation impossible, but they are muffled by the great outflowing of federal debentures that steadily increase the growth of our already mountainous debt.

Our basic need is to adopt self-interest as the key to our foreign policy. This will quickly end foreign gifts and loans with part of the saving being devoted to our own problems. Certainly it will impell us to stop supplying arms on anything less than a cash basis to countries that may at any time become our enemies, and keep our military advisors on this side of the oceans. Trying to establish order in Central America may be justified but doing the same thing on the other side of the world is foolish meddling. Whether we do it to maintain a grandiose image of ourselves or whether it has merely become an addiction is a moot question. Certainly all the countries we are aiding are our debtors at the expense of our own solvency and the welfare of our own people.

Russia does not want war with us. Surely we wish no nuclear confrontations and certainly we cannot win a conventional war on the other side of the oceans against so powerful an adversary. Conversely they do not wish to engage us here, so with our great ideological differences we should content ourselves with being coolly polite.

While we have been meddling in their backyard we have seriously neglected our own. The Monroe Doctrine was well conceived and if we deviate from it, it should be only to reach out to the remaining English-speaking countries who have been our allies in World Wars I and II—Australia, New Zealand, South Africa, and Great Britain. With these friends and Canada we would form a large homogeneous block and as none of us have any expansionist aspirations we should be a stabilizing factor in the world. Surely we do not lie in the path of any Russian expansion plans unless we believe they will not be content until they have conquered the world. If that is in their minds they cannot hope to implement it in this century and if it does come up later we will be better able to counter it if our own house is in order and we have withdrawn from the frictions of Europe and Asia.

I am sure many reading this will say, "But we need the Arab oil." That is hardly a valid assumption. Mexican and Central American oil fields are as promising as those of the Persian Gulf and our substituting them should minimize the chance of Russian friction and should leave us in much better shape if the Near East erupts.

Obviously any change in our foreign policy which puts our own interests ahead of those of other nations will call for our withdrawal from the United Nations. We contribute much more heavily than any other nation, receive no benefits, and our delegates must spend much time listening to representatives of the third, and second, world powers as they gain personal pleasure and gather "Brownie Stars" at home for their tirades against us. To make it more absurd, each has the same voting power in the General Assembly that has been granted to us.

CHAPTER XXI

Our Military Concepts

We came out of World War II with a superior economy, the military prestige and power to dominate the world, with all but a few communist and war-battered nations anxious to be our friends, and with a heartily patriotic population. Yet the last thirty-five years seem to have been devoted to cultivating the seeds of disaster.

Those seeds of our decline had already been planted at Yalta and in the mass of New Deal legislation. They have been constantly nurtured with a lavishness that not even Roosevelt could have envisioned. Our generosity to enemies and to our theoretical ally, Russia, has made the former our industrial superiors and the latter our military peer. To compound this disastrous international picture we have engaged in two wars that we could have won quite inexpensively but which we elected merely to prolong. These not only wasted our human and industrial resources, but also seriously damaged the nation's morale and the patriotism on which it was based.

In short, we seem to have been dedicated to our own destruction and to that end have left few stones unturned during these thirty-five years. We persuaded England to dismantle its empire, gave lavishly of our substance to the resulting fragments and to the fragments of other disintegrating empires both directly and via the United Nations, an organization which like the League of Nations was founded with noble purposes, but to which others have contributed little except rhetoric, and which is now controlled by the least civilized yet most numerous nations with much assistance from the Russian Bear.

It is high time that we adopted a military posture designed with our own defense in mind, and stop scattering our military resources around the world. This obviously increases our vulnerability and makes it almost certain that if we tangle with Russia it will be in its backyard where the great distances from our land will fractionalize our effectiveness. In fact, if we engage in a conventional war it will allow the Russians to chew up our detachments as we deliver them to the arena.

If we adopted a policy of self-interest we will withdraw our conventional forces from West Germany, except for those needed to protect our nuclear institutions. The Germans are fine fighting men and will acquit themselves well if their country is attacked. Indeed the extra deterent we are now providing is measured primarily by our nuclear potential and this factor can remain in place and be generously reinforced by Pershing II missiles. The detachments we allow to remain with these installations should be put on a war footing with both officers and men instructed to send their wives back home. As a matter of morale this should be balanced by limiting their tour of duty to a single year.

As soon as arrangements are made to secure sure access to the Mexican and Venezuelan oil we should also withdraw from the Persian Gulf, from Korea, and possibly from the Philipines. The only countries in that area worth defending and where we can count on the full cooperation of the inhabitants are Australia and New Zealand. Like the Germans they have fine fighting men and the support given them could well be confined to sophisticated equipment. The same is true of South Africa. Their standards have changed much less than ours since World War II and they then rallied to the allied cause so willingly that their per capita casualties were higher than those of any other allies—even those of the United Kingdom itself. Further their location is a strategic one and they have natural resources that supplement our own and which will be critical if we have a war of long duration. To date we have treated them shabbily and with England have destroyed Rhodesia, which also was a staunch military ally in in the 40's and could have been one in the future. Indeed its mineral potential can be an invaluable asset to any nation having access to it.

With our troops withdrawn from the eastern hemisphere our standing army could be allowed to shrink proportionately and we could easily match the Russian nuclear arsenal even while drastically reducing our defense budget.

A step of equal importance and perhaps greater urgency is having a Kennedy-type showdown with Cuba. We should require the elimination of their missiles and other sophisticated weapons, then follow through to make sure they remain a safe neighbor. They clearly are part of the Russian arsenal and we cannot afford to have them on our flank in any real or threatened military engagement. Even if they made no overt moves they would immobilize a large fraction of our war machine. Once the military situation is faced we should go a step further and insist that they stop all subversive interference in the affairs of other western nations. We have been shutting our eyes for too long and have reached a point where each month adds to the danger of the situation. We should also include the right to patrol their waters for drug runners.

We must bear in mind that Russia, in spite of its belligerent attitude is no more desirous of military confrontation than we; however, our ideas are very different from theirs and our best chance of comfortable co-existence lies in minimizing our contacts.

The troop withdrawals I have suggested certainly will be a step in this direction. There, of course, will be people who will criticize a substantial revival of the Monroe Doctrine and abandonment of our forty-year posture of being everything to all races as letting down our allies. The answer to that is best supplied by recognizing that these nations, from Germany to France to Indonesia, do not regard us as a real friend, but merely as a convenient source of assistance and protection, but it is quite safe to say that should we be the nation attacked there would be no chance of our being supported by any but the English speaking races, and this together with our self-interest should be the key to our foreign policy.

We all know we have been living under the threat of nuclear war for many years and that our grace period seems to be due to the realization that east and west can destroy each other. Sadly this balance may be upset at any time by the development of new weapons, but there is a greater, yet never mentioned, factor that should stand as a permanent deterent. A war that destroys either east or west will surely turn the world over to the Asiatic and African races that even now are many times as numerous as the Europeans and Americans.

Within our own country we have a somewhat similar long-range problem. It surfaces when we compare the high birthrate of our burgeoning minorities with that of the Euro-Americans which has fallen so seriously. The blacks, the mestizoes and orientals are all extremely fertile races and they find our generous welfare allowances most encouraging to the production of large families. The outlook is ominous—a country under the control of a minority coalition within the life span of many adults now with us. Our dwindling breed may then be oppressed as no group has been burdened by the ruling class since the Civil War.

At the turn of the century a quite distinct American racial type had developed. The melting pot had completed the assimilation of most European races, and that of the Mediterranean and semetic groups was well on its way. They came to this country determined to become Americans, asked no special favors, and attained their goal—

often in a single generation. Now our immigrants ask and receive much aid from our government—aid not to speed their assimilation but to ensure their comfort. The melting pot cannot function as it did in the past and the ranks of the minority coalition swell day by day.

I have infinitely less knowledge of nuclear warfare than our military men, but even here I think it would be prudent to let logic enter the picture.

Apparently we have reached a point at which we are struggling to be able to reply in a somewhat punishing fashion to a Russian first strike and are planning to invest many billions in Wyoming installations the efficacy of which is a point of controversy even in military circles. It is quite clear that if we fire our missiles before those of the Russians have a chance to hit us their damage would be quite unacceptable. Our early-warning system is supposed to be fine, but surely could be made better at a small fraction of what we contemplate spending on the MX.

Why not do this and extend the authority to dispatch our missiles to a group large enough that at least one could be on duty every hour of each day instead of letting it remain the president's sole responsibility? When and if that time comes, seconds not merely minutes will be crucial. Surely this strategy adjustment and minor investment seems much more sensible than hoping that some of our missiles will survive a Russian attack and be able to retaliate, and it certainly would be a much more powerful deterrent.

Anti-ballistic missiles around our cities and our most important military installations might also be a good investment, but that is for the experts to determine. I can only judge their effectiveness by the outcry from the Russians when we contemplated their construction.

CHAPTER XXII

Crime and Our Judicial and Penal Systems

I think we are all aware that our courts are creaking under an overload of technicalities. Unfortunately, correcting this will be both laborious and time-consuming. This will be especially true because the present system has been largely constructed and abetted by the country's attorneys.

Criminal restraints have been so emasculated by the courts in recent years that they are no longer effective deterrents. To the credit of our law enforcement machinery, arrests continue to be made, but from there on "Due Process" seems to become a game for lawyers to play. I don't think anyone aligned on the side of law and order can fail to feel that the rule revisions effected in the last fifty years have been designed to protect (and over-protect) the criminals rather than the victims. How many of these can be over-ridden by legislation and how many must be corrected by the Supreme Court, I do not know, but certainly there should be no delay in getting the program under way.

In the interim much good could be accomplished by making both trial and sentencing as nearly instantaneous as possible. Prosecutors should move for trial as soon as they have the necessary evidence at hand and all dates should be set within a week from the receipt of the requests. In setting the dates, time allotments should be determined and determined economically. This should be a matter of hours for most cases, and never more than a week should be allowed for the requesting and scheduling of appeals (this week to be spent in jail), with punishments being carried out within seventy-two hours of the denial of an appeal.

Probation should be abolished, but except for horrendous crimes sentences should be much shorter. To make these shorter sentences effective they should be designed for punishment, not for pleasure and rehabilitation. I would even advocate continuous confinement to a cell for the duration, with no communication with other prisoners (except for cellmates where private cells cannot be assigned) or with the outside world. Gang formation and prison violence would be eliminated and the hardened criminals would be unable to leave their impress on the newer men.

This should be punishment to remember and to deter others. Further, the yearly expenses would drop from the twenty-odd thousand per man I have seen quoted to a tenth of that; and, as the sentence length could be halved or quartered, billions would be saved by obviating the need for new prisons through the foreseeable future.

Special consideration for the insane criminals is a long-established part of our jurisprudence but that does not keep it from being completely fatuous. The mentally unbalanced have a minimal chance of becoming safe and useful members of society and usually repeat crimes similar to those for which they were committed soon after being given their freedom. This is especially true of rapists and they should be castrated whether adjudged sane or not. This, and the threat of the penalty, would reduce the number of offenses, make our streets safer, and effect a major saving.

While I have indicated that sentences could be made much shorter with no loss of effectiveness if our prisons were less attractive hostelries, criminals still will not be properly inhibited as long as they do not think of punishment as something immediate. So many technical loopholes exist that the average man expects either acquittal or a light sentence. Certainly both lawyers and the courts have given more thought to the protection of the rights of the criminals than of the victims. Probably we need more judges than those now sitting, but the simple expedient of giving each lawyer a somewhat miserly time limit would result in better and quicker verdicts. The attention spans of all people are limited and this is especially true when you have juries who do not understand the material being presented.

The situation is worsened by the fact that when a man is sentenced to death he need only find one sympathetic judge to secure a stay. A law requiring that all appeals be made within a week of conviction should eliminate this. Surely no federal judge should be allowed to interfere with a state conviction.

The procedure for civil cases should be streamlined in similar fashion with the time allotted each attorney for the presentation of his case being strictly controlled and the limits adhered to. The privilege of appealing should be extended less frequently, briefs limited in length, and the cases disposed of promptly. I am confident that in both criminal and civil cases, the imposition of time limits will allow cases to move quickly enough that few, if any, additional judges or jurists will be needed, but where required they should be provided.

Lawyers will, of course, oppose this streamlining but I am quite sure few additional salient points are developed in long trials and there would be less danger of juries (and even judges) losing track of the important factors, either because they are obscured by unimportant ones, because their attention span falters, or they weary.

It is important that damage awards be held to reasonable levels. I have advocated that awards be set by judges—not jurors, but this mandate should be accompanied by guidelines that limit all awards to reasonable amounts. Amounts in personal injury cases should never exceed the earning capacity of the injured through the remaining life expectancy. Where incapacity is total and the remaining years must be spent in an institution, the award should not be available in a lump sum, but there should be a requirement that the defendant pay the institutional costs as they are incurred—of course, posting a bond for performance.

When one of my workmen was killed in the late 20's, the award was for between two and three thousand dollars. Recently I noted a case where the basis of a woman's suit had been that she attributed the birth of a sub-normal child to her physician having prescribed medication during her pregnancy which the medical profession later suspected might have serious side effects. In sharp contrast her award was about seven million, and was followed by a multimillion judgment against Ford in favor of the parents of a girl killed in a traffic accident in which a Mustang fuel tank was ruptured. A recent judgment against a Florida hospital was even more outrageous. Apparently it was based on improper administration of anaesthesia which resulted in brain damage. The award was for eleven million with four million added for attorney fees. This was a Broward County award and was topped within a few weeks by one in Dade. This latter case concerned a man crippled by an engine room explosion. His compensation was set at $25.8 million!! These are merely three cases that have come to my attention recently, not the result of research. This strongly indicates that the total iceberg has the weight to seriously impact our economy—especially since each such award incubates additional suits and encourages each new jury to apply for a place in the record books.

Civil damage awards should be strictly limited to a fair appraisal of the damage incurred. Punitive damage awards should be terminated. If criminal action is involved, any additional redress should be sought in that direction.

The underlying thought here is not just that excessive awards are unfair to the defendant, whether individual or corporate, but to the country as a whole. These awards and the legal and insurance protection they mandate become business expenses that in the case of a corporation either result in higher product prices or lower stockholder dividends. With both corporations and individuals a high percentage of awards are paid by insurance companies; thus excessive automobile awards boost the insurance costs of all and malpractice awards increase the premiums to be paid by physicians and hospitals. In some surgical specialities these premiums run to the fifty thousand level and this is passed on in the form of higher medical charges.

Another antidote for this heavy load would be to limit the percengage that attorneys can claim as contingent fees. Certainly the figure should never be over ten-percent, or five-percent plus costs in cases where this figure proves to be the greater.

A point of especial concern is that while our founding fathers intended our judicial and legislative branches to be entirely separate, more and more of our recent laws and regulations have been written or rewritten by our courts. Some of these such as school busing and affirmative action directives remain highly controversial and it might be well to have everything of this nature implemented since World War II compiled and submitted to a special session of congress for each item to be approved or disapproved.

Plea bargaining has become increasingly widespread and does much to defeat the ends of justice. True, it means less work for prosecutors and jurists but it also means that a high proportion of our sentences do not fit the crimes for which the people are tried. Abolishing the practice could be a simple, prompt, and effective cure.

CHAPTER XXIII

Drugs

The drug trade provides one of the most menacing clouds on the social horizon. It is a menace that destroys the health of millions and makes criminals out of hundreds of thousands. It has overwhelmed our law enforcement departments and corrupted our courts. It spares no age, but youth seems to suffer most, perhaps because those who embrace the habit when young seldom reach middle-age; unless they are able to overcome the addiction.

Further, the profits of the trade are astronomical and are reaped by the underworld. It is these profits that spawn the corruption, and as the men who reap them never include them in their income taxes, billions are lost to the national treasury. Needless to say all drug expenses are highly counter-productive and siphon off more billions.

The flow can be stopped only by an all-out campaign that includes all law enforcement departments, the coast guard, the navy, the army, and the courts.

Penalties must be made more severe, the technical loopholes closed, diplomatic immunity invalidated when it interferes with enforcement, and all cases given top priority in our courts. In addition we should end trade and travel relations with any nations who fail to cooperate. It is a major threat to our security and we must pay the price of a maximum effort to stop it.

We have long concentrated on the apprehension of dealers but that is only one side of the picture, and perhaps of lesser importance than deterring the users directly. Prohibition demonstrated quite clearly that when the demand is there the underworld will contrive to fill it.

I am quite sure the way to stifle the demand is to apply the newly developed and relatively simple drug tests to all involved in automobile accidents as we do now with drivers who are suspected of having imbibed too generously. In addition we should authorize all law enforcement officials, welfare workers and military officers to require similar tests upon suspicion of use. Further there should be routine, but unscheduled tests for military personnel for it is obviously vital to the safety of their companions and to the country as a whole that they be in full command of their faculties at all time. Modified procedures should also be made available to school officials.

When users are uncovered they should be confined, if not in a prison at least in a place maintaining a prison-like atmosphere for a period of their addiction. This would be dreaded much more than a fine or commitment to an institution that would try to wean them gradually and it would be much less expensive. Some records probably should be kept to distinguish new hands from old, but I would suggest that it not be a criminal record per se, for most probably are as much sinned against as sinning, and if they are real addicts the abrupt withdrawal will be severe punishment in itself.

Repeaters should be given much longer sentences and third offenders treated as pushers. A favorable by-product would be the deathblow it would deliver to a large sector of the underworld.

CHAPTER XXIV

Education

I have always held that every ambitious and able child is entitled to a good education, but by trying to provide higher education to all who elect it even when they lack these qualities, we have lowered our educational level. The volume of this poor material required our colleges and universities to expand faculties far beyond the limits of the supply of competent and dedicated teachers. The expense of furnishing these unmerited free rides is astronomical and most of the riders come out ill-equipped to fill the positions for which they have been trained, yet unwilling to do the less prestigious work available to them.

Of even greater concern is the academic disintegration at all levels—the elementary student commonly is allowed to flounder without a grasp of phonics and accordingly with a painfully limited vocabulary that often expands but little in high school and college and continues to handicap him throughout life. Thanks to our long courtship of the abstract ideas of modern math the situation in this field is almost as bad. Sadly even the concerned educators who do attempt to effect repairs are frequently thwarted by the fact that most of today's teachers were trained in the shadows of those philosophies and are unable to re-orient themselves.

Indeed the educationists have established a powerful and incredibly ubiquitous bureaucracy that seems to have a stranglehold on the institutions that train our teachers, on the public schools of most communities, and on a great number of the private schools.

The trend first came to my attention in the physical education field. The early physical education schools were profit-making institutions that found it financially expedient to recruit their students without regard for their athletic potential. The natural sequel to this was a teaching philosophy that relegated the importance of the embryonic teacher's performance to the limbo of the curriculum.

As the social ship flounders with no one at the helm, our schools and parents must share the responsibility. Schools have made bigger and better buildings and higher salaries their chief concern, but the efforts of the few dedicated and high-minded teachers have been disastrously diluted by the addition of more young teachers who have been prepared in modern schools with liberal and lazy faculties. As educators they rationalize their failures and blame the parents. To compound this situation students commonly go forth unequipped to do the work of college graduates and unwilling to take a "menial" job. In short they stand ready to increase the welfare army, an army that is surely getting more than enough recruits from its own offspring who skip high school and follow in the footsteps of their parents and grandparents, enlisting as soon as they are old enough or being signed up in infancy. When you realize the welfare army also has millions of recruits from legal aliens, as well as from those whose entrance has been illegal, the day of reckoning must be very near.

Recently many communities have sounded a call for a return to basics, but school boards who try to implement this laudatory objective find it difficult to secure teachers whose knowledge of English equals that of students graduated from high school in the 20's, 30's, and 40's, and good basic mathematic teachers are equally hard to find. Even the letters of application and resumes of "potential" English teachers are frequently laced with errors.

The system that produced the present generation of teachers—more educationists than educators—may take long to destroy, yet its eradication is a pre-requisite for healthy education systems. A good start might be to require an AB with a major in English and a minor in mathematics for entrance into teachers colleges, and let those institutions give masters in education at the end of one year and doctorates in special fields two years later—those two years being devoted exclusively to the degree subject, not to teaching methods.

An alternate approach for teachers who do not expect to secure their masters could be three years of liberal arts followed by one of teaching methods. Such of these as later wish to secure a masters should have their work based upon subject study, not upon teaching methods.

We should also keep in mind that education as a whole is badly clouded by the immense number of hours spent in front of the TV. Not merely is this time lost from studies, athletics, and worthwhile reading; it mesmerizes the senses and distorts the life picture while glamorizing the distortion.

While proper teachers are being trained, we should make a careful reevaluation of the ones now serving, terminate the poorest, compliment the best, and require the intermediate group to spend at least ten weeks per summer studing their subjects in colleges or universities. All with inadequate English should study that as well as their specialty. Those teaching in cities with universities that give night courses should take these also. As soon as their progress warrants, these teachers should be recertified in their specific fields and allowed to teach in no other.

Of course, tenure should be denied or revoked for all of this retraining group until they are certified. Indeed it would be most salutary if tenure were abolished and salaries stepped up on the basis of performance, not length of service. Many teachers relax and start to deteriorate once they have the protection of tenure. An obviously important factor in a rebuilding program is a clear understanding that any strike will mean prompt and permanent dismissal so teachers may regain the highly honorable status they once held in their communities.

Second only to stronger teaching staffs is the abolition of quota busing. There is no more justification for requiring a child to spend additional hours on a bus than for having teachers extend their days without additional compensation. It robs them of both playtime and study time, distorts the home routine, and is disliked by both blacks and whites. A child should be assigned to the nearest school. If parents prefer another, they should provide the transportation and the transfers should be limited to cases where it will not result in an oversize class.

Today's schools labor under another serious handicap. Most lack adequate discipline. This will be helped by the end of quota busing (less tired and more homogeneous pupils), but much of the fault lies in faulty organization and the lack of uniform expectations.

The college picture is quite as bad as that in the grades. In good part this is because nearly all institutions have concentrated their energies on rapid growth that in most cases has diluted faculty quality.

Even more disasterous has been the quality of the students who have filled these expanded facilities. In part this drop has been due to the recent practice of trying to route each high school graduate (many of them unable to function at a sound eighth grade level) to college.

This has been done in part by lowering entrance standards, waiving them in some cases, and giving preferential treatment to minorities in most admission offices. Another instrument to this end is our ill-conceived pattern of student aid. Most is given on the basis of declared need (many families who can ill afford current tuitions are too proud to declare themselves paupers and either bypass college or attempt to work their way through). This used to be a big feather in a student's cap. It still is but the funds that must be acquired today put it beyond the earning power of most—no matter how ambitious. Community colleges are extremely important to this group, and an initial two years there can allow them to build up a reserve that will enable them to negotiate two years in a university which they must attend as a boarder. Of course, if they live in a university town the problem is much simpler.

The low tuitions of my day (less than $500 for room and board and tuition in my prestigious Hamilton) presented no hurdle to any ambitious student, but the increase has been many times the inflation rate and controlling this would be much more helpful than loans and scholarships. This is not to suggest that there is anything wrong with scholarships per se, but to be effective they should be given strictly on merit and winning one should put a student in a position to be envied, not on the charity fringe. Some such remain but they are a small fraction of the whole. The advantage of this type of scholarship is that it gives the best exposure to our best brains and fosters their development for the public good.

Athletic scholarships are on the disasterous side and should be outlawed. Not merely do they open the doors to numerous students without ability but they bring in many with no interest in study and most are assured of passing without effort. Further, they change the character of sports and in effect close them to many amateurs. If we wish to pay for the higher education of our youth we should make it available only to our most competent with many being sidetracked at Grade VIII and others when they finish high school. Most of these less competent students will profit more from technical training at these levels.

Few people seem to realize the extent to which our educational institutions also are being damaged by the preferential treatment the affirmative action policy inspires. Schools take unqualified students and their graduates are accepted by colleges and universities even when it is obvious they cannot do the work normally expected. Their presence in classes lowers the general level and requires more teachers, a demand that has been augmented by the current opinion that all would-be students are entitled to as much education as they want. Properly qualified teachers have not been available to effect the necessary faculty expansions without serious lowering the quality of the instruction and all students suffer. It is suffering they pass on to their communities when they return unable to do the work properly expected of graduates and unwilling to work at the lesser jobs they normally would have filled. It is no wonder our per capita production no longer leads the international list, and that without the tariff protection of earlier years our markets are flooded with foreign products and our welfare and unemployment rolls swollen.

CHAPTER XXV

Medical Costs

The years that have been the worst for our country as a whole have been the time of medicine's greatest progress. Polio has been eliminated, diabetes, tuberculosis, and most contagious diseases, except those in the venereal category, are well under control, and surgery has taken tremendous strides; but unfortunately those gains have been matched by increasing costs.

Medicare is doing much good but in combination with other health insurance it has increased the cost of medical and hospital care to a point where the average expense for the individual approximates the charges prevailing before its inception. This has generated a medical bonanza that must be controlled. It can be done by revising downward the Medicare price shedule. $10–$15 should cover office visits, and hospital days should be in the $50–$75 range with other charges limited proportionately. This will mean that some sophisticated equipment will be available at fewer institutions but the men operating them will have more practice and become more skillful.

Recently a friend whose brother went to a hospital for terminal attention and for whom no operation or special treatment was attempted spent six weeks in the hospital and incurred a bill in excess of thirty-two thousand dollars. When she protested, she was advised not to be concerned since he was well covered by insurance. I assumed this to be quite atypical but casual conversations on the subject in the last few months seem to indicate that similar experiences are not uncommon, and certainly indicate that a cap on all medicine costs to be prudent both as protection for the public and to forestall campaigns for state medicine.

Placing a carefully worked-out but all-inclusive limit on malpractice awards would reduce the insurance costs of both physicians and hospitals and lessen the impact of a lower price schedule. Malpractice premiums were an insignificant part of a physician's budget prior to World War II, but now run over fifty thousand dollars for some of the surgical specialties.

A less direct medical cost has been boosted to unreasonable heights by the "saving" of babies that can never be normal and by prolonging the lives of patients who must vegetate or suffer to exhaustion and who would not themselves elect such an ordeal. The latter is often a heavy financial burden for families to bear, but it is of shorter duration that that of parents presented with a seriously defective child. Physicians should be authorized to allow adults to die, after getting family consent; and obstetricians should be empowered to make such decisions in the delivery room.

In short we should make an effort to have our medical objectives tied more closely to the welfare of the patients and be less concerned with the prosperity of our insurance companies, our hospitals, our attorneys, and the medical profession.

CHAPTER XXVI

Welfare

Every legislator knows that our burgeoning welfare rolls are an albatross around the nation's neck. Further by raising millions in comfortable idleness it is doing much to weaken the work ethic for them and for others who observe their life style. Of course, we cannot let our citizens starve but we are under no obligation to support them at the TV and automobile level, nor should we give them anything when they refuse to work at a job for which they are physically qualified.

We talk at length about the financial burden of maintaining our military, but our politicians seldom zero in on the mushrooming welfare budget. I am quite sure this is because they fear reprisals at the polls and the answer to that seems extremely simple, yet I have never heard it suggested. It is merely to take welfare out of politics by disenfranchising all recipients until they have been self-supporting for at least two years—and then been required to pass a literacy test. This will be highly effective, first by making it impossible for recipients to vote on welfare measures, and second by leaving legislators free to use their best judgment without fear of voter reprisal and without expecting extra ballots to carry their names at the next election because their vote was deemed favorable.

A simple and obvious way to reduce costs would be to warn all welfare families that they must have no babies until they become self-supporting and that allotments will not be increased to provide for any children born more than ten months after notification. Notification can be simply effected by memos attached to all welfare checks issued after the legislation or executive directive becomes effective. Advice to all later welfare enrollees should be given at the time of their enlistment. The next step should be to weed out all false claims and disqualify all aliens. Then all recipients under sixty should be advised that their checks will shrink to a subsistence level, not a luxury level, by gradual steps spread over a twelve-month period. If the minimum wage laws are not repealed, these people should be issued a six-month or one-year exemption card to simplify their getting back into the productive world. Of course, all recipients guilty of making false claims should be dealt with severely, and denied future assistance.

I am sure food stamps were a well-intentioned gesture, but one only needs to do the family shopping in our supermarkets for a few weeks to sense its wide-spread abuse. Stamp holders buy the most expensive items, and frequently carry them out to comparably expensive cars.

While these people are preparing to literally live off the fat of the land, many elderly who are proud but impoverished mentally recheck the contents of their baskets to see if they have enough money to pay. Frequently they miscalculate and must leave part of their intended provisions at the counter.

When you add to this the number who give false data to secure their stamps and the 1981 disclosures of privately printed stamps being literally "cashed" with the connivance of store managers, it becomes clear that the system is a most inefficient one.

My suggestion is that this sector of our bureaucracy be wiped out, and that we substitute a simple system for free distribution of cheese, powdered milk, and grain products. All could be drawn from our surplus stores and the last could include flour, cornmeal, cornstarch, oatmeal, and shortening. With but minor supplements the list could provide a palatable and health-sustaining diet.

CHAPTER XXVII

Social Problems

Our war babies and everyone born before that time must have a first-hand consciousness of the country's moral disintegration. Those of us who are older cannot avoid part of the responsibility for allowing the standards to deteriorate so badly. To a large extent the key to the whole situation has been the weakening of family ties and family discipline, but unfortunately many of the young are themselves disgracefully culpable and this makes it difficult for even some suitably concerned families to maintain proper moral and work levels in the face of the examples of the others, and to lead their children upstream against the horrendous peer pressures of the day.

These pressures are most serious in the areas of sex, drugs, respect for authority, honesty, patriotism, and willingness to work—so serious that without a reversal our society may need no outside help for its destruction. The process is being speeded up by the growing proportion of working mothers. A house with a part-time mother is like a school staffed exclusively with part-time and frequently absent teachers. It is, of course, essential that some mothers work, but that is no excuse for those who do it because they have career urges or merely wish to augment already-adequate incomes. Most destructive of child values are the divorced parents with live-in companions.

Our judges and lawyers must bear much of the responsibility for this frightening picture for they have so twisted our laws that they give encouragment to our malfactors. The contrast between now and the early nineteen hundreds makes it hard to understand how a people could allow its society to unravel in this fashion, but it surely must be corrected and stop-gap measures will avail little.

Our young people seem unconscious of the all-pervasive deterioration, but the subconscious of many is more astute and at this level the awareness is lethal rather than helpful and results in a deadend outlook and a much-less-than-happy live-for-today philosophy. Good camps and schools could be an antidote against the development of this attitude, but they are too few to salvage the situation. In terms of today a special concern must be the lack of joy in the lives of our young people—a lack apparent to all who can remember the bright faces of earlier teenagers.

Articles on, and discussions of, our moral decline are frequent and they seem always to blame parents, schools, and television. Undoubtedly they are at fault, but I cannot help feeling that our clergy are equally culpable, and this is especially sad for it is in their direction we should always be able to look for moral guidance.

Most choose to ignore this area and to my mind they are neglecting a major, perhaps the major, duty of their calling when they do this. More unfortunately there is another group that openly condones or commends practices against which they should be campaigning. A recent occurrence is clearly documented by the letters reprinted here. The name of the clergyman and his parish have been deleted, but except for this the letters are reproduced in toto. His reply to my letter was primarily a response to my final paragraph. It stated that when a priest introduced a resolution which declared homosexual acts to be sinful in all instances at a diocese meeting, the bishop took the unusual step of turning the chair over to the chancellor so that he could himself enter the debate to defeat the motion.

14 July 1982

Dr. G. H. Longstaff
Eagle Point Road
Eagle Bay, NY 13331

Dear Dr. Longstaff:

Greetings to you and your wife. I trust you had a good winter. People have said even Florida was unusually cold.

I have wished we had had a chance to talk, following the service at ▮▮▮▮. It was so nice that you came, and I hope you will again.

You said you were surprised by my remarks about our attitudes toward unmarried couples living together. I had the feeling that you too would have liked to chat more at length about the matter. I hope you caught my statement that it is our hope and prayer that all such couples will grow to know the beauty and holiness of Christian marriage.

Meanwhile, what is to be our attitude? Tradition looked askance upon such a situation until very recently. I recall - I think in the late 60's - that a couple had been discovered living together at Columbia University, and it made headlines all over the country. Now it is so common, the census bureau has made provision for this classification. My daughter has been living with a much younger man for quite a few years; Jean and I visited his family in Houston, and stayed overnight with them. We both wish they would marry. They sleep together when they come to our home, or go to his parents'. Most of the couples I have married in the last ten years have been living together. When six to ten fellows and girls come to someone's house for a night or more, it is futile to tell them where to sleep, or assign rooms. Jean and I just had to give up. I have heard the same from other parents. And in two cases amongst our adult friends, a long-time divorcee and a recent widow each moved in with her man a year or more before the wedding. We visited in the home of one of them before their wedding, and the other couple were here at our island before theirs. What are you going to do???

All of these are just as fine people as any I know. So should the Church take the stance of condemning, and drive them out of its fellowship? I think this would only deepen the serious misunderstanding of the Church that is widespread, and is confirmed every Sunday morning on TV, where a very distorted Christianity is presented.

One of the couples present at that service at Blue have a son who is living with a girl, and it troubles them very deeply. I wanted them to know it is better to trust these young people and believe in them. Then we may hope that someday they will come to see the richer meanings of the Church and its sacraments, including Holy Matrimony.

I do hope you and Mrs. Longstaff will be with us again at our annual service here on 1 August at 4 pm. Warmest regards to you both.

Sincerely,

July 17, 1982

Dear ▮▮▮▮

I fear I must judge your thoughts as morally corrosive and to my mind your position makes them doubly dangerous and doubly culpable. Certainly the banning of adultery lies at the heart of Christian morality, yet when the breach of the ban is condoned from a Christian pulpit it is seriously vitiated. Indeed even if I could join you in considering the Bible and its teaching obsolete I would feel compelled to protest vigorously the damage to the family. Further, if that were not a factor and we judged only by the resulting physical damage, there would be cogent reasons to oppose it: the innumerable bastards resulting, the irreparable physical damage done by the prolonged use of contraceptives, disease flourishing as never before (for it is fatuous to think that extra-marital affairs do not breed promiscuity).

Unfortunately, it is clear that the promiscuity extends to the very young and you need only to talk to a gynecologist to secure evidence that many girls are rendered unfit for motherhood before they even reach high school and as teenagers. Further, men loose much of their incentive to marry as they realize "socially acceptable" girls are readily available as bedmates. Certainly the best will be unwilling to settle for a sexually experienced girl as a lifetime companion. Even when one is attracted and impressed to a point of overlooking this facet of a girl's character, he is almost certain to have many bitter hours wondering whether or not marriage really changed her. To complete the picture we must add to these that the many who "play around" so long, children are no longer possible.

If the clergy does not take a solid stand against this moral and physical collapse, where is succor to be found? The occasional parental heartache you seek to assuage is miniscule compared to the damage you and other maverick priests can do.

I know that reading this letter must be painful but I doubt if gentle measures would be productive and only pray that this admittedly cruel approach will. Incidentally, the role of devil's advocate does not become you.

You also condoned acceptance of homosexuals in your sermon and I am certain that letting them out of their closets is doing great damage to our young and gaining many recruits for the former closet dwellers.

Sincerely yours,

With views such as these expressed in the cleric's letter emanating from some of our pulpits, open defiance of the old conventions by adults, television glamorization of sex, and peer pressures, the alarming rate of teenage pregnancies is quite understandable—but that makes the effects no less devastating to the child-mothers, to their parents, and to the babies. National statistics indicate that ten percent of our pregnancies occur in the teenage group, with many in the eleven to fourteen-year bracket. The direct social damage is horrendous and the economic picture serious. Our report estimates the proportion receiving welfare assistance at seventy-five percent. This often means government must raise a child to maturity at a cost that averages one hundred thousand dollars, and then have this child grow up to become a permanent welfare client. These various facets explain the heat of my letter to the encouraging minister. A survey by a large Orlando, Florida agency indicates that seventy-five percent of their clients gave their own or their sexual partner's home as the place where their problems started. I hope this and other statistics may plant serious doubts in the minds of such working mothers as do not desperately need the extra money.

Still another aspect of our present mind-boggling horrors is the number of educated couples who viewing the situation elect not to produce children. This contrasts ominously with the great number of black, Asiatic and Latin-American babies with whom we are being presented. In the past our melting pot has worked well largely because all who came were anxious to embrace America and its ways. Unfortunately, this is no longer the case.

Part of the solution to our social problems will be effected automatically when we improve our law enforcement and destroy the drug culture. Separation of church and state is well established in this country, but I feel we would not be violating this if we enacted laws that would proscribe public utterances such as those made by the cleric whose letter is reproduced here. Of course, such a law should apply to others, not merely to clerics, but I would like to see churches devote some portion of each service to current behavior and moral values."

In school we should lead required and classroom reading back to the old pattern that extolled virtue, hard work, and their rewards. Also, teachers should not attempt sex education until the approach of the critical years and then have it deal, not with the mechanics, but with the danger of disease and the almost certain forfeiture of their chances for a happy and productive marriage.

Girls and boys, of course, should be instructed in separate classes. Less time could be given to the boys, but they should be impressed with the venereal potential and warned they should never marry "experienced" girls if they wish a happy marriage of mutual trust and healthy children.

Aids to proper conduct should cover a much wider field than the merely sexual and this should start in the grades and be reinforced by effective and constant discipline. Parents should be urged to take the quite Victorian attitude of not letting their children play with those of parents whose life styles they disapprove.

We cannot bring Will Hays to life but we should establish effective movie and TV censorship and bar from the air all stations unwilling to conform. Since all operate under government license this would present no mechanical difficulties.

Such twelve-to-eighteen year olds as disregard our laws should not be given preferential treatments in the courts and more reform schools should be established to accommodate the younger ones. Those sixteen to eighteen should be sentenced as adults with short terms and cell-confinement and required to work or study for eight hours a day.

Certainly no minimum wage should apply to the twelve to sixteen groups and they should be encouraged to find employment. Undirected leisure breeds mischief and today much of this is serious.

For adults the prompt and severe punishment without parole and with no more than one quick appeal, which I have advocated, should be surprisingly effective. Of course, the liberalization of divorce laws that put offending parents on a par with their moral partners strikes at the very heart of the secure home and the well-protected child.

This should be reversed, the penalties of earlier years for adultery revived, and cohabitation no longer recognized as a basis for financial claims. Beyond restablishing these simple legal precepts I think we must hope that a general return of morality will bring about a very different outlook in the adult world. Revitalization of the family could be expedited by dropping personal exemptions from the income tax structure but retaining and increasing the allowance for legitimate minor children. Certainly the need is great and strong families can be invaluable in solving many of today's critical problems.

CHAPTER XXVIII

Patriotism

Another ominous factor with which the country must contend is the critical shortage of what in the past has been its greatest resource—patriotism. We now make heroes out of draft dodgers and lure men with negative loyalties into the service by high wages and fringe benefits. This represents a full circle and a most debilitating one.

Some men may have been reluctant to sign up for World War I, but I never heard any contemplate avoiding service. My own alma mater was a good example. All of its two hundred-fifty to two hundred seventy-five students volunteered for the Student Auxiliary Training Corps. Many had enlisted before the S.A.T.C. was formed and some of our 1918 group realized their hopes of being transferred to the Plattsburg Officer's School in the two months before the Armistice. The World War II picture was quite similar though I viewed it from a different perspective. Except for physicians few of my age were desired, but most of my Cedar Isles staff volunteered. At no time did I hear any younger man express a hope that he might not be called. In these years I was not in touch with the prime military generation, but I am sure few sought unmerited exemptions.

When we came to the Korean War the numbers were not large but the men called went willingly, and the only grumbling I heard after their return concerned Mac-Arthur's not being allowed to win the war and our shabby treatment of our Nationalist allies.

You all know the Vietnam story: the same unwillingness to win a war which we could have ended overnight, even without the use of our nuclear arsenal, generated much discontent.

Now we have a largely illiterate mercenary army with an unhealthily high percentage of minorities and are spending the country into the poorhouse to maintain it. We ended World War II with the might to dictate the actions of the world indefinitely, but now we are in second place and shorn of the confidence and, except for the British Commonwealth, of the friendship of the world.

Any corrective action designed to rebuild patriotism and respect for the law will take years, not months, for to do this we must start in the grades. We must begin with histories and novels that feature worthy heroes and high ideals. Further we must censor motion pictures and television productions to replace the glamorizing of crime and sex with Hardy Boys and Horatio Alger types. The college-level follow-up will be more difficult but it should not be neglected. Also, we need concerned and available parents who set proper examples. Further, we must insist that our public schools teach all classes in English. In many sections of the country they are under pressure to conduct their classes in Spanish, but one look at the situation in Canada should be convincing proof of the folly of bilingualism. There its corrosively divisive effects threaten to tear Quebec out of the nation—a move that may be followed by the withdrawal of the resource-rich British Columbia and Alberta.

While I have long been aware of the Hispanic pressures, I had not considered black English to be an even remotely comparable threat until a Midwestern TV station recently broadcast a discussion between the affirmative action, or equal opportunity, administrator of a Michigan university and a woman teacher who had majored in English. The teacher related how she had obtained an undergraduate degree in English from a state teachers college and applied for a public school position only to be rejected because she still spoke black English. She returned to college to learn white English (her phraseology) and secured both her masters and doctorate. The gist of her complaint was that her original native language, that of the American black, was not acceptable for teaching in a white school. The interviewer, who also spoke black English, was equally indignant and the program ended with a unanimous conclusion that black English should be taught to all black children and that they should not be expected to master the English taught in the white schools—apparently a black plea for segregated schools. They deemed the language part of their culture and felt it should be preserved.

Chapter XXIX

Perspective

There certainly are people in the country better qualified to speak about our major national problems, but since none seem to be presenting the country with a comprehensive survey and solution, I have taken this opportunity to set forth my own views. Most of the solutions I have suggested will fall into a pattern for which precedence can be found in our history, but there are two major ones of which this is not true. The first is the concept of abolishing the income tax and letting planned inflation supply the government funding needed to fill the resulting void. The other is substitution of a uniform old age pension tied to the country's average income as a substitute for Social Security and other retirement payments. I feel both concepts to be sound and to fit into two goals for the country that I believe should have high priority—the shrinking of our bureaucracy and the trimming of federal expenses. Both would be giant strides in this direction and would eliminate vast amounts of paperwork thus releasing billions of man hours for productive use. Certainly I am on sound ground when I attach great weight to shrinking the unproductive portion of our citizenry and expanding the productive segment.

In this context the word "productive" should not be confused with "important." Police and firemen and millions of government servants do important jobs, but they do not add to the country's production or income and thus represent a load, albeit a most proper one, for the productive sector to carry. It is now clear that the load is an excessive one and that trimming it must be an essential objective for any comprehensive solution of the country's problems.

Of course all my ideas run counter to those of the political and economic intelligentsia. Theirs are well epitomized by the latest end-of-the-year report of the Research Institute of America. It concludes that the U.S. can no longer be competitive in the heavy industries such as steel, autos, machine tools, and construction equipment—nor even in computers and home appliances. It says that "smokestack industries" will *never* come back and that we must expect to live with permanently high unemployment. This is to necessitate lower living standards that will include smaller homes and "stingier" cars.

After this "shakeout" it pictures a predominantly service economy with 80% of our jobs being provided by that sector, and predicts that we will become primarily suppliers of capital and industrial design.

The difference between the perspective of this rapidly growing and increasingly vocal group and mine is simply that they are willing to settle for an America that is just another spot on the map while I feel we should make the efforts needed to return to the days when living here were so very special—both exciting and rewarding.

The chance of all my correctives being adopted is insignificant, but I am confident that adoption of a few of the most important ones would do much to give the country a happier and safer future. I would let my VARIABLE TARIFF head the list. Its effect on industry and employment would be felt as soon as it was announced, and we would quickly move from the most seriously unfavorable trade balance in our history to one that favors us. In the process the import taxes, even though based on a sharply lowered volume, would swell our federal coffers in a most salutary fashion, and both business and labor would be convinced that government was at last in their corner.

The writer of an economic short recently estimated that each billion dollars of exports provided forty thousand jobs. Conversely his calculations would mean that if we shrink the estimated trade imbalance for the coming year to zero, we would gain four million jobs. This estimate may be a generous one, but surely there would be enough to lead us out of our current doldrums.

The Variable Tariff would also inspire a rush by oriental and many other countries to buy American products in campaigns to hold down our important duties on their goods. In most cases their purchases would be largely of farm products and thus would aid the most deserving sector of our economy.

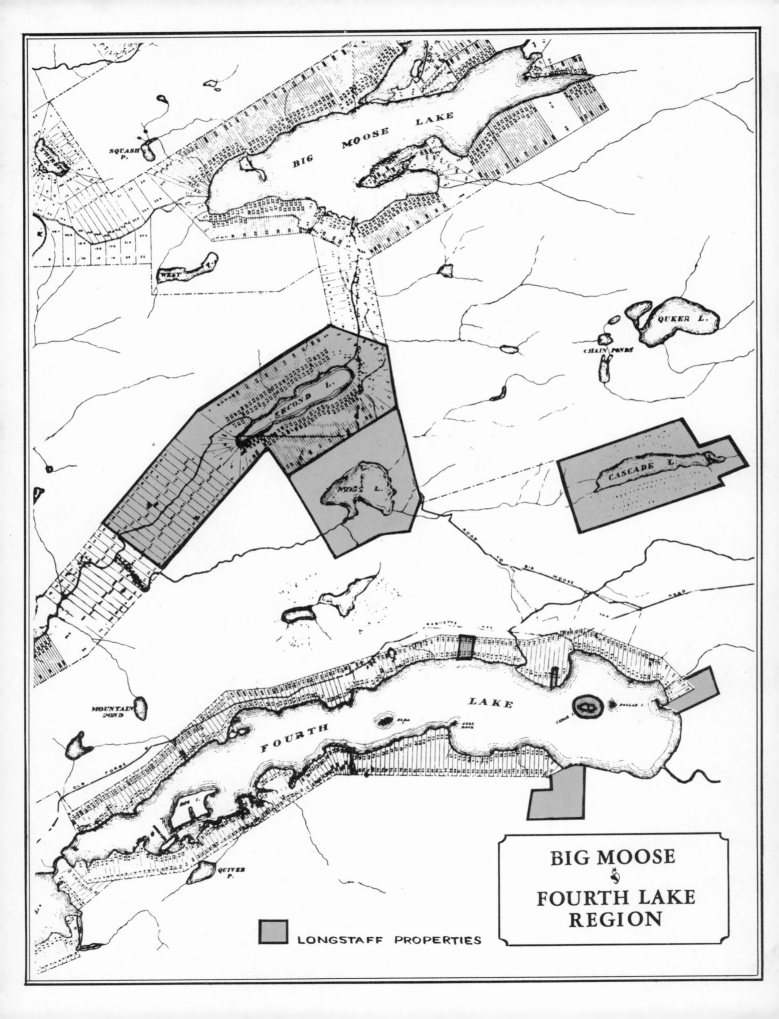

BIG MOOSE
&
FOURTH LAKE
REGION

LONGSTAFF PROPERTIES

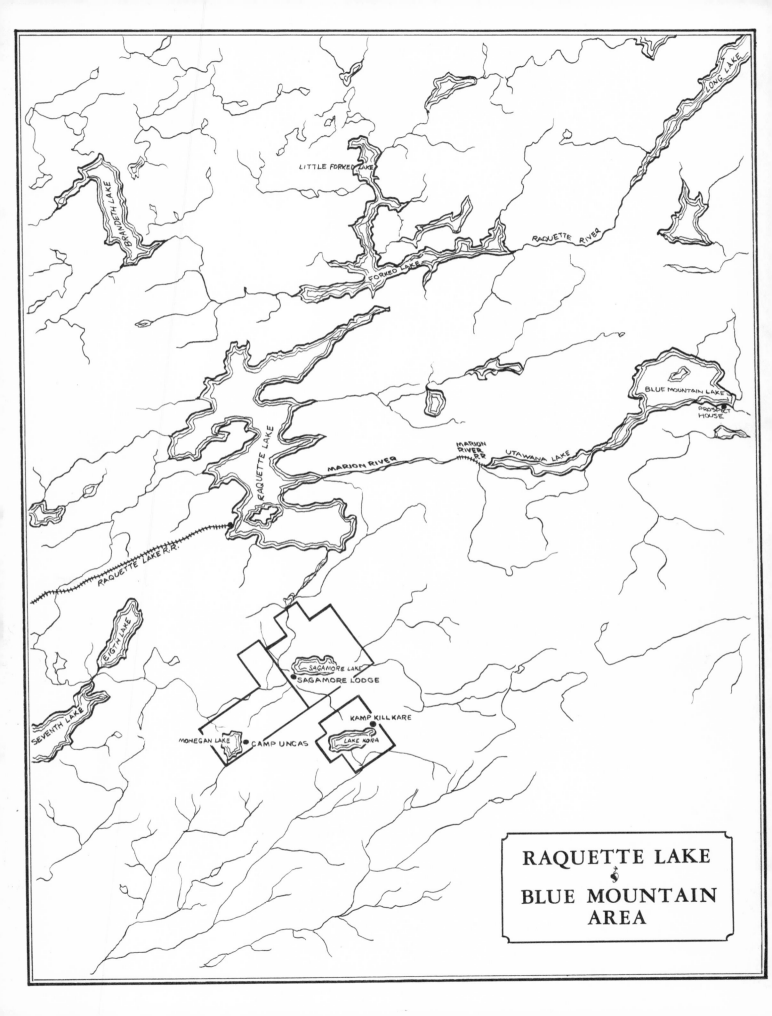

LONG LAKE

LITTLE FORKED LAKE

BRANDETH LAKE

RAQUETTE RIVER

FORKED LAKE

BLUE MOUNTAIN LAKE

PROSPECT HOUSE

RAQUETTE LAKE

MARION RIVER R.R.

MARION RIVER

UTAWANA LAKE

RAQUETTE LAKE R.R.

EIGTH LAKE

SEVENTH LAKE

SAGAMORE LAKE

SAGAMORE LODGE

KAMP KILL KARE

MOHEGAN LAKE · CAMP UNCAS

LAKE KORA

RAQUETTE LAKE
&
BLUE MOUNTAIN
AREA